The Complete Y2K
Home Preparation
Guide

W9-CCD-866

ISBN 0-13-014306-5

9 780130 143068   90000

The Complete Y2K Home Preparation Guide

Ed Yourdon and
Robert A. Roskind

Prentice Hall PTR
Upper Saddle River, New Jersey 07458
http://www.phptr.com

Editorial/production supervision: *Joanne Anzalone*
Cover design director: *Jerry Votta*
Cover design: *Scott Weiss*
Manufacturing manager: *Alexis R. Heydt*
Acquisitions editor: *Jeffrey Pepper*
Marketing manager: *Dan Rush*
Editorial assistant: *Linda Ramagnano*
Photos by Jim Foreman Photography, Boone, NC

Prentice-Hall International (UK) Limited, *London*
Prentice-Hall of Australia Pty. Limited, *Sydney*
Prentice-Hall Canada Inc., *Toronto*
Prentice-Hall Hispanoamericana, S.A., *Mexico*
Prentice-Hall of India Private Limited, *New Delhi*
Prentice-Hall of Japan, Inc., *Tokyo*
Prentice-Hall (Singapore) Pte. Ltd., *Singapore*
Editora Prentice-Hall do Brasil, Ltda., *Rio de Janeiro*

To our children,
Alicia Roskind
Julie Mattera
Jennifer Yourdon
Jamie Yourdon
David Yourdon
who, more than their parents, will inherit
the post-Y2K world

Contents

ACKNOWLEDGMENTS

We would like to thank the people that helped make this book possible:

Jeffrey Pepper, our editor at Prentice Hall, who believed in the book and kept it on a fast track;

Jim Foreman, our photographer, who gave us great photos and good jokes;

Harley Levitt, for his research and finding every fact, no matter how obscure;

Judith Gadd and Anna Pepper, who kept everything going while the book was being created;

Julia Roskind, for her support throughout, and

Joanne Anzalone of Prentice Hall for an excellent job of quickly pulling this book together.

INTRODUCTION

Mammoth productive facilities with computer minds, cities that engulf the landscape and pierce the clouds, planes that almost out race time—these are awesome, but they cannot be spiritually inspiring. Nothing in our glittering technology can raise man to new heights, because material growth has been made an end in itself, and, in the absence of moral purpose, man himself becomes smaller as the works of man becomes bigger. Gargantuan industry and government, woven into an intricate computerized mechanism, leave the person outside. The sense of participation is lost, the feeling that ordinary individuals influence important decisions vanishes, and man becomes separated and diminished.

When an individual is no longer a true participant, when he no longer feels a sense of responsibility to his society, the content of democracy is emptied. When culture is degraded and vulgarity enthroned, when the social system does not build security but induces peril, inexorably the individual is impelled to pull away from a soulless society. This process produces alienation-perhaps the most pervasive and insidious development in contemporary society

—Dr. Martin Luther King

The biggest problems and opportunities with the Y2K bug are not going to be food storage, debugging code, or power outages, but how people react to the situation: how we treat each other; how much we help each other through this; what kind of creative, appropriate responses we meet the challenge with will determine whether we build and bring together our local communities or whether things degenerate into mob rule.

—Michael Connolly, WizCity (http://www.wizcity.com/)

Owing to past neglect, in the face of the plainest warnings, we have now entered upon a period of danger. The era of procrastination, of half measures,...of delays, is coming to its close. In its place we are entering a period of consequences...We cannot avoid this period, we are in it now...Unless...,this House resolves to find out the truth for itself, it will have committed an act of abdication of duty without parallel

—Winston Churchill, November 12, 1936, Testimony to the House of Commons: Debate on National Defense Posture

DO I REALLY NEED TO PREPARE FOR Y2K?

No one knows what will really happen in the first few hours, days, weeks, and months of 2000. This includes the authors of this book, government and business leaders, computer experts, "Y2K wishful thinkers," "Y2K doom and gloomers," the press, and your brother-in-law. None of us really knows what will happen. And it is because of this one central fact that complete preparation is essential.

Our world will enter the new millennium with everything it takes for modern life to function at risk. How this risk will turn out is, and will continue to be, the subject of much debate and controversy. However, everyone agrees there is the risk. People just disagree as to how much risk there really is. But when your health, your comfort, your food, your water, your heat, maybe even your life, is at risk, no matter how great or small, it would be wise and reasonable to prepare. If the risk does not go your way, you have too much to lose.

You should start your preparations as soon as you can. In late 1999, if not earlier, there may be a shortage of preparation supplies. By starting early, we help the situation as suppliers can ramp up to meet the demand. As early as late 1998, preparedness food delivery was taking 2-4 months instead of the usual weeks, orders for large generators were taking several months, wood stoves were selling at triple their normal rates, some solar products were getting hard to find—all because of Y2K preparedness. And in late 1998 only 2% of the people surveyed believed Y2K would be a serious problem. What happens when this grows to 10%? 25%? 50%? 100%? As the old saying about preparing goes, "It is better to be five months early than one hour too late."

Needless to say, as Y2K approaches, fears will increase. Also denial and wishful thinking will be factors. As we look out at this well-oiled technological machine, humming right along, and an unconcerned population, we keep asking ourselves, "Is this really going to happen? Will our post-Y2K world really be that dramatically different and if so how?" As we lower our fears, our perception becomes clearer and our decision making becomes more effective. Remember Benjamin Franklin's thoughts, "Failing to prepare is preparing to fail."

IF Y2K IS POTENTIALLY SO SERIOUS, WHY DO MOST OF THE WORLD AND ITS LEADERS SEEM SO UNCONCERNED?

This is the first question that springs to mind whenever someone is told they need to prepare for Y2K. The answer is not as obvious as it might seem. Nothing like Y2K—nothing so big, so total, so innocuous—has ever occurred before. For the last 40 years we have spent trillions of dollars and person-hours building an almost unseen global computer system that runs much of our world, for the most part with few failures or disruptions.

Where there was once a typing pool with many people, there is now one person and a PC; where once hundreds of men manually directed trains at switching stations, now chips and mainframes direct them from one central location; where there was once a highly staffed accounting department, there are now a few computer operators. The system is global and affects almost every aspect of modern human life. And until now it was considered safe, dependable and effective. The entire system is broken and must be fixed by a set deadline. There can be no extensions.

Because of the size and scope of this problem, it creates denial that it is there—both in everyday citizens and leaders alike. If the only issue were that the phone systems might fail, or TV transmission, or water delivery, or accounting systems, or billing systems, or traffic lights, or medical devices, or con-veyor belts, or oil refinery pumps, or food delivery systems, or paychecks, or residential heating systems, etc., we could look the problem in the face and fix it. But when the problem is so complex, so costly, involving so many areas of our lives and businesses, it is much easier to shut down, ignore the evidence, and assume it will get fixed—somehow.

Also, computer stories are inherently boring to the general public. The recent coverage of the Microsoft court case can attest to this. The press does not really know how to cover Y2K. All there is to report is everyone's opinion as to what will happen. There is no event yet and the media is event driven. With the massive onslaught of information delivered daily, the Y2K story does not rise above the other stories. In fact it sinks. The implications of the problem are too massive to assimilate easily.

Many people believe there will be a "quick-fix" that will fix every computer in nanoseconds. However, even IBM and the U.S. government have admitted this is impossible. Add to that the issue that it is almost ludicrous to believe that a small two-digit year date could collapse this magnificent machine called modern life, and you have a disaster in slow motion.

John Kenneth Galbraith, one of the great writers and observers of capitalism, could only find one inherent flaw in the system.

> *Long-run salvation by men of business has never been highly regarded if it means disturbance of orderly life and convenience in the present. So inaction will be advocated in the present even though it means deep trouble in the future. Here, at least equally with communism, lies the threat to capitalism. It is what causes men who know that things are going quite wrong to say that things are fundamentally sound.*

It is this possible threat, the only one Galbraith could find in our system, that may manifest through Y2K. Not so much because of the threat itself but rather from our incapacity to maturely deal with it once detected. Many business leaders are concerned that if the public knew they had Y2K problems their stock price could drop. Many government leaders worry about everything from terrorist threats to a run on the banks to stockpiling weapons. All of these fears could keep us from dealing with the issue or announcing the truth to the public. However, as the quotes from leaders throughout this book will show, many have already spoken out of their deep concern about Y2K.

THE FIVE STAGES OF Y2K

Many people feel accepting the reality of Y2K is like the five stages of dying outlined by Dr. Kubler-Ross, the well-known death and dying researcher. Her five stages were denial, bargaining, anger, depression, and acceptance. Let's take a look at how these five stages would apply to Y2K.

First, in denial, we may tend to deny that we could have done something so stupid, that "they" could let this happen, that technology could really fail us to this degree, that something so small could cause something so large. In the bargaining stage we are likely to feel if we just do enough work, or if we are lucky enough, the risk will dissipate. In the anger stage we will feel anger toward programmers, computer companies, the government, Bill Gates, Bill Clinton, and maybe anyone who warns us about the problem.

In the depression stage, where we have accepted that Y2K is really a threat that could cause us much pain, collectively and individually, we may become despondent, almost incapacitated to take action. It seems too big, too overpowering. What can we as individuals do? Preparation for an event of this potential size seems too overwhelming.

Finally in the acceptance stage our emotions start to level out and we are moved to action. We realize that no matter how much time is left, a certain level of preparation is definitely possible and appropriate. We move from "this can't be happening" into "what do I need to do." This is the stage of positive action and hope. It is the stage that we need to get to as quickly as possible.

Also, realize that Y2K will continue to create moral dilemmas for everyone. Do I need to store food for others who do not prepare? Should I leave my home if I do not feel comfortable there if Y2K problems are major or long lasting? Do I buy a gun? Do I take my money out of the bank? Do I tell others of my preparation plans and maybe help them or keep quiet so no one will ask me for food if they need it? Do I take this thing seriously at all, spend all this effort and expense, when it just may roll over without any major problems or am I a fool for not preparing when potential risk is undeniable?

No one can answer these questions for you. Everyone who has looked this thing in the face has gone through these decision making processes. Many know the feeling of laying in bed at 3 AM, with your family safely sleeping around you, and wondering what to do (or as one Y2K expert said, "If you're sleeping well at night, you do not understand the scope of the problem."). Some questions will bring up deep issues of self-interest versus group interest, of generosity versus self-preservation. Other questions will bring up issues of how much ridicule and loss of stature in another people's eyes you are willing to risk to emphatically encourage others to prepare—even when their eyes continue to glaze over when you mention Y2K. The only advice that we can offer is, as much as possible, to make peace with your fears and be willing to let go of your attachments, and then trust your heart as to what you feel guided to do. We are well aware that this is much easier to write than to do.

HOW LONG SHOULD I PREPARE FOR Y2K?

How long to prepare is the subject of raging debates. Some say days, others weeks, others a year or more. As an example,

How Long to Prepare

Red Cross	3-7 days
FEMA	3-7 days
U.K. government	2 weeks
Canadian government	2-3 weeks
Most Y2K experts	1-12 months
Authors of this book	1-12 months

As you can see there is a tremendous range. If budget is not a big issue, prepare for the high side. If it is, prepare for as long as is financially feasible. It may not be that those who prepared will eat while others starve but rather they may have more choices as to what they eat and more convenience in getting their food. Or they may be able to stay home while others need to go to a shelter or relatives. Or they may be able to shower when others sponge bathe.

Between now and the New Year, read every article about Y2K with discernment. Ask if the writer or spokesperson has a hidden agenda or ulterior motives. Adjust your preparation plans as we near the event if you feel that information or events call for it. Be conservative. Prepare for the top end of your estimate. In the end, the decision is yours.

WHOM SHOULD I INCLUDE IN MY PREPARATIONS?

You cannot get very far in the preparation process before you begin to realize that no matter how completely and cleverly you plan for your family's needs, all it takes is a few relatives, friends, or neighbors—who didn't prepare—to show up on your doorstep and spoil those well-laid out plans. Of course your option is to remind them that you encouraged them to prepare, slam the door in their face, and send them away cold or hungry.

If things get too bad, everyone of us may need to make those kinds of decisions. There just may be too many people in need. However, if the breakdown is moderate or slight (the most likely scenario), though we can't help everyone, we might be able to help some. It may be best to decide to prepare not only for your family's needs but for several others—if you can afford to. At worse, you'll have to shop less often in 2000; at best you may rescue a friend or relative from a painful situation.

This event may well stretch us in many ways, especially in our willingness to serve and give to others. Maybe that's the beauty of Y2K, that the only way to repair our world will be through tremendous cooperation between countries, between companies, between communities, between neighbors, between friends.

WHERE DO I SPEND THE WEEKEND OF JANUARY 1, 2000?

Many people are giving a lot of thought to where they want to spend the weekend of December 31, 1999-January 1, 2000. People are reconsidering the "Millennium Celebration" in exotic places (much to the concern of the travel industry). Many are opting to celebrate at home in a well-Y2K-prepared home, surrounded by loved ones. Whatever your choice, a good rule of thumb is celebrate that weekend knowing that wherever you are, you may be stuck there for awhile—perhaps without essential services and supplies. A Caribbean island may seem like a great place to be stuck in early 2000 but not when you realize that almost everything they need to survive must be brought in—from a fully functioning outside world.

No one really knows how the airline, cruise, train and other transportation industries will make the transitions. Many top officials such as Senator Chris Dodd, co-chair of the federal Year 2000 Committee, recommend against being on a plane. Cruise ships are floating computerized worlds, needing the rest of the world to supply them at every port. Trains are now totally computerized and track switching is controlled from one centralized location. Add to this the threat of terrorist attacks, in and outside the United States, and maybe the weekend is best spent at home.

Another option is to be prepared to go to a safe shelter provided by local emergency agencies. However, these might become overcrowded, straining their resources if conditions are too difficult. Be sure you ask the agencies the location of the shelters, whether they will be prepared for a large crowd. Also ask them what items they recommend people bring and if there are provisions for pets.

You may want to make preparation for everyone you feel responsible for (even the loved ones who laughed at you for preparing) and invite (almost insist) that they spend the weekend with you. It should be a fascinating night as the entire world focuses on one thought, "What will Y2K bring?" The rollover will begin in Fiji, 17 hours ahead of New York time, and roll across the planet toward us. The news of Fiji, New Zealand, Australia, etc., will be carried worldwide as the first countries roll into the new millennium. It will be a night like no other in history.

Of course all this makes sense unless your home is on the 70th floor of a high rise in New York City or Chicago, or a half mile away from a large chemical plant. These are serious issues and not to be made light of. If New York City, or Chicago, or Boston, with all their inner city high-rises were to lose power, then there could be serious problems. Even if the entire city did not lose power but the microprocessors and computers controlling the elevator in a tall high-rise failed, people could become stranded high up in buildings. (Elevators will not plummet due to Y2K failures but may slowly descend to the basement believing they need to be serviced. Elevator companies are saying they are OK for Y2K.)

Living in a large city during a major Y2K failure will be quite a different experience from living in a suburban or rural area. Large cities are much more reliant on computer-controlled essential services, have less space to store food, water, fuel, etc., and often have a criminal element which may take advantage of an overtaxed police force. In late 1998 Canada announced Operation Abacus. The Canadian federal government plans to have tens of thousands of troops and their warships standing by in major ports, in case the computer problems in 2000 bring civil chaos. And they plan to have them there from December 26, 1999 to March 15, 2000.

There are no easy answers for this situation. It is not feasible for millions of people living in large inner cities to abandon them, even for a weekend. If you can leave for vacation, to visit a relative, to a second home, it may be wise to do so. If you cannot, do what you can to prepare within the limits of your situation and start calling the power companies, water companies, building owner, mayor, police and fire chiefs, to keep the pressure on them to be prepared. As late as December 1998, 13 months before the event, local governments, including 911 response teams, police, fire, essential services, etc., were woefully behind. (Check the "Y2K Books" section in the reference section for preparedness books geared toward city dwellers.)

CAN I BELIEVE THE NEWS
ABOUT Y2K?

Until 1998 almost all the information about the Y2K situation was coming from the ever-growing community of professional computer scientists who were involved in trying to fix the problem. For the most part their reports were alarming. The more they delved into the problem, the bigger it seemed to be. First there were the mainframe problems, then the desktop computers and networks were recognized as problematic, and then finally it was discovered that 1-3% of the small microchips and microprocessors (embedded systems) may fail. The percentage seems low but there are estimated to be 30-50 billion microchips running the world. And you must check them all to find the faulty ones.

In 1996 and 1997, the computer experts all agreed that there was still time to avoid real problems *if* the governments and corporations of the world would get on the stick and take it seriously. By 1998, it became clear this was not happening. Only 24 countries had a Y2K program. Only 50% of all counties had started. Eighty percent of small to mid-sized businesses had not begun and 50% said they did not plan to. By mid- to late-1998, many of the experts began predicting disastrous scenarios and were quickly accused of being "doom and gloomers," who had no trust in the human spirit and potential to fix the problem in time. They were, and are, in fact realistic.

By late 1998, it became obvious to anyone looking at this problem that not enough work had been done and the risks were now great. By then many government and corporate people were becoming concerned that the public needed to be reassured to avoid a public loss in confidence in the banking system, the stock market, the government agencies, etc. More and more government and corporate Y2K spokespeople have come forward with comforting statements that everything will be fine. It is becoming harder to distinguish whether this is the truth or a conscious (or unconscious) decision on their part to reduce the fears of the public.

As an example, the House Committee studying the Y2K problem, chaired by Rep. Horn of California, has consistently been giving the federal government an overall grade of "D" or "F" in their Y2K preparation. Yet in January of 1999, days after receiving another "D," John Koskinen, the federal Y2K Czar and the person in charge of getting the federal agencies ready, said the following:

> *Based on the data we have seen thus far, we are increasingly confident that there will not be large scale disruptions among banks and in the power and telecommunications industries. But one thing is clear: everyone has a lot of work left to do. We are most concerned about organizations that don't have the Y2K problem as a high priority. They are the source of our greatest risk.*

In the November 27, 1998 edition of *USA Today*, Sen. Robert Bennett, R-Utah, co-chair of a Senate Special Committee on Year 2000, stated that there was improvement among agencies. "There aren't as many people lying to us as there used to be." As you can see, no one really knows how to call this one.

In reality, the true state of affairs will become more and more difficult to determine as we approach the event. Fear will increase and the stakes are very high. One day you may read a report that makes you wonder if you need to prepare at all. The next day a report may have you running to your grocery store to stock up. Perhaps the best approach is to follow the time-tested advice of "hope for the best but prepare for the worst."

xxx The Complete Y2K Home Preparation Guide

HOW DO I CONVINCE OTHERS TO PREPARE?

Once you begin to take Y2K seriously and prepare, your natural inclination is to tell other people you care about (and even perfect strangers) to do the same. This can be a frustrating, humiliating, and trying experience. A man recently called our office from a small town in Texas. He had been a community leader for 30 years and was concerned about Y2K. However, the more he talked to his friends and fellow leaders, the more discredited he became. It had even begun to affect long-term friendships as people accused him of becoming a "doom and gloomer." He wanted to know what to do. Should he press on, further alienating himself from his community or should he keep quiet, while fearing a coming storm. He had no answer and we had no answer, other than to trust his best instincts.

When talking with others, using articles and quotes from reliable sources is the best way to make your case. Steer clear of hearsay information or rumors. And always stress that no one will know how bad things will be until after the event. Also mention the good that could come out of this event. Y2K may allow us to rethink our priorities and it may serve as a wake-up call for other technological problems (nuclear weapons, El Nino, global warming, etc.). What you are trying to alert them to is not a prediction of definite problems, but to a risk, a very real risk that everyone, "doom and gloomers" and "wishful thinkers" alike, agrees is there. And it is because of this risk that everyone should prepare.

Our observation has been that many people have to be told of the problem many times, and from many sources. Family and friends are often the least credible source. If your brother-in-law needs to hear it from 28 sources before he takes it seriously, you do not know if you're #1, #14, or #28. It's really like picking tomatoes. When tomatoes are green it is a struggle to pick them. They hold tenaciously to the vine. But when tomatoes ripen, they fall into your hand with the slightest touch.

The following quote from Douglass Carmichael's article "Social Psychology of Y2K: Trying to Understand the Denial," explains why the acceptance process may be slower than we wish.

> *Y2K is very hard to come to terms with. Each of us who encounters it, dances around it for quite a while before figuring out what to do with it. Often we experience months of rollercoastering in and out of intense anxiety. Those of us who see Y2K as an opportunity may find ourselves going especially high and low. The unconfrontability of Y2K makes it awkward to talk about with those who don't share our understanding of the problem. Some people will just brush it off, to our intense frustration. If someone was unaware of the threat, we may feel like we're messing up their lives by waking them up to it. And they may turn away from the subject (or us), or make fun of it (or us). And, if we want to motivate them to DO something about it in their communities, we often find they have been sent into a spin by their fear and confusion. It may take quite a while before they get their "Y2K sea legs" and can finally function in the face of such an unsettling future.*

WHAT CAN INDIVIDUALS DO TO HELP?

For many, a desire to help, to be part of the solution, will emerge as you become Y2K-aware. The question will then arise as to what can you do to help. The obvious thing that arises is to contact the appropriate companies (power, water, fuel, phone, banks, brokers, etc.) and government agencies (police, fire, emergency response, etc.) to push them to correct enough of the problem to continue service uninterrupted. In early 1999, this is probably worth doing as many companies and agencies still may not be taking it seriously. By late 1999, this may be of little value.

In many areas, Y2K support groups are forming to share info and resources and to lobby government officials and key companies as a group. The Cassandra Project (www.cassandra-project.org) is a nonprofit Y2K group that list groups around the country. Their site is also an excellent resource for community preparedness. Also the Co-Intelligence Institute has an excellent Web site with suggestions for both personal and community help at http://www.co-intelligence.org. (See "Community Y2K Groups and Resources" in the Reference section at the end of the book.)

In addition to a Y2K group, consider getting your churches, synagogues, civic groups, boy and girl scouts troops (be prepared is the boy scout motto), etc., involved as well. Be prepared to encounter some degree of resistance about preparing. Just keep reminding everyone that all experts agree that the risk is real, and therefore contingency preparation plans are wise. Even the Red Cross and FEMA (Federal Emergency Management Agency) are now advising one to two weeks of preparation, though this length of time may increase as the event gets near (see "Red Cross and FEMA sections in Reference section at the end of the book).

WHAT TO DO MONTHS BEFORE Y2K

❑ Prepare as outlined in this book

❑ Turn off the power and do a dry test run to be sure you have everything you need

❑ Spend three days eating from your stockpiled food to be sure you have what you need and what you like

❑ Encourage neighbors, friends, relatives, and strangers to prepare

WHAT TO DO NEW YEAR'S EVE DAY
(or before)

❑ Fill the cars with gas; make sure they are tuned and serviced.

❑ Fill sinks, bathtubs, pots, pools, containers with water.

❑ Get some cash.

❑ Know how to turn off gas and water.

❑ Bring out your flashlights and other alternative lighting.

❑ Get you alternative heating ready.

❑ Get your alternative cooking equipment ready.

❑ Get your stored food ready.

❑ Call to wish loved ones Happy New Millennium.

❑ Be sure everyone knows what to do if the power goes out.

❑ Be sure you have a fire extinguisher handy.

❑ Install your battery-operated smoke and carbon monoxide detector.

❏ Wash all your dirty clothes.

❏ Fill all you prescriptions.

❏ Post a list of items inside on the refrigerator and freezer doors.

❏ Get all your important papers and financial papers safely stored.

❏ Prepare a travel kit in case everyone needs to take shelter elsewhere for a few days.

❏ Settle back with your loved ones and see what happens.

WHAT TO DO NEW YEAR'S DAY

If the power is off:

❏ Check to see if you need to turn off gas or water.

❏ Call (if possible) to see when power can be expected.

❏ Begin to use your Y2K preparations as outlined in this book.

❏ See if the phone, gas, and water are working.

If the power is on or off, check to see if the following are operating properly:

❏ Cars

❏ Heating and air conditioning systems

❏ Security systems

❏ Phones

❏ VCRs

❏ Sprinkler system

- ❏ Coffee maker
- ❏ PC
- ❏ Fax
- ❏ Copier/ scanners
- ❏ Cell phones
- ❏ Pagers
- ❏ See if your on-line banking is working.
- ❏ Call loved ones to see how they are doing.

AN INTRODUCTION TO THE PROBLEM

"The problems that we created cannot be solved at the level of thinking that created them."

—Albert Einstein

"I know of no safe depository of the ultimate powers of society but the people themselves, and if we think them not enlightened enough to exercise control with a wholesome discretion, the remedy is not to take it from them to inform their discretion..."

—Thomas Jefferson

SATURDAY MORNING, 11:00 AM

Your head throbs as you roll out of bed. It was quite a celebration last night—the celebration of a lifetime—and you've slept through your alarm clock. But now it's Saturday morning, and you always call your dear old mom in North Carolina every Saturday morning. So you shuffle past the kitchen, pause briefly to snarl at the coffee machine that failed to brew your morning coffee as usual, and slump into the living room sofa to conduct the weekly hi-Mom-howya-doin' ritual. You pick up the phone, and after a moment, snarl again—there is no dial tone.

1

Shuffling back to the bedroom, it becomes obvious why you didn't hear the alarm clock—there's no electricity. And, when you step into the shower to wash away the headache, there is no hot water. You're in a worse mood when you step out again. Snarls have given way to soft curses, but you realize that you need to sound pleasant and cheerful when you talk to Mom, so you force a smile onto your face as you head for the living room again. You pick up the phone again, and after another moment of silence, all attempts at civility vanish-still no dial tone. You hold the phone in front of your face and curse in loud, angry terms at the telephone company.

There's still no dial tone at 1 PM, and the coffee maker still won't work. To make matters worse, the refrigerator has stopped too, and the freezer is now leaking water onto the floor. You've gotten dressed in the interim, and even though you've frequently criticized the coffee at the corner deli, you now decide that it's better than no coffee at all. As you reach the front door of the apartment building, you remember that you ran out of cash during the celebrations last night, so you stop at the bank on the corner to get a few dollars out of the ATM machine—but the machine gobbles up your bank card and refuses to give you any cash at all. When you reach the deli on the corner, you find it even more curious that their phone is also out of service, and that they're operating without electricity. And when you return to your apartment, you still find silence rather than a dial tone when you pick up the phone.

More silence on Sunday, and again on Monday. It's now been three days since you've had working telephone service, and it's no longer funny. Not only have you been unable to reach Mom in North Carolina, but you also haven't been able to communicate with any of your friends and business associates.

We won't continue the vignette any further—you get the point. If your phone was out of service for three days, it would be somewhat annoying, and there could possibly be some important consequences. But suppose that it wasn't just your phone that was inoperable, but every phone in your building... in your neighborhood... in your city... in your state... in the entire country? Suppose that nobody could call anybody else for three days? Would civilization come to a screeching halt? Not likely, but there would be a lot of grumpy people, and there would inevitably be some financial consequences.

Let's make this vignette more serious: Suppose the phone outage persisted not just for three days, but for a full month. No phone calls for the entire month of January; nobody has a dial tone. Don't just nod your head when you read this sentence: Think about it. Suppose you couldn't call anyone, and no one could call you because nobody in your city had a working phone, and as far as you could tell, nobody in North America, Europe, or anywhere else where phones were taken for granted had viable telephone service. (It's worth noting, by the way, that approximately 50% of the human race, particularly in large sections of China and Africa, have never made a phone call, so not everyone would be affected!)

Obviously, a month without telephone service would be pretty serious, but what if it was a full year? Could your employer survive for a full year, let alone a month, without phone service? Could your city? Could the national government of whatever country you live in? A century ago, all of what was then considered "modern society" functioned quite well without telephones—but would that be possible today?

Lest you think that we're concocting stories to pick on the phone company, remember the other events in the vignette above: Your bank's ATM machine doesn't work and the lights are out. And, let's expand our vignette a bit: What about your car? Suppose you turned the key in the ignition and nothing happened? Or, to put things into the proper perspective: Suppose you were driving home a little early from the New Year's Eve festivities, and just at the stroke of midnight, all the red lights and alarm signals on the dashboard begun to flash and beep at you? Now what?

Welcome to the Year 2000 problem. No, this is not a joke, and it may not be an exaggeration. New Year's Eve falls on Friday December 31, 1999. And when the clock strikes midnight on that very special Friday night, every computer system in the world will encounter a "rollover" phenomenon that may or may not be fatal. In the best of cases, your phone will still work on Saturday morning, January 1, 2000 (indeed, the major telephone companies assure us this will be the case), and so will your car, the electric utility company, and all of the other machines and devices that you've come to depend on, often without even realizing that there's a computer inside.

But in the worst of all cases, the rollover phenomenon that occurs when 1999 changes to 2000 could cause consequences that make the vignettes above seem quite tame by comparison. The computer industry is planning to spend between $300-600 billion in the course of fixing the problem in an attempt to avoid this problem, and some experts are already warning that this estimate is too low. But as we write this book, it's becoming increasingly clear that the vast complex of computer systems will not be completely modified and upgraded to deal with what has come to be known as the as "Year 2000" or "Y2K" software problem.

Because of the magnitude of the Year 2000 problem, hundreds of technical articles have already been published in computer journals, and dozens of computer conferences have been held to offer advice to computer professionals and managers. Numerous articles have appeared in *Fortune, Forbes,* the *Wall Street Journal,* the *Economist,* and other business publications to warn senior managers of the impact of the problem. Articles have even appeared on the front pages of the *New York Times,* the *Boston Globe,* and *Newsweek.* And, several technically oriented Year 2000 books have been published—with more on the way.

The technical books and articles warn the computer professionals: "The Year 2000 problem could be really serious if we don't do something about it. We need to get started right now in order to avoid a major disaster!" But this book asks the question: What if the computer industry doesn't manage to fix the Year 2000 problem successfully? How serious a problem could it be, and what should your fallback plan be? What would be the economic consequences of a telephone outage for a day, or a month, or a year, or a decade? The telephone, of course, is only one form of communication; what if we didn't have FedEx, the Post Office, or the Internet available? What if the Year 2000 problem knocks out electricity for three days, or the water supply for a month, or access to your bank account? Then there's the field of transportation: What are the personal consequences of failures with cars, buses, trains, and airplanes? What about credit cards and the stock market? What about newspapers, radio, and television? Hospitals, access to medicine, access to doctors? Food supplies? Welfare? The Internal Revenue Service? The Defense Department? Schools and universities? Oh yes, one last question: What about your job?

If you've never heard of the Year 2000 problem before, the notion that every aspect of our social infrastructure could shut down for even a single day seems preposterous. And when it's presented in such simplistic terms, it is preposterous; Year

2000 problems won't happen in the same way, at the same time, in all of these areas. It's highly likely, for example, that when you pick up the phone on January 1, 2000, you will get a dial tone—because it's one of the most fundamental, obvious, high-priority aspects of telephone service that AT&T, MCI, Sprint, and the regional Bell operating companies are working on. However, we're far less confident about all of the tiny telephone companies that have sprung up since the telecommunications industry decentralized; indeed, we're not even sure that the larger phone companies will succeed in converting the other aspects of their operational systems. What happens, for example, if you get a phone bill on January 31, 2000 for $325,914,166.14? What happens if every telephone customer in your city gets an equally preposterous bill? What happens when every customer tries to call the phone company's customer service department, on the same day, to complain about his or her bill? What happens when the phone company's computer systems decide to cancel everyone's service because of nonpayment of his or her bill?

Why do we think something like this could happen? Not because we think the phone company is incompetent, but because the effort to fix the software is a massive job with a very immovable deadline. Most of the large telephone companies have a "portfolio" of computer programs and systems with a total of some 300-400 million program instructions that need to be examined for possible corrections for proper operation after January 1, 2000. Banks are dealing with equally large numbers, and the federal government is dealing with an even larger software portfolio. Unfortunately, the computer industry has been notorious for being substantially behind schedule and over budget, even on projects that are a hundred times smaller than the Year 2000 project. Not only that, programmers have a notorious record for innocently injecting "bugs" into the complex software systems they create. If the statistics about the error-prone nature of "normal" software development is any indication, Year 2000 project teams will still be fixing their mistakes in 2005.

Even if individual companies are able to solve their own Y2K problem, there is still the "domino effect" problem that can occur if a relatively simple error in, say, the computer systems of banks "ripple" into the credit card systems, and then into the Wall Street stock market systems, etc. This is a variation on the "chaos theory" argument that says a butterfly flapping its wings in Tokyo could cause a tornado in Wichita, Kansas.

The "meat" of this book is a discussion of the contingency plans we should be making. One aspect of this contingency planning is to assign reasonable levels of probability to different levels of "severity" of Year 2000 problems. Do you think the most likely scenario is a rash of Year 2000 problems that will last for two or three days? Or, do you think the most likely scenario is a massive decade-long collapse reminiscent of the Great Depression of the 1930s? We personally believe that a majority of the Year 2000 problems will be of the minor variety, though there could well be some "minor" problems that render such critical systems as banking, telecommunications, and utilities inoperable for a few days. We also believe that a significant minority of the Year 2000 problems—perhaps as great as 25-35%—will be of the "moderate" variety, causing failures that will take a month to solve; invoicing and billing systems within business organizations are a prime example of this category.

Unfortunately, we also think that a small percentage—perhaps in the range of 5-10%—of the Year 2000 problems could be of the "serious" variety, i.e., requiring a year to repair. In many cases, this will occur because the "cleanup" process can be time-consuming and tedious. A hurricane usually lasts for only a day, but the hurricane recovery can easily take a year if the damage is extensive; we believe the same situation will occur with a small percentage of the Year 2000 software bugs.

Here's an example: Your local bank runs afoul of the Year 2000 problem and begins generating wildly incorrect banking statements. Panicked customers begin withdrawing their cash, and after a few days of attempting to cope with the crisis, the bank has to shut down operations. Assuming that you have a standard bank account (as opposed to uninsured certificates of deposits), and assuming your balance is less than $100,000, your account is insured by the Federal Deposit Insurance Company (FDIC). Assuming that several banks have the same problem, and that all of their banking records are corrupted by Year 2000 bugs, how long do you think it will be before the FDIC gives you your money? Many of us would be grateful indeed if it only took a year—but attempting to carry out our day-to-day business without the funds in that frozen account could be a problem indeed.

Finally, we think that a very small percentage of Year 2000 problems could be sufficiently devastating that it could take a decade to recover. A decade, by the way, is approximately the length of the Great Depression; we won't try to draw any parallels between the events of 1929 and 1999 at this point, but we do want to emphasize that not all problems can be fixed or forgotten overnight. Our primary concerns in this area are the massive government agencies and systems that are in shaky condition already. Two that come to mind are the Internal Revenue Service (IRS) and Social Security Agency (SSA), though several other federal agencies were experiencing Year 2000 difficulties as this book went to press. It's possible that the political fallout of the Year 2000 problem could lead to both the IRS and SSA being abolished in their present form, and being replaced by something fundamentally different. For those who have based their life's plans on the assumption that income and savings would be taxed in a certain way, or that retirement funds would be available at a certain age, it could well take a decade to recover from such a shock.

With this kind of framework, minor, moderate, serious, and devastating failures could occur in each of the major aspects of society mentioned up to this point: communications, utilities, transportation, banking and finance, news broadcasting, travel, medicine, social services, education, government, and employment. Chances are that you'll ignore certain categories. Parents of school-age children, for example, might be thrilled at the prospect of television disappearing from their lives for a year. But, there are likely to be a few categories that represent life-and-death risks. If you're a diabetes patient, the notion that insulin might be unavailable for a month is not a joking matter.

Of course, a far more pleasant Year 2000 scenario would be to assume that nothing will go wrong at all. In the best of all worlds, $300-600 billion will be spent by the world's government agencies and private corporations, the computer problems will be quietly taken care of, and we'll all enjoy New Year's Eve in 1999 with nary a hiccup. Another scenario you're likely to hear is: "Well, it may be a problem for a few of the big companies with those old-fashioned mainframe computers, but it won't be a problem for small companies with their modern PCs; and in any case, most individuals don't depend very much on computers for their day-to-day lives." Perhaps this will turn out to be true, in which case we'll be justifiably criticized for needless scare-mongering. But even though both authors are optimists in our day-today lives, our investigation of the Year 2000 situation leads us to believe that it's very unlikely that we'll escape serious problems so easily.

If nothing else, the issues raised in this book may lead you to ask the appropriate officials—i.e., the spokespeople and managers of the various organizations that provide critical services—whether they can confidently promise that their organizations will be Year 2000-compliant. When former Senator Alphonse D'Amato asked this question of the Federal Reserve Bank in his capacity as head of the Senate Banking and Finance Committee, the answer he got was, "No comment." What will you do if you get that answer from your bank... or your phone company... or your automobile manufacturer... or your local doctor and hospital?

What most people will do, in the final analysis, is nothing. After all, the prospect of a moderate, serious, or devastating collapse of the nation's socioeconomic system is too awful for many people to accept. And the actions that would be required to protect oneself from such a disaster would require too much of a sacrifice for most people to accept in advance. This is rather puzzling, because our society has long accepted the notion of paying for insurance associated with crises it hopes will never occur. We pay hundreds of dollars per year for automobile insurance, but nobody wants an auto accident. We pay for medical insurance, and then hope that we won't have to use it for operations or serious illness. And even though each of us must accept the inevitability of our eventual death, we certainly don't expect it to happen next month or next year—yet most of us realize that it's important to plan for it by purchasing life insurance. The Year 2000 planning that we discuss in this book is, in a sense, just another form of insurance; unfortunately, we aren't very optimistic that most people will see it that way.

In researching this problem for the book *Time Bomb 2000*, we found a wide range of opinions about the ultimate impact of the Year 2000 problem. Some of those asked said, "If you really think it's going to cause another Great Depression, put yourself on the line and say so." And a few readers criticized us for alarmist exaggerations, implying that perhaps we were doing it in an attempt to generate more sales of the book. Especially when communicating with noncomputer-savvy readers, we consider scare-mongering to be the moral equivalent of shouting "Fire!" in a crowded theater—and we did our best to avoid it. But if an occupant of such a theater smells smoke, there's a moral obligation to say so. And if the theater is constructed of wood and other flammable materials, we also think it's appropriate to shout, "There are no smoke detectors or fire sprinklers in this building!" and then let people draw their own conclusions.

We don't know what's going to happen when the clock strikes midnight on December 31, 1999; nobody else does either. Some have suggested to us that by making the decision to write a book, we have created an obligation for ourselves to find out, so that we could state the future with certainty. That is not possible. We don't have the "answer" to the Year 2000 problem, and given the complexity of the problem, we think it's pretentious for anyone to suggest that he or she does.

Ultimately, what we think, and what other people think or do, is not your problem. What you do is the real issue—in the final analysis, you're responsible for your own actions and for the health and happiness of your family and loved ones. The issues we're writing about in this book are of direct concern to our family, and it forms the basis for our own plans for the Year 2000.

Endnotes

1. Paul A. Strassmann, "Numbers Add Up to a Bigger Year 2000 Disaster," *Computerworld*, June 13, 1997.

2. See, for example, William M. Ulrich and Ian S. Hayes, *The Year 2000 Software Crisis: Challenge of the Century* (Prentice Hall, 1997).

FOOD AND HOW TO
STORE IT

*The press tends to characterize Y2K as one of two extremes:
they either focus on the most dire Y2K predictions or they
summarily dismiss Y2k as a non-issue. Both approaches are
wrong. The first road leads to public alarm, or even panic,
the consequences of which could be even worse than those
caused by the Y2K technological problem itself. The second
road is equally dangerous. Deceptively smooth and far easier
to traverse in the short term, it leads to a precipice that will
not be seen until there is no time left to change direction.
Each day brings us closer to the brink, and there are no
brakes on the vehicle in which we are traveling*

*Y2K is an event that has potentially massive and unpredict-
able economic, social, and geopolitical ramifications. Our government is not going to get all of its critical systems fixed in
time for the century change. State and local systems that process
Federal benefit checks are not likely to be fully remediated.
County-operated "911" systems may have failures. Many companies, like Chevron, and General Motors, are now conceding
that they cannot guarantee their service as of January 1, 2000.
Even John Koskinen, Chairman of The President's Council on
Year 2000 Conversion, has publicly acknowledged that the
time to begin Y2K remediation is past. Everyone—business
leaders, politicians, community leaders, and families—needs
to begin calmly and rationally preparing.*

*Our challenge as a nation and a world community over the
next 338 days is clear. We must acknowledge that we are, indeed, facing a crisis. We must look at each component of the
problem and act rationally to find acceptable solutions. This*

is certainly not the time to begin bunkering down with propane tanks and money-stuffed mattresses, but we should begin treating the century date change as the real, but manageable, crisis that it is.

And because the precise dimensions of this problem will not be know until the stroke of midnight on December 31, 1999, we must focus on contigency planning. Most importantly, we must face this crisis together, at the community, national, and global level.

—Senator Robert Bennett (R-UT) Chairman of the
Senate's Year 2000 committee

It's my understanding that many cities still only have a 72-hour supply of food within their borders.

—Senator Gordon Smitt (R-OR) February 1999

THE PROBLEM

There is a growing concern that Y2K failures could cause disruption of the food supply to your local supermarkets. This could make food limited and/or expensive. Most food is inventoried and distributed through a long supply chain of computer systems. For example, when you buy a quart of milk, the grocery store computer tracks this sale and automatically sends reorders to their main office and on to the main distribution center and then on to the wholesale supplier. From there, this order is delivered to the dairy manufacturer and then over to a trucking company—all by computer. If one of these computers has a Y2K problem, many other computers may respond to that as an error and simply eliminate the order all together. This may not sound like any big deal to correct unless it's happening in many places at the same time. Keep in mind, most supermarkets only have a three-day inventory.

Much of our food must be shipped from hundreds or thousands of miles away. This means our transportation system must be functioning effectively. Over 40% of our fruits and vegetables come from South American countries, which are woefully behind in their Y2K remediation (manana, manana). When one high official was asked what his country was doing about the Millennium Bug, his answer was, "No problem. We are spraying everywhere."

In December 1998, 13 months before the event, the United Nations announced that only 24 countries in the world had an organized Y2K program. For the supply of foreign food products to continue into this country, their fertilizer plants, farm equipment, transportation system, ports, and ships of foreign countries must all operate effectively. It is doubtful this will be the case in early 2000 (no more watermelon in February 2000 in Ohio).

In late 1999, people will begin stockpiling food. FEMA and the Red Cross, as well as the governments of the UK, Canada, and Australia, have already told citizens to store food and water (1-3 weeks). If the food companies have not accounted for this, shortages may occur before the event. In late 1998, the storage food industry companies that package freeze-dried and dehydrated food to last 20 years were running low of supplies. Deliveries of storage foods that used to take weeks are now often taking months. The owner of one company told me by March 1999 he would not be able to take any new orders.

It may seem ludicrous that a country like the United States could have a food shortage. We can almost understand food shortages in other countries (in some areas of Russia people no longer greet each other with "Hello" but with "Do you have food?"). Here we have such an abundance of everything and large grocery stores are a testament to our food abundance. Remember, in three-days, fewer if people get scared, shelves could be empty. Perhaps the greatest risk is that of hoarding. Hoarding is one of the most likely outcomes of the year 2000 problem. This event is like no other potential disaster that has ever occurred. It may not hit one region and disable a small part of the infrastructure. It has the potential to affect many, if not all, regions and collapse many pieces of the infrastructure. With this in mind, store your food early. This will also help everyone as it will give the food companies more time to ramp up to meet demand.

THE SOLUTIONS

In the event of a possible Y2K-related disruption of infrastructure (power, water, transportation, etc.), we recommend a minimum of 4 to 8 weeks' supply of food be stored. However, with the possibility of a longer disruption, higher prices or greater inconvenience in obtaining food, you may want to consider 6 to 12 months of food supplies.

There are two main approaches to food storage. These include

- Storing nonperishable foods that you normally eat
- Storing dehydrated and freeze-dried foods

YOUR IN-HOME GROCERY STORE

Storing Nonperishable Foods
That You Normally Eat

Perhaps the least disruptive and most palatable approach is to simply increase your normal supplies in your pantry. For instance, you may now have a week supplies of canned and packaged foods in your pantry. If you want to store enough food for 3 months, just increase your supplies and increase your storage space as needed. Then each week or two, just replace the food you have eaten, always eating the oldest food first. Most foods off the grocery shelf have a 6- to 24-month shelf life. If you constantly eat from your pantry and "rotate" the food, it will never be out of date. Another advantage of this system is if Y2K does not create food shortages, the food you've stored won't go to waste. You just won't have to shop as often after the event. (Figure 2.1)

Figure 2.1 This pantry is stocked with all off-the-shelf grocery items. This food should last four people several months.

You may want to include the nonperishable versions of foods that are often stored in the refrigerator or freezer, such as canned and nonperishable meats (some canned hams need no refrigeration and are good for 2 years), canned and powdered milk, etc. Also be sure to include "treats and sweets" (cookies, candy, gum, chips, etc.) as these are always appreciated in times of increased stress. (Figure 2.2)

Figure 2.2   Almost all grocery items have a one year+ shelf life. Many are good for several years.

The advantage to this approach is that it allows you to eat in a near normal manner during any disruption and should you decide to no longer store the food, you can eat it as you normally would. Think of your home, apartment, or other safe storage space as your personal in-home grocery store. Imagine having supplies of food and other necessary items on hand from which you can draw continuously for up to a year. Imagine everything in constant stock rotation—items consumed are replaced periodically and new items added as they are discovered and enjoyed. Think about having quality foodstuffs to prepare wholesome and nourishing meals, very similar to the meals you are accustomed to eating.

There are several disadvantages to this approach. Because off-the-shelf grocery items are not dehydrated (though you can buy a few dehydrated products, such as potatoes, from the grocery store), they contain water and weigh more and take up more space. They are often not as nutritious as dehydrated or freeze-dried foods. Their shelf life is 12-24 months compared to the 10 to 20 years of their dehydrated or freeze-dried cousins. Grocery items have a broader selection than the other options and will cost less than freeze-dried foods and the same or more than dehydrated.

Planning for 4 to 8 weeks' supply of food takes time, thought, and money. Planning for a 6-12 month supply of food takes a lot of planning, thought, and money. It should start with a family meeting of everyone who will be eating the food to decide what you really want to store. Listen to everyone as each person has different eating habits and stressful times are not the time to force eating preferences on anyone. As you start to form your order, do not be surprised if you start to resist and think, "Do I really need to be doing this? Surely this is really not going to happen." Do not let the effort or cost stop you from preparing. It may be difficult at times for the entire family to remember why they are going to such extremes to prepare when the rest of the world has so little concern. The risk is very definite and real. It is wise to prepare for Y2K. It is foolish to ignore it.

The cost of storing 1 to 6 months of food for a family may be difficult for many of us to arrange. However, given the seriousness of the problem it is necessary. Remember this is not a wasted expenditure. You are simply spending your early 2000 food money in advance. You may want to get together with some neighbors, friends, and relatives and try to buy together in volume to get lower prices. With Y2K the best personal preparation is a well-prepared neighborhood.

Purchasing canned and nonperishable foods in volume should not be viewed as the same as shopping in greater volume at the corner groceries. Considerable money and time can be saved by purchasing from discount price clubs, such as Sam's Club, Price Club, etc. Also, many food wholesalers that sell to restaurants, hospitals, colleges, etc., will sell to the public. They usually require a minimum dollar amount paid in full when you get the food. Many of these companies will even deliver to your house. Check your local yellow pages under "Food Wholesalers." The best approach is to start immediately since some supplies could run short or become more and more expensive.

Building Your In-Home Grocery Store

You'll need to analyze for yourself how much food to store. Given the possible Y2K problems, we would suggest a bare minimum of at least 4-8 weeks' worth. It may be a good idea to store for as long as a year's worth; then you are covered for anything that might happen. And it may save you from having to wait in long lines or from not being able to get the food you want.

The important thing is to keep it simple. You don't need to go out and buy unfamiliar food to prepare an emergency food supply. So, in other words, you don't need to do anything weird. If you like tuna, just buy more of it. You can use regular canned foods like canned tuna, soups, fruit, vegetables, dry mixes, and other foods that you normally use. Other things to include could be pastas and grains. Buy foods that your family will enjoy but are high in nutrition. Also, canned foods don't require cooking, water, or any special preparation.

Just remember, you want to store foods that require no refrigeration and minimum preparation or cooking. Other nonperishable foods can include, crackers, fruit bars, granola bars, bouillon cubes, peanut butter, trail mix, tea bags, coffee, and powdered milk. Be sure baking items require no eggs unless you plan to have powered eggs stored. You can buy powered milk in airtight containers which prevents oxidation. Typically, we don't give this a lot of thought but realize that much of the food at the grocery store that you buy everyday has a year shelf life or more, so you are really okay with a lot of the things you're used to.

Also get a good supply of dried beans, peas, rice, wheat, etc. These can be bought in bulk and are inexpensive, easy to store, and nutritious. If you are getting whole wheat, be sure you have a quality hand-operated grinder.

Also get a good supply of sprouting seeds (alfalfa, adzuki, lentils, mung, peas, triticale, wheat, etc.). Get organic beans from your health food stores. Sprouts, being a live food, are an excellent source of vitamins and minerals. Sprouts contain enzymes that aid in digestion, as well as needed protein, vitamins, and minerals. It's like having a garden in your kitchen. Seeds are small and easily stored until you sprout them. You can sprout easily at home and if you don't know how, your health food store probably has a pamphlet or book. This is perhaps the best of all stored foods.(Figure 2.3)

Stock up on spices, too. Food need not taste bad just because you are operating in a disaster mode. Also, keep an extra supply of multivitamins and other nutritional supplements around. The idea is to keep everyone's spirits up, so you don't want just a bunch of canned tuna and oatmeal. Be sure to get some enjoyable snack food and treats too, like chips, cookies, and candy. In fact, familiar foods are important in times of stress and disaster. This helps keep morale strong and lessens tension and anxiety. You also may want to consider purchasing a food dehydrator to dry your own fruits and vege-

Figure 2.3   Sprouts, easy to store and full of vitamins and minerals, are perhaps the best stored food.

tables. You can even make your own jerky. But remember an electric dehydrator may not be usable if the power is down. There are also many books available on canning, curing, and smoking that you can look into.

Keep in mind any special dietary needs such as food for infants or the elderly. Nursing babies may need liquid formula in case they are unable to nurse. Canned dietetic foods, juices, and soups may be helpful for the ill and elderly. Whatever you do, don't forget pet food! They're completely dependent on us.

As you build up your inventory, you always want to rotate your foods, so you are constantly using and replacing your foods until you can't anymore. Try and use your foods when they are freshest; even canned goods gradually deteriorate. So rotate, rotate, rotate.

The best thing to do is to mark and date your foods so that you always know which foods to use at any given time. The best way to do it is to color code your foods according to the

"Use by" date stamp, not the date you purchased it since different types of foods have different "use by" dates. Most non-perishable grocery store goods will last one year but you still want to rotate as much as you can.

You can use different colored markers or get different colored paper dots at any stationary store. (Figure 2.4) Then, create a color chart and allocate a different color to a different "Use By" month. So, say January is blue; put a blue dot on all the foods you have that should be used by January, a green dot for February, a red dot for March, etc. Or you can have different areas of the pantry shelves set aside for the different months. This way you always know that your foods are providing you with the best nutrition and taste possible. Always eat the food with the closest "use by" date. Unfortunately "use by" dates are not standardized and codes are hard to dic ipher. You may need to just mark them for the month you bought them. Check our www.walton-feed.com/grain.faqs/default\.htm for more storage info).

Figure 2.4   Put colored dots on each product. Each color should represent a different "use by" month. Eat the oldest food first.

GARDENING: You may want to give some consideration to putting in a good garden as soon as the weather allows. Much of our fresh fruits and vegetables come from South and Central American countries, which are very far behind fixing their Y2K problems. You may want to buy and store all needed tools, fertilizers, seeds, insecticides (go organic), etc. When buying seeds, get nonhybrid seeds. Nonhybrid seeds regenerate—the seeds created from their plants can be stored and reused the next year. Hybrid seeds, a genetically altered seed developed and heavily promoted by seed companies to make more money, will only grow once. The seeds from their plants are sterile. Fresh seeds will last 5-10 years if kept cool and dry (which many seeds available in stores have not).[1]

FREEZE-DRIED OR DEHYDRATED FOODS

Another way to store your needed foods is to order what is called "preparedness," "reserve," or "emergency" food from a company specializing in these products.[2] These foods, which are either freeze-dried or dehydrated, offer several benefits in food storage. (Figure 2.5) These advantages are

• Lightweight (as they contain little water).

• Compact.

• More nutritious than many canned foods.

• Their shelf life is often 10 to 20 years.

• They can be as a complete system, in prepacks of one week to one year.

- They are delivered to your home packaged and ready to store.

- Most reputable companies are careful to supply all the needed calories and nutrients.

Figure 2.5   Freeze-dried and dehydrated (low-moisture) foods are often packed in #10 cans. You can store more food in less space with these products.

Perhaps the biggest drawback to this option, other than the cost of the more expensive freeze-dried packages, is that if you do not need these foods, if your normal food supply is not interrupted or quickly restored, then you may not want to eat these foods that are not as tasty as what you are used to.

The purchase of a system represents an investment of between $300 (for basic dehydrated) to $2500 (for better tasting freeze-dried) per person per year. Also, some products are "taste challenged," so be sure you test a few samples before ordering. Also, as early as late 1998 many suppliers were already taking months to fill orders. If you order in late 1999, it may be too late to get your shipment by 2000. If you get a shipment date, be sure it is a real date.

Dehydrated and freeze-dried packaging involves storing dehydrated, dried, and freeze-dried foods in prepacked cans, cartons, etc. Compared to typical consumer food prices in the supermarket, many dehydrated food storage items may be less per serving than the grocery store. Buyers making selective choices normally find great value in dehydrated, dried, and freeze-dried foods in prepacked cans or bulk foods. Virtually every food storage supplier has the capability of selling a pre-packaged plan or "program" of selected fruits, grains, meats, or simulated meats, and vegetables in #10 cans or in bulk. These "programs" can be "one person/one year" or "family of four/six months," etc. These suppliers also provide individual food items from open stock.

Be sure to deal with a reputable company. This is not a large industry. With Y2K increasing demand, many new-comers are entering the market. It can be very difficult to evaluate the different food programs. Costs and claims of "feeds family of four for a year" can be confusing. You can buy a one-person, one-year package for as little as $298 but it is almost all rice, grains, beans, and other staples. True, you won't starve that year but you won't look forward to any meal that year either. You really need to analyze each food package to see how much is your basic staples and how much is the better tasting freeze-dried or dehydrated products. This can be rather complex to do.

SELECTING A FOOD RESERVE SYSTEM

Some day you may actually need to depend on a food reserve system. The purchase of a system represents a sizable investment. The consumer should be discriminating in selecting the manufacturer. The questions and information below provide a valuable process by which one can identify and determine the most suitable food reserve system.

The following questions will assist you in identifying a system for you and your family:

1. Under what scenarios do you anticipate the need for using food reserves?

2. Will you be mobile?

3. Will food preparation facilities, supplies, and fuel be available?

4. Have you determined the length of time you desire the system to sustain you and your family?

5. How many people will be depending upon your food?

6. Are there special nutritional requirements?

7. How important is ease of preparation?

8. Have you considered your budget?

9. How many calories do you require per person?

Considerations

1. PURITY OF INGREDIENTS — Are foods all natural with no artificial preservatives, flavorings, colorings, MSG, or white sugar?

2. FAMILIARITY — Your food system should be familiar everyday foods easily recognizable and reflect a balanced diet offering good taste.

3. PREPARATION CONVENIENCE — Can food systems be prepared with a limited amount of fuel and water?

4. SHELF LIFE — Shelf life of any food reserves is always critical. Excessive heat will shorten the shelf life of all products. A rule of thumb: the cooler the better.

5. PROPER ROTATION —It is important to rotate food reserves into your daily diet.

PACKAGING

Most freeze-dried and dehydrated products are packed in #10 size cans (approximately one gallon) or #2 1/2 size cans (approximately one quart). These cans are heavy-gauge metal and enamel coated both inside and out. Nitrogen-flush (inert gas) and the use of a "state of the art" oxygen absorber in #10 size cans are often used to eliminate oxygen. Both procedures insure the very best in shelf life. Resealable plastic lids are often included in all systems.

See endnotes at end of chapter for recommended food companies.[2]

FREEZE-DRIED FOODS

For instant or quick rehydration of certain dried foods and for products which retain their shape and texture, freeze-drying is the preferred method.[2] (Figure 2.6) The first step in freeze-drying is to rapidly freeze the food. The water content, now frozen, is turned directly into a gas and withdrawn from the food during the next steps, vacuum and heat, thus avoiding the shrinkage. Freeze-dried products include grains, beans, fruits, meats, seafood, pastas, vegetables, and eggs. Often these ingredients are packaged as a complete meal, such as beef Stroganoff or chicken Alfredo, and you just add boiling water.

Figure 2.6   Freeze-dried foods can last 10-20 years. They look and taste like the real thing but can be a little costly. Note smaller one-meal packages.

Freeze-dried foods, the most expensive of the preparedness foods, are also the most flavorful. Many of the meals are quite enjoyable and remain very close to their original food in taste, smell, and texture. If they are not needed for Y2K, you can keep them stored for 10-20 years in case of other problems, or eat them as part of your standard diet.

Advantages of freeze-dried products:

- Retain the original taste and nutritional value of the food.
- Foods are quick and easy to prepare.
- No waste.
- Ideal method for maintaining flavors of meat, poultry, and fish.
- Extends the shelf life of the product.
- No preservatives are necessary.
- Results in a super-lightweight/compact product.
- A wide variety of foods are available.
- Can be packaged as complete meals—not just individual dishes.

Disadvantages of freeze-dried products:

- Can be expensive.
- Some may be "taste challenge."

DEHYDRATED FOODS

The standard method of dehydrating vegetables and spices is to place the items on a conveyor belt and run them through an oven at a high temperature for a relatively short time.[2] (Figure 2.7) Between 90% and 95% of the moisture is removed. Drying is the oldest known form of food preservation. For example, the Egyptians sundried various foods in three days for the Pharaohs; a roasted meal called Pulmenturh was the principal field ration of the Roman legions: and, our American Indians had their pemmican and jerkies. While the technical reasons may have escaped those earlier generations, they all discovered that dried foods kept better and were the only way they could keep variety and quality in their diets.

Figure 2.7   Dehydrated foods will store for 10-20 years and are relatively inexpensive. Be sure you try some samples as some of the products are excellent, others "taste-challenged."

In the raw state, fruits, vegetables, and most other foods contain 80% to 90% water. That water, in combination with heat and/or oxygen, is the principal cause of food spoilage. Hence, the elimination of most of the original moisture from foods extends their shelf life and natural goodness. Since all minerals are stable during heat, oxidation, and storage, the major changes in the nutritional stability and values of foods occur in vitamins. Acidity, alkalinity, heat, light, percent of oxygen, storage temperature, and time are the principal factors that affect the stability of vitamins. Low-moisture foods that are packed in sealed containers from which most of the residual oxygen has been removed and replaced with nitrogen usually retain or sustain higher levels of vitamin stability than is possible with other forms of food. That stability is further protected when such low-moisture foods are stored at constant temperatures of 72°F, or lower.

Some vegetables are more suited to this form of drying than others. This means that with the addition of water, the product rehydrates back to its original state more easily. Preferable items include onions, bell peppers, tomatoes, celery, carrots, and mushrooms. Dehydrated items such as peas, corn, and green beans do not rehydrate as well as freeze-dried. Dehydrated meats are not available so many dehydrated food companies use a vegetable substitute that is flavored to resemble various meats.

You can dehydrate many of your own foods with an air or electric dehydrator. (Figure 2.8) However, sometimes this can be more costly that purchasing the food already dried. Also remember the electric units may be worthless in early 2000.

Low-moisture (dehydrated) foods that are purchased in quantity and used frequently as components in everyday meals are as economical and often times more so than other forms of food when the following factors are considered:

- No seasonal price or quality variances.

Figure 2.8   This electric unit lets you dehydrate many of your own foods. However, electric units may be worthless in early 2000.

- Require no refrigeration or freezing.

- No leftovers or waste.

- No spoilage.

- No peeling, coring, trimming. or washing.

Advantages of dehydrated products:

- Foods are quick and easy to prepare.

- No waste.

- No preservatives are necessary.

- Results in a super-lightweight/compact product.
  - — Long shelf life
  - — Cost-efficient food option

- No peeling, coring, trimming or washing.

- Provide year-round fresh like appearance and taste.

- Require no refrigeration, freezing, or other expensive, energy-dependent storage.

- Require much less space than other forms of food.

- Are not subject to infestation or bacteria growth.

- Are easily and quickly measured into precise servings that eliminate leftovers and waste.

- Are ideal for most kinds of special diets.

Disadvantages of dehydrated products:

- Some may be "taste-challenged"

- A limited variety of foods are available

- Can be slow to reconstitute

Proper Food Storage

STORAGE: The preferred method of storing foods is to store everything inside in your living space. These keeps them dry, away from extreme heat and cold, and hopefully rodents (not

Figure 2.9   MREs (meals-ready-to-eat) are another option. However, these are expensive, costing from $4-6 per meal per person. They require no cooking.

above 70 degrees and not below freezing). You can make use of normal pantries and closets and then consider other storage areas. There is a lot of room under beds, under furniture, on top of kitchen cabinets, in a corner, in a guest room, etc.

If storing inside is impossible, garages and sheds can be considered but extreme heat, cold, moisture, and rodents may make some foods unusable—a harsh reality if you ever need them. Can goods should do OK in an unheated garage if temperatures can be moderate, even if it means a small heater on bitter cold nights. (Figure 2.10, Figure 2.11) Always leave your canned goods in cardboard boxes, if they came in them. It helps insulate the food. If your area is very cold, you may want to buy the styrofoam that comes in sheets like plywood and wrap it around your stored food to help prevent freezing. A deep freeze that lasts several day may burst a canned product in an unheated garage. However, if the canned goods freeze even a little, their nutritional value is diminished.

Figure 2.10 If you must keep your food in the garage, protect it from freezing, extreme heat, and rodents. These large plastic storage sheds may

Figure 2.11   Each storage shed can hold approximately one-year supply of preparedness food for two people. Water in background is two-month supply.

Your canned and jarred products can store easily for as long as the "sell by" or "use by" date listed on each. Even after this date, they can be consumed safely for quite awhile. The "sell by" date has a large margin of error in these types of food. Foods that are packaged in plastic or paper bags or boxes should be stored unopened in plastic buckets or boxes to further protect them from moisture and rodents. (Figure 2.12) You may want to place a moisture or oxygen absorber in each bucket. Keep food covered at all times.

Figure 2.12 Bulk foods can be stored in plastic buckets like these. Also leave all foods in their original packaging. The lid in front is a "screw-on" type, which makes opening much easier.

Basically, there are four storage deterrents to keep in mind:

- Temperature
- Light
- Humidity
- And vermin infestation

STORAGE TIPS

- Foods should be kept dry and cool, in a dark area, if possible (not above 70 degrees and not below freezing).
- Keep food covered at all times.

- First In-First Out (FIFO)

- Do not place directly on cold floor or against exterior walls

- Open food containers carefully so that you can close them tightly after each use.

- Crackers, cereals, cookies, and breads should be kept in plastic bags, then in tight containers.

- Store packages of sugar, dried fruits, and nuts in screw-top jars or airtight cans to protect them from pests.

- Put other boxed foods like cereals in tightly closed cans or metal containers.

- Inspect all food containers for signs of spoilage before using.

- Rotate foods as you can, dating your food supply. Inspect your food periodically.

REFRIGERATION: Needless to say, if the power goes out, so will you freezer and refrigerator. However there are some things you can do to keep your foods cold. Food can stay usable in both the freezer and the refrigerator for several days, if the doors are not opened too often. On New Year's Eve (before midnight), make a list of everything you have in the refrigerator and freezer and where in each they are located. This will allow you to keep the door open for as short a time as possible. If the power goes out, wrap blankets around the freezer or refrigerator. This will help insulate them and keep the food even longer.

It would be a good idea to have several large picnic-type coolers. (Figure 2.13) You can place food in these and set them outside in colder areas and this will keep food cold. Also there are refrigerators available that run off propane (LP) gas. These are available through your propane dealer. If you have one of these and a 500-1000 gallon above-ground or buried tank, you're set for refrigeration without electricity.

Figure 2.13   The cooler on the right will work better than the refrigerator if the power goes out. You can buy propane refrigerators which do not need electricity.

HOUSEHOLD SUNDRIES

It takes more than food to supply yourself with everything you need to make meal preparation run as smoothly as possible. For example, make sure you have a nonelectric can opener, a grain grinder, and disposable utensils. (Figure 2.14)

Figure 2.14 A good grain grinder would be a good item to add to your food collection.

Here are some other items to include on your shopping preparedness list:

- Nonelectric can openers (3)

- Paper plates, napkins, cups to reduce the need for washing dishes

- Aluminum foil (better than dirtying pans)

- Heavy-duty Ziplock bags of all sizes

- Measuring cups/spoons

- Trash bags

- Disposable baby bottle liners, if needed

- Several nonelectric can openers

Endnotes

1. Seeds Blum Co., 800-528-3658, www.sseedsblum.com

2. We recommend the companies listed below as they have been in the industry for many years and have a known product.

RECOMMENDED FREEZE-DRIED FOOD COMPANIES

- FOOD PLUS (distributors for AlpineAire), 1-877-FOOD-PLUS, www.foodplusonline.com. (Be sure to ask for the "Y2K discount or free gift" for readers of this book.)

- NITRO-PAK, 1-800-866-4876, www.nitro-pak.com (Be sure to ask for the "Y2K discount or free gift" for readers of this book.)

RECOMMENDED DEHYDRATED FOOD COMPANIES

- FOOD PLUS (distributors for AlpineAire), 1-877-FOOD-PLUS, www.foodplusonline.com. (Be sure to ask for the "Y2K discount or free gift" for readers of this book.)

- PERMA-PAK, 1-877-353-FOOD, www.permapak.com. (Be sure to ask for the "Y2K discount or free gift" for readers of this book.)

- NITRO-PAK, 1-800-866-4876, www.nitro-pak.com. (Be sure to ask for the "Y2K discount or free gift" for readers of this book.)

- MILLENNIUM III FOODS, 1-888-883-1603, www.millennium3foods.com. (Be sure to ask for the "Y2K discount or free gift" for readers of this book.)

- AMERICAN HARVEST FOOD, 1-800-500-3858, www.americanharvestfoods.com

KITCHEN CHECKLIST

(Courtesy of Y2K Women, www.y2kwomen.com)

Pantry

Variety of Beans

- ❏ Great Northern
- ❏ Kidney beans
- ❏ Lentils
- ❏ Navy
- ❏ Pinto

❏ Red beans

❏ Sprouting peas, etc.

❏ _____

❏ _____

Rice and Grains

❏ Barley

❏ Cold cereals

❏ Corn (popcorn and field corn)

❏ Flour (wheat, white, and other varieties)

❏ Instant hot cereals (oatmeal, Cream of Wheat, etc.)

❏ Oatmeal

❏ Rice (brown, white, or combination)

❏ _____

❏ _____

Meat and Fish

❏ Chicken

❏ Corned beef

❏ Salmon

❏ Soy protein—Taco filling, BBQ Beef, etc.

❏ Spam

❏ Tuna

❏ _____

❏ _____

Oil (Cooking Agents)

❏   Baking powder

❏   Baking soda

❏   Oils

    ❏   Butter-flavored Crisco

    ❏   Shortening (like Crisco)

    ❏   Olive oil (stores best)

    ❏   Vegetable oil (canola stores well)

❏   Mayonnaise (small jars if there is no refrigeration)

❏   Yeast (in a pinch you can use sourdough)

❏   _____

❏   _____

Salt

❏   Iodized

❏   Rock salt

❏   Sea salt

❏   _____

❏   _____

Sugar (Sweeteners)

❏   Brown sugar

❏   Corn syrup

❏   Equal or Sweet N'Low (just to have on hand for us die-hards!)

❏   Honey

❏   Maple syrup

❏   Molasses

❏   Powdered sugar

❏   White sugar

❏   _____

Pasta

❏   Macaroni

❏   Shells

❏   Spaghetti (with jars of heat-up sauce)

❏   _____

❏   _____

Dairy Products

❏   Dry Buttermilk

❏   Milk (canned evaporated)

❏   Parmesan cheese

❏   Powdered butter/margarine is available (like Butter Busters)

❏   Cheese powder (This sounded gross to me until I realized it was what was in the boxes of prepared macaroni and cheese!)

❏   _____

❏   _____

Eggs

❏   Powdered eggs

Vegetables

Dehydrated vegetables

❏   Beets

❏   Broccoli

❏   Cabbage

❏   Canned and bottled vegetables

❏   Carrots

❏   Celery

❏   Creamed corn

❏   Green beans

❏   Instant mashed potatoes

❏   Peas

❏   Soup and stew blends

❏   Spinach

Fruits

❏   Apples

❏   Applesauce

❏   Apricots

❏   Bananas

❏   Canned and bottled fruit juices

❏   Flavored apples

❏   Fruit cocktail

❏   Lemon juice (bottled does not have to be refrigerated)

❏   Oranges

❏   Peaches

❏   Raisins

❏   Small boxes of juice for kids

❏   Variety of dehydrated fruits

❏   _____

Soups

❏   Canned chicken/beef stock

❏   Cream of Mushroom, broccoli, etc.

❏   Soup starter

❏   Variety of canned soups (Chicken Noodle, Tomato, etc.)

❏   Vegetable soups

❏   _____

❏   _____

Spices and Flavorings

❏   Baking cocoa

❏   Basil

❏   Bouillon (beef and chicken)

❏   Canned tomatoes

❏   Chili powder

❏   Cinnamon

❑   Garlic (powder, minced, salt)

❑   Green peppers

❑   Ketchup (Tomato products are a regular in most American kids' diets and they will often eat things with ketchup on them they wouldn't otherwise! Ketchup is high in sugar and kids are almost addicted to it!)

❑   Mustard

❑   Onions (powder, flakes, salt)

❑   Oregano

❑   Pepper

❑   Salad dressing

❑   Salsa

❑   Soy sauce

❑   Teriyaki sauce

❑   Tomato paste

❑   Tomato powder

❑   Tomato sauce

❑   Vinegar (plain and flavored)

❑   Worchestershire sauce

❑   Bay leaves (I've found bay leaves are great for keeping bugs out of flour and cereal so you might want to get an extra large bottle!)

Seeds for Sprouting: (essential for vitamins)

❑   Alfalfa, mung, radish, sprouting peas, lentils, etc.

Fresh Root Vegetables

❑ Butternut squash

❑ Potatoes (kept in cool, dark place)

❑ Waxed rutabagas

❑ _____

❑ _____

Odds and Ends

❑ Biscuit mix

❑ Canned mushrooms

❑ Cans of nuts (peanuts, cashews, etc.)

❑ Cereals

❑ Crackers

❑ Pancake mix

❑ Pickles

❑ Salad dressing mix (Italian, Ranch—Good Seasons type)

❑ Waffle mix

❑ _____

❑ _____

Beverages

❑ Coffee (vacuum sealed but already ground if there is a problem with electricity)

❑ Gatorade

❑ Hot chocolate

❑ Individual coffee bags

❏   Instant coffee

❏   Noncarbonated drink mix like Tang, Kool-aid, etc.)

❏   Nondairy creamer

❏   Sodas (I have lots of friends who say they won't survive without Diet Coke!)

❏   Tea

❏   Wine in boxes with Mylar bags

❏   _____

❏   _____

Quick and Easy to Prepare Foods

❏   Canned chili, canned soups, canned meats, peanut butter, etc.

❏   Freeze-dried or dried or no-cook foods

❏   Instant soups (like Ramon or any soup you just add water to)

❏   Macaroni and cheese

❏   Spaghetti sauce

❏   _____

❏   _____

Psychological Foods or Comfort Foods

❏   Brownie mixes

❏   Cake mixes

❏   Cheerios

❏   Chocolate chips

❏   Chocolate milk mix

❏   Crackers

❏   Dream Whip

❏   Hard candies

❏   JELL-O

❏   Jelly

❏   Popcorn

❏   Powdered drinks (with added vitamin C like Tang)

❏   Puddings

❏   _____

❏   _____

Baby Food and Formula

(Note: I absolutely encourage breast feeding! However, if a woman is under stress from a crisis, it is very possible for her not to have an adequate milk supply. Supplementation may be necessary!)

❏   Powdered formula (A pediatrician I spoke with said canned formula wouldn't last as long and was more expensive. Have some bottles of sterile water on hand to mix with the formula.)

❏   Pureed fruits and vegetables

❏   Hand grinder to puree table food

❏   _____

❏   _____

Vitamins

❏   Children's liquid or chewable vitamins

❏   Liquid dietary supplement (like Ensure)

❏   Mineral supplements (like calcium)

❏   Multivitamins

❏   Vitamin C

Water

❏   Drinking water

❏   Distilled water

❏   Soda water

❏   Water for cleaning and bathing

Remember, as James Steven's says, "Buy what you eat and eat what you buy."

Cupboards

Cooking utensils

❏   French press coffeepot (the kind you add hot water to, let steep, and then press the grounds down)

❏   Pressure cooker

❏   Kettle

❏   Cast iron cookware

❏   Skillet

❏   Dutch oven

❏   Bread pans

❏   Waffle iron

❏   Griddle

❏   Wok

❏   Plastic storage containers

❏   _____

Checklist Garage

❏   Dog/cat food in airtight containers (like metal garbage cans) to keep rodents out

❏   Kitty litter

❏   Pet supplies (vitamins, pet medications like heartworm preventative, flea and tick treatments, chew toys, shampoo, etc.)

❏   Bug extermination

    ❏   Ant, roach spider killer

    ❏   Bee/wasp killer

    ❏   Rat/mouse traps

    ❏   Fly traps

    ❏   _____

    ❏   _____

STORING AND TREATING WATER

You wouldn't want to be in an airplane, you wouldn't want to be in an elevator, and you wouldn't want to be in a hospital...(government and business leaders) are not thinking about the contingency plans that they ought to be thinking about today, not waiting a year from now...(these) need to be put into place to minimize the harm from widespread failures.

—Sen. Chris Dodd, Year 2000 Tech Committee,
Senate Hearings into Y2K, June 12, 1998

When microprocessors at Coff's Harbor's water storage facility were tuned in to 2000 dates in a simulation, the entire chemicl holdings—normally used in carefully regulated amunts to purify water—were dumped into the water in one hit. Experts say this would have the potential to kill the town's entire population.

—From the *Sun Herald*, an Australian Newspaper,
April 26, 1998.

We believe that the Year 2000 problem is a lot bigger than the President and the Administration have admitted. We think it will cost more than 4 billion dollars (approved by Congress) to solve it. There are estimates as high as 30 to 40 billion.

—Rep. Newt Gingrich, CNN, June 21, 1998

55

THE PROBLEM

Nothing is more essential than water. Without it we would die in several days (as compared to weeks without food). Without it disease is born and spread, cleanliness becomes impossible, modern life degenerates quickly. It is assumed that unless Y2K disruptions are so catastrophic as to cripple all governmental services (a possible scenario but improbable) any interruption of our water supply will be quickly restored (obviously this may not be the case if you use your own well. See "wells" at the end of this chapter). However, the water delivery may be only for several hours per day and the water may not be safe. And there is always the possibility of no water at all for awhile. Therefore, you must have clean, drinkable water stored and available to you before the event

Local water companies may draw on a water source hundreds of miles away. This requires computers and pumps and valves, many with microprocessors and chips (embedded systems) that are needed to keep the water flowing. Water treatment, such as the addition of chlorine, is controlled by computers. If the computers or chips in these systems fail due to Y2K, the system can stop or become contaminated. When we asked a local North Carolina water company if they were prepared in late 1998, they did not know their pumps had chips that needed to be checked and after one week, no water. Maybe after 1 minute if their chips failed.

Another problem that may occur if we lose heat and/or water in the middle of winter is that the pipes can freeze and burst. When the water is restored and the pipes thaw, you can flood your house. *Be sure to turn off the water into your home and to drain the existing water in your system by opening the lowest faucets if your pipes are in danger of freezing.* Also be careful in using the water immediately after water service is installed.

The first supply coming through the system may be silty or contaminated. Don't use it as drinking water until local officials have declared it safe.

Using contaminated water for drinking or cooking can lead to problems which range from a minor upset stomach, such as you'd have with the flu, to life-threatening illnesses, such as amoebic dysentery, viral infection, cholera, typhoid, or hepatitis. Also, Y2K may lead to environmental pollution. Chemicals may get into our water supplies from storage yards, manufacturing plants, etc., that experience a computer failure. A chemical leak in Bhopal, India several years ago killed 1200 people and devastated a community. In fact if you live near a potentially dangerous environmental threat (chemical, nuclear plant, etc.) you may want to spend the New Year's weekend with friends or relatives until you know your area is safe. Therefore, you must have a stored supply of clean water *and* a way to treat more water until normal water delivery is restored.

THE SOLUTION

WATER STORAGE

As with food, in the event of a possible Y2K-related disruption of our infrastructure (power, water, transportation, etc.), we recommend a minimum of 2-4 weeks' supply of clean, drinkable water, for each family member, be stored. However, should you feel that more storage, say for 6 to 12 months, is best, there are water storage products on the market for large-volume storage of water. Be sure to store water that you are used to drinking, water from your own tap. This will avoid any problems created by adjusting to new water. Before the event this is rather an easy and inexpensive task to do. After the event, who knows.

Drinkable water should be stored in new, thoroughly cleaned, heavy-duty, plastic containers with tight-fitting lids. Be sure your containers are food grade and approved for water storage by the FDA. If you are also storing water for bathing and clothes washing, this can be stored in any uncontaminated container (new large garbage cans will work and are very cheap). Clean glass containers can also be used but breakage (especially if the water freezes) and weight are a problem with these. Avoid metal containers as they can rust. For drinking water, avoid reusing light weight food grade containers, such as used milk and drink containers. Milk containers will leave a taste. These containers can freeze and burst and often leave a residual taste. However, cleaned two-litre drink containers can be used if freezing is not a factor and the budget is (see Figure 3.1). Also be sure water is stored away from paint, chemicals, fertilizers, and petroleum products; the objectionable odors can penetrate the "breathable" bottles. Water should not be stored where it will get over 100 degrees, freeze, or be in direct sunlight. Before using any containers, even new ones, wash them out with baking soda and warm water and rinse with clean water.

Store the water you are presently drinking so no adjustment will be necessary. You will need 1 gallon per person per day for drinking and cooking (more for children, nursing mothers, people with illnesses, in hot areas, or when doing physical exercise). For staying cleaner, extra water is needed. Another gallon per day per person is recommended for cleaning (and yet more if you plan to flush toilets). Remember pets will also need water. If you are a family of four, storing water for 2 weeks, you will need to store 4 people x 1 gal/day x 15 days=60 gallons of water. Another 60 gallons is recommended for improved cleaning. That's 120 gallons. This can be accomplished with 120 one-gallon containers, 25 five-gallon, 4

Figure 3.1   If necessary, water can be stored in clean two-litre drink bottles. However, these can freeze and burst. Heavy duty water containers are preferred.

thirty-gallon or 1 one-hundred and twenty five-gallon. (Figure 3.2) As with food, rotate the water on an ongoing basis so that it keeps its quality and taste.

The choice of what size containers to use depends on several factors. Spacewise, a large 250-gallon may not work. If a tank this large is stored on a deck or second floor, be sure it can hold the weight. These large tanks are cumbersome to use but most have spigots so you can easily draw off smaller amounts. Large water tanks can be placed outside or in the garage (if it does not freeze), inside the house, or in the attic but only directly over a load bearing wall. You can get these in rigid tanks for $200-500

Figure 3.2   Water containers come in everything from 5 to 50,000 gallons. These 5- and 55-gallon containers work well for residential use.

or in inflatable bladders for about $100.00. (Figure 3.3) They have a 200-gallon FDA approved inflatable bladder for about $100.00. You can even get a large bladder that hold 700-2000 gallons. Waterbeds can be used (around 350 gallons) but use these only for washing and bathing, not drinking, unless it is a new waterbed without algacide in the water.

Mid-size water tanks, 30-100 gallons, are also very affordable. (You can get a FDA approved 55-gallon drum for $38.00. Figure 3.4) Rubbermaid and several other plastic companies make 5-6 gallon water cans for around $8-10. (Figure 3.5) Try to find one that is stackable so you can save space. If you are using the larger tanks, be sure you buy either a hand pump or a battery-operated pump to transfer the water to smaller containers. (Figure 3.6)

Figure 3.3 These 200-gallon water bags cost only $90. They store enough water for 4 people for 50 days.

Figure 3.4 Fifty-five-gallon water drums cost under $40. Note hand pump for transferring water to smaller containers. Also note metal lid opener.

Figure 3.5   Five-gallon containers work well and are often stackable.

The 5- or 35-gallon plastic drums are not particularly portable. There are flexible 5-gallon plastic water containers that have the advantage of folding up completely when empty and some flexibility when full. (Figure 3.7) If you need to travel, these are a good idea. There are also portable 5-gallon showers available in most camping sections of department stores.

In many areas, where rainfall is scarce, people use cisterns. A cistern is usually a tank built into the ground that catches and stores rainwater that has been diverted from rooftops, porches, etc. (a 2"-rain can collect 150-300 gallons). By building it into the ground, it keeps the water cool, which in turn prohibits the growth of bacteria. Though earlier models were built from brick or mortar, you can now use plastic or metal containers.

Figure 3.6 Small water pumps can be hooked to a car battery and used to transfer water from large containers to small ones.

Since most houses are already equipped with a gutters, a cistern system can actually be quite easy to set up. You can just divert your gutters into 55-gallon drinking water drums, tanks, waterbeds, or even into a large plastic swimming pool. Many people choose to divert the first few minutes of the rainwater away from the cistern; this washes away dirt, debris, pollutants, bugs, etc. Put some fine screen over the ends of the gutters or hoses to filter out large particles, and then treat the water for drinking as outlined below. Also cover it from sunlight, which promotes growth of algae.

As you store your water, you may want to add aerobic oxygen to it. This has stabilized oxygen molecules that kill anaero-

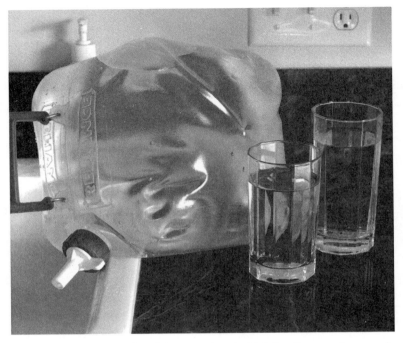

Figure 3.7 These collapsible water jugs hold 2.5 gallons and are easily stored when empty.

bic (infectious) bacteria while leaving untouched bacteria that are harmless or good for you. It also aerates the water by adding oxygen to it, which keeps some harmful bacteria from growing in it. The added oxygen is also considered a health benefit when the water is consumed. You can store water for up to 10 years with aerobic oxygen added to it but it is a little costly at about $14.00 to treat 50-75 gallons. (Figure 3.8) It is not really needed if you plan to store your water in late 1999 and use it in early 2000. On New Year's Eve, you should also fill up every bathtub, hot tub, pot, and other container in the house. Keep them filled for a few days and if everything is OK, celebrate by pulling the plugs.

Figure 3.8   You can add stabilized oxygen to your water to help kill bacteria. A good option but a little costly.

Normal Water Usage	
Drinking and Cooking	1 Gallon
Shower (1 per day)	25 Gallons
Toilet Flush (10 flushes @ 3 gallons each)	30 Gallons
Hand Washing (Twice @ 2 gallons each time)	4 Gallons
Brushing Teeth (Twice @ 1/2 gallon each time)	1 Gallon
Total	61 Gallons

Minimal Water Usage	
Drinking and Cooking	1 Gallon
Shower (1 solar shower or sponge bath every other day)	2 Gallons (optional)
Toilet Flush (with use of boat potty, composting toilet, etc.)	1 Gallon
Hand Washing (Twice @ 1/4 gallons each time)	1/2 Gallons
Brushing Teeth (Twice @ 1/8 gallon each time)	1/4 Gallon
Total	4 and 3/4 Gallons

LOCATING AND TREATING WATER

If a disaster catches you without a stored supply of clean water, you can use water in your hot-water tank, in your plumbing and in ice cubes. As a last resort, you can use water in the reservoir tank of your toilet (not the bowl), but purify it first.

Water beds hold up to 400 gallons, but some water beds contain toxic chemicals that are may not be fully removed by many purifiers. If you designate a water bed in your home as an emergency resource, drain it yearly and refill it with fresh water containing two ounces of bleach per 120 gallons. You may use the water for toilet flushing only.

To use the water in your pipes, let air into the plumbing by turning on the highest (elevation) faucet in your house and draining the water from the lowest one. To use the water in your hot-water tank, be sure the electricity or gas is off, and open the drain at the bottom of the tank. Start the water flowing by turning off the water intake valve and turning on a hot-water faucet. Do not turn on the gas or electricity when the tank is empty.

Do you know the location of your incoming water valve? You'll need to shut if off to stop contaminated water from entering your home if you hear reports of broken water or sewage lines. Also, in cold climates, frozen pipes may burst if there is no heat. Shut off the water and drain the pipes if there's a strong possibility of this occurring.

If you need to find water outside your home, be sure to purify the water before drinking it. Avoid water with floating material, an odor, or dark color. Use salt water only if you distill it first. You should not drink flood water. Outdoor water sources include rainwater, streams and rivers, ponds and lakes, natural springs, and snow.

Locating additional water may be as obvious as looking around the house. Before New Year's Eve you may want to fill all sinks, bathtubs, hot tubs, pools (even inflatable pools can hold a lot of water). Your hot water heater can hold 30-50 gallons. Local creeks, ponds, lakes, springs, etc., are also sources of water, though obviously this water must be treated before it is consumed. (Figure 3.9)

Never drink questionable water unless it has been properly treated. Contaminated water can threaten your health, even your life. Bad water can cause anything from stomach problems to such life-threatening illnesses as amoebic dysentery, cholera, typhoid, hepatitis, viral infection, etc. Symptoms can include nausea, vomiting, diarrhea, fever, feelings of general discomfort, fatigue, and weight loss.

To treat any questionable water you can either boil it, chemically treat it, or run it through a water purifier. Remember just because water is clear does not mean it is safe. You can get water from any stream, creek, lake, etc., and if properly treated, it will

Figure 3.9   Water from most lakes, creeks, and springs can all be used for drinking if properly treated.

be perfectly safe. Be sure you have identified possible sources of water before the event. No matter which option you choose to go with, be sure you understand how to properly treat water. Your health or life may depend on it. Getting sick early in 2000 may be problematic if medical facilities are strained. There are several approaches to treating water:

- Water purifiers and filters

- Chemical treatment

- Boiling

WATER PURIFIERS AND FILTERS

We highly recommend a quality water purifier or filter. However, the water filters that can be purchased at many retail stores, are not as effective as quality water purifiers and filters and most are not suited for emergency preparedness. The standards of filters sold in many retail stores must meet, are much lower than those for purifiers. Some good water purifiers (*General Ecology*, Katadyn, British Berkefeld)[2] can remove not only chemical contaminants like pesticides, insecticides, PCBs, etc., but they also can remove many pathogens and bacteria, such as Giardia and Cryptosporidia. Cryptosporidia, or Crypto, is the most frequent cause of water-borne illness in the United States today. In 1993 in Milwaukee it caused 400,000 illnesses and more than 100 deaths. Though Crypto can be killed by boiling, it will not be killed by chlorine or bleach-treated water. "Purifiers" (as opposed to filters), by U.S. federal guidelines, are required to protect against all three types of disease organisms including those caused by viruses.

It is probably a good idea to put a permanent water purifier attached to your water line under the kitchen sink. However, for Y2K you may want to get a portable unit in case no water is coming out of your tap and you are using stored water. Water purifiers come as portable units ($75.00, Figure 3.10), under-the-counter units ($200-500, Figure 3.11), and even an under-the-counter unit that can be used with a hand-pumped emergency preparedness kit with a $150.00 adapter if your tap water stops running. With these units no boiling or chemical treatment is required. Be sure to get extra cartridges when you buy your unit. The manufacturer will specify how many gallons can be purified with each cartridge.

Figure 3.10 Portable hand-pumped water purifiers like these effectively treat any water by passing it through a filter. This model removes all harmful contaminants and bacteria.

Figure 3.11 Under-the-counter water purifiers work fine, as long as the water is running. This unit will be installed under the sink and can also be used with a hand pump, shown in foreground.

BOILING

Boiling is a common approach to treating water. You must bring the water to a rapid boil for at least 10 minutes (15 in higher altitudes)—and this can use up a lot of precious cooking fuel. Boiling water will also leave a flat taste that can be improved by adding a pinch of salt and aerating the water by passing it from one container to another. Also though boiling will get rid of bacteria, it will not remove pesticides, insecticides, and other chemical pollutants. (Figure 3.12)

Figure 3.12 Boiling water will kill pathogens that cause disease but will not remove contaminants that water purifiers do.

CHEMICAL TREATMENTS

Water can be treated chemically to remove dangerous bacteria and viruses but not Crypto, Giardia, or other larger pathogens. As with boiling, chemical treating will not remove pesticides, insecticides, and other chemical pollutants. Chlorine, in the form of fresh (less than one year old) regular household bleach (5.25% solution), is the most common chemical added to the water. Be sure no soap, phosphate, or scent is added. Use 8 drops per gallon for clear water, 16 drops for cloudy (for 55 gallon use 1 oz. if clear, 2 oz. if cloudy). The water will have a slight chlorine odor at first but let it stand for at least 30 minutes. It may seem strange to be adding chlorine to your drinking water but remember that's what they are doing at your local water treatment plant. (Figure 3.13)

Figure 3.13 Common household bleach (unscented) can effectively treat water. Bleach contains the same chlorine that is used to treat city water.

Treating water with household bleach
(5.25% sodium hypoclorite unscented)

Water Quantity	Water Condition	Bleach
1 quart	Clear	2 drops
1 quart	Cloudy	4 drops
1 gallon	Clear	8 drops
1 gallon	Cloudy	16 drops
5 gallons	Clear	1/2 teaspoon
5 gallons	Cloudy	1 teaspoons
55 gallons	Clear	1 ounce
55 gallons	Cloudy	2 ounces

Use bleach less than one year old!

You can also purchase tablets that are specifically made for treating water wherever camping goods are sold. These are usually a 2% tincture of iodine. Just follow the instructions on the bottle. You could buy tincture of iodine (2%) and use 3-5 drops per gallon. However, iodine usually leaves a taste (you can add a little Kool-Aid) and odor and should not be used by nursing or pregnant women or people with thyroid problems. Also, it can be rather expensive treating large amounts of water with iodine. Iodine, like chlorine, is not effective against Crypto. (Figure 3.14)

Figure 3.14 Iodine tablets can also treat water but leave an unpleasant taste and smell.

WELLS

Many people do not rely on central water systems but rather have their own wells (Figure 3.15). Unless there is a major environmental disaster nearby that pollutes the underground water table, this water should be fine. The problem is getting the water out of the ground without electricity. You can get a generator that you can hook to your well pump. Just be sure you know how to hook it up and that the generator has the capacity to drive the pump (many of which are 220 volts).

Figure 3.15 Wells are a good source of water if you have electricity to power the pump.

There are small buckets available that allow you to take the pump out and lower a small bucket to manually draw out the water but this can slow and exhausting (unless you have energetic kids around). However, pulling a submersible pump can be a major chore. There are manual pumping systems that are easier and systems that can use a pump that can run off solar or wind power.[2] Also it may be a good idea to replace your existing 50-100 gallon pressurized well storage tank with a larger one so that each time you fire up the pump it will store more water.

WHERE TO FIND PRODUCTS LISTED IN CHAPTER

1. Watertanks.com: www.watertanks.com, 1-877-420-8657. They have tanks from 55 to 50,000 gallons.

2. Jade Mountain, 1-800-442-1972, www.jademountain.com. (Be sure to mention #241 and get your "Y2K discount or free gift" for readers of this book) The Survival Center, 1-800-321-2900, http://survivalcenter.com

3. General Ecology, Inc., (1-800 441-8166, www.general-ecology.com).

CHECKLIST FOR WATER

❑   Water

❑   Water containers

❑   Aerobic oxygen (optional)

❑   Water pumps (manual or battery-operated)

❑   Iodine—2% (optional)

❑   Water purifier with extra cartridges

❑   Bleach (5.25 percent sodium hypochlorite unscented, less than 1 year old)

HEATING

The magnitude of the potential Year 2000 problem in the regulated energy industries (electrical, gas, etc.) is not yet known....Compilation of this information is inadequate...Without testing, the potential impact of Year 2000 errors could cause...a ripple effect across a portion of the grid.

—Kathleen Hiring, Chief Information Officer, Federal Energy Regulatory Commission (FERC)

A survey conducted in June (1998) by the US Senate's Y2K committee found that only 20% of companies involved in power generation, transmission and distribution had completed a Y2K assessment. At least one-third of all telecommunications companies may experience at least one failure of a mission-critical system, resulting in sporadic interruptions of service.

—cio.com (Website for *CIO Magazine*)

Let's stop pretending that the Y2K isn't a major threat to our way of life. There is too much at stake for such uninformed wishful thinking. Perhaps, the time has come as though we are preparing for a war. This may seem extreme and unnecessary. However, if we prepare for plausible worst-case Y2K scenarios, then perhaps we can avoid at least some of them.

—Ed Yardeni's keynote address to Bank for International Settlements, April 1998

THE PROBLEM

In areas where the weather will likely be cold in January, alternative heat must be provided in case there is a loss of electrical power or an interruption in coal, oil, or gas deliveries. The concept that losing power in cold climates can threaten lives was brought home on January 8, 1998, when parts of the United States and Canada lost power for several weeks in an ice storm. Emergency efforts were strained trying to rescue people trapped in their homes in freezing conditions. Many had resorted to burning valuable furniture in energy-inefficient fireplaces. Three to five million people were without power, some for as long as 22 days—all in freezing conditions. Twenty-two people died as a result of the storm.

Should Y2K failures cause large areas of countries in cold climates to lose the ability to provide heat to their citizens, people may not be able to rely on the usual emergency efforts to help them. We must go into this event assuming we will have ourselves, our neighbors, and our immediate community to help. Remember even if your fuel suppliers assure you that they will be Y2K ready, they may not be able to predict their supply chain. Will the Mid-East, a major source of our petroleum products, catch up as they are far behind on their Y2K repairs? Will ships and ports operate effectively? As early as January 1999, one major U.S. oil company (Chevron) has already announced they will not finish in time and disruption may occur at their refineries. Oil platform have thousands of embedded systems that may cause problems. Will they pump oil in early 1999?

Even if we can get refined petroleum products to every country, will their transportation systems (trains, trucks, planes, etc.) be able to adequately distribute the fuel, both to homes for heating and to electrical plants for power generation. And finally, each household must determine two other potential problems. Even if we have heating fuel, will a loss of electrical power disable our central heating systems, most of which will not operate without power. The other problem is that embedded chips in our wall thermostats or heating system itself may not properly roll over.

Even if the equipment manufacturer assures you they are OK, are you willing to risk your comfort, and perhaps your life, on their guarantee? Therefore, it is imperative that every person living in a cold climate, provide enough fuel, and a nonelectric heating system, to keep warm through their winter of 2000. In extremely cold climates, where life can be threatened, we would even recommend a back-up system (two kerosene heaters, two propane heaters, etc.) should your main alternative system experience problems.

Finally, there will almost certainly be the problem of hoarding and increased demand on suppliers. You need to make sure you oil tank is full and do not leave filling the tank to the last second. Your oil supplier may be too busy in December 1999 to get to you.

Another problem that may occur if we lose heat and/or water in the middle of winter is that the pipes can freeze and burst. When the water is restored and the pipes thaw, you can flood your house. *Be sure to turn off the water into your home and to drain the existing water in your system by opening the lowest faucets if your pipes are in danger of freezing.* Also be careful in using the water immediately after water service is installed. The first supply coming through the system may be silty or contaminated. Don't use it as drinking water until local officials have declared it safe. Also be sure you know how to turn off your gas and electrical power as well.

THE SOLUTIONS

In order to be assured of heat for space heating and cooking, you must find a source of fuel that does not rely on delivery to you after Y2K (perhaps even shortly before when the rush is on). That means storing enough fuel, in a secure, safe, and dry area, on your property or otherwise accessible to you, to last as long as the cold weather might last. You do not have to heat the entire home, but just enough of it to effectively live in. And remember that may be larger than you think. You may be taking in friends and relatives who are in need.

Everyone who thought you were nuts when you warned them to prepare, will remember that you are Y2K-prepared. Yes, they were wrong, and may have insulted us with their laughter, but we can't leave them out in the cold. So you may want to get ready to know your neighbors, friends, and relatives more closely than you would otherwise. However, looking back on this period, this building of relationships with so many different people, as we prepare for and experience Y2K, may be one of its great blessings. Modern life has driven us apart as a society. We are in our homes watching TV, on the Net, playing with our computers. Y2K may be just what we need to bring us back together. A study found that when survivors of the years of London bombing during WW II were interviewed 30 years after the bombings, over 60% said that period was the best years of their life. People suffered together, worked together, helped each other, served each other. Life had meaning, where so much of our modern life has become trivialized.

In evaluating your options, and in determining how much fuel to store, you must decide on what your "comfort zone" and your "Y2K prognosis" are. "Comfort zone" means how much of your home do you plan to heat, for how many hours of the day, to what temperature. The whole house? One room? One day room and one night room? 60 degrees, 65, 70? Heating an entire house, 24 hours a day to 70 degrees will require much more fuel than one large room for 16 hours at 62 degrees. However, the thought of living in one room with all your relatives, may convince you that storing enough to heat two rooms is well worth the money. Be aware that storing enough fuel to get through winter may involve large amounts of fuel, which may mean a substantial investment and wise planning for safe secure storage.

"Y2K prognosis" means how long do you believe a Y2K-related emergency might last, and therefore how much fuel do you want to store, though there is no way to predict the duration of Y2K-related disruptions, or if there will even be any. However, in situations that may be life threatening, not just inconvenient, err on the side of caution. If cold weather could threaten your life, not just make you uncomfortable, have enough fuel for the winter. Also food, water, and essential prescription medicines and medical equipment must be planned assuming a one-year interruption.

THE OPTIONS

Their are six common sources of fuel that will work in this situation:

• Propane heat

• Generators

• Wood heat

• Kerosene heat

- Oil heat
- Coal Stoves
- Solar heat

NOTE: In addition to the above options make sure you have a generous supply of warm clothes, gloves, wool socks, caps, scarves, blankets, and sleeping bags around. Also you may want to keep some rolls of plastic around. You can cover the windows inside and out and this will cut much heat loss.

PROPANE

Propane gas (also called LP gas) is perhaps one of the best alternatives as it is often used to heat homes in normal conditions. Propane should not be confused with NG gas (or natural gas). Propane is stored on your property in large tanks (often buried in the ground). (Figure 4.1, Figure 4.2) NG is piped into your home from a central source which might be affected by a Y2K problem. The advantages of propane are many. It is a clean, efficient source of heat that can easily be stored in large volumes (5-1500 gallons) in buried or above-ground tanks that are provided at a nominal charge from the gas supplier. The larger tanks are enough for almost any winter. It can be used as your sole source of heat, both in normal and electrically challenged times. Its only real disadvantage is that burying or storing gas in above-ground tanks may not work in every home.

Figure 4.1   Large propane tanks like these can hold 500-1000 gallons which can last a full winter in many areas. There are above-ground or in-ground tanks.

Figure 4.2   Once buried, the propane tank is barely noticeable.

If you have central propane heating, your heat may not work if the power is out as these central units require some power for blowers and ignition systems. To solve this, there are two alternatives. Check with the heating manufacturer to see if you can hook your system in to a small generator to provide this power. You can even hook up propane generators ($4-10,000.00) or propane refrigerators[3] to your propane tanks.

Or perhaps the best option is to install small wall propane heaters that do not require electricity. (Figure 4.3) These can be installed in place of, or in addition to, the central propane system. These small units can be installed for $300-500 each and can heat one room or several if strategically placed. They do not require any electricity and with several of these with 500 to 1000 gallons of propane in your tank, your heating problem is solved. Unvented propane spot heaters can easily be installed in any room except the bedroom. In bedrooms most states require using a small (6") vent pipe to the outside. You can even buy these units that look like fireplaces with gas logs. You may also want to consider adding energy-efficient propane gas logs to your existing fireplace. There are also small portable propane heaters. Avoid the ones that use the small cylinders and get the ones that can hook to 5-gallon tanks. (Figure 4.4)

GENERATORS: Many people, when they think about power outages, immediately think about getting a generator. This may be a good idea to power some appliances (lights, freezer, TV, washer, fans, blowers for central heating systems or gas hot water heaters, etc.). However, using a generator to creater heat, either for cooking or space heating, requires a large generator and a large supply of fuel. This is a very expensive option, often requiring large storage tanks and expensive gen-

Figure 4.3 These propane wall heaters require no electricity, as will a propane furnace. Wall heaters can produce up to 30,000 BTUs—enough for a small house or several rooms.

erators professionally wired into your electrical system. Even then, it is an inefficient way to heat a home. (For more, see Generators in the Lighting chapter.)

WOOD HEAT

Wood heat is a pleasant and inexpensive option, though not practical in every situation. Its advantages are that in many areas wood is abundant, inexpensive, safe to store. It is pleasant, healthy (if moisture is added to the air), and obtainable in some areas for free by the homeowner with the proper equipment. And once a wood heating system is installed, it can be a

Figure 4.4   There are also small portable propane heaters. Avoid the ones that use the small cylinders and get the ones that can hook to 5-gallon tanks.

source of ongoing enjoyment and wise contingency planning after the Y2K problems are resolved. However, it has several disadvantages. It is not practical in all homes (New York City co-ops may object to wood stoves retrofitted into their buildings), it is expensive to install, and the heating source cannot be moved from room to room.

You can have several cords delivered to your property in early 1999 (before the rush). Be sure that it is good dry hardwood, the proper length for your stove or fireplace, and can be stored in a secure, dry area where theft will not be a problem. A cord (4' feet wide by 4' tall by 8' long or 128 cubic feet) can cost anywhere from $40-120, depending on location and the quality of the wood and whether it is stacked neatly or dumped. (Figure 4.5) Wood pellet stoves are also a possibility. These use small processed wood pellets, instead of chopped wood. These can be very efficient but be sure you store enough pellets. They may be impossible to find in early 2000.

Figure 4.5   If you plan to use wood, be sure you store enough for the winter of 2000.

It is difficult to give general rules as to how much wood you will need. In varies according to the stove, the wood, the size and outside air infiltration of the space being heated. The best thing to do is to test your stove or fireplace and then calculate from there how much wood you will need.

If you are depending on wood as your heat, also have the following:

- A chainsaw with fuel

- A secure storage area

- Kindling and fire starters

- A gas jet in your fireplace to start the fire (optional)

- Newspaper

- Wooden, waterproof matches

- Log carrying bag

- A good grate

- Fireplace heat deflector (optional, but a good idea with energy-inefficient fireplaces)

- Fireplace tools (brush, shovel, bellows, poker, etc.)

FIREPLACES: There are several options as to what type of wood heater to use. However, be careful in thinking that your existing fireplace will provide much heat. Typical wood fireplaces in residences are mostly decorative and 80-100% of the heat goes up the chimney. Some even make the house colder as they burn by drawing cold air into the home to feed the fire with air. Energy-efficient inserts and heat reflectors can be installed in these types of fireplaces to increase their efficiency but typical wood burning fireplaces are still not an effective way to heat the home. However, you may add a very energy-efficient set of propane gas logs to your existing fireplace, to make it a viable alternatives. These logs are 80-95% efficient compared to the 0-20% of most fireplaces.

You can get energy efficient fireplaces or inserts that work much better. Two companies make energy-efficient built-in fireplaces.[1] (Figure 4.6) Units cost from $1200-2000 plus installation. Instead of 0-20% efficiency, these units can give 50-70% efficiency. The units have optional electric blowers that can spread the heat around, but these require electricity, which may require a generator if the power is off. However, these more efficient units must be either built into a new home or installed after an existing unit can be removed. This can be very expensive or impossible, in which case, going to a wood stove is advised for wood heat.

Figure 4.6   This energy-efficient wood fireplace is 50-60% efficient compared to 0-20% efficiency of standard residential wood fireplaces.

WOOD STOVES: Wood stoves are by far the preferred way to heat with wood. They are less expensive, easier to install, more efficient, and more available than energy-efficient wood fireplaces. (Figure 4.7) There are some excellent energy-efficient wood stoves that can be installed in most existing homes. Be sure you get a serious wood stove, not one made mostly for decorative purposes. Compare pricing, features, efficiency ratings, how much wood they burn, etc. Get an efficient stove that you can damp down and burn though the night, so it only requires stoking in the morning. There are even small portable wood stoves on the market that can be moved with a small 3-4" flue pipe poked out a window.[3] (Figure 4.8) However these are good as emergency backup only as they burn a lot of wood and usually will only heat a small room.

If you are having a wood stove retrofitted into your home, either follow the instructions carefully or leave it to a professional. The last thing you want is to proudly walk over to your wood stove if the power goes off in 2000 and light her it up and burn your house down. And remember the local fire department may have a somewhat slower response rate in the early post-Y2K world (like days, instead of minutes).

WOOD STOVE ACCESSORIES: Should you decide to go with a wood stove, you may want to consider several options that can be fitted on to some wood stoves. There are water heater units that will allow you to heat your water as you heat your house. Also there are oven units, often inserted into the flue pipe, that will allow you to bake with the waste heat going up the flue. There are even heat exchangers, which capture the heat going up the flue, that can be inserted into your flue pipe to capture the waste heat.

Figure 4.7   A good energy-efficient wood stove can heat several rooms or a small house. Some only need to be refueled every 12-24 hours.

KEROSENE

In the past kerosene was seen as a smelly, dirty way to heat a home. However, in recent years odorless, sootless kerosene heaters have made kerosene heating a viable alternative. (Figure 4.9) As with all open flame heating, there is a greater fire risk, but this is negligible if you follow the manufacturer's

Figure 4.8   Small, portable wood camp stoves require only a 4" flue and can be moved.

safety instructions. If used properly, they are safe, inexpensive, efficient, and give out minimal odor. The advantage of a portable kerosene heater is that they can be moved from room to room as your needs change during the day. It can be placed in the living room during the day, the kitchen at meals, and in the bedroom at night. The disadvantage is that it cannot provide whole house heating without operating units in many rooms and fuel storage can be a problem.

Figure 4.9   Kerosene heaters are safe, odorless, and can be moved from room to room. Be sure to follow manufacturer's safety instructions and directions to avoid fire and burns.

Be sure to check the specification sheet with the heater to see how much kerosene it burns per hour. Then calculate how many hours each day times number of days you want to store to calculate your fuel needs. For instance, a typical portable kerosene heater produces 23,000 BTUs by burning 1 gallon every 6 to 8 hours. So if you use it 16 hours a day you will need 2-3 gallons/day. This may not seem like a lot but if you have four months of winter you will need 240-360 gallons. That's lots of 5-gallon cans or one large storage tank. And that only heats one heater for two-thirds of the day. Storing flammable fuels should always be done away from the house and not in attached garages or sheds. Most manufacturers recommend that the kerosene be less than 6 months old, so you may not want to start storing until late summer of 1999, or add a fuel additive to extend its life. (Figure 4.10)

Figure 4.10 This is enough kerosene to run one heater, 24 hours per day for only 20 days. You will need much more to get through the winter in many areas.

When using these alternate fuels be sure you have three safety devices:

* Fire extinguisher
* Battery-operated or photoelectric smoke detector
* Battery-operated or photoelectric carbon monoxide detector

(Kerosene stoves are safe when used as instructed but all open flames use oxygen and give off carbon monoxide. And all open flames have inherent fire risks.)

OIL HEAT

Many older homes are heated with heating oil through central furnaces. The oil is stored in large tanks placed outside the house, usually above ground. (Figure 4.11) Some of these will work without electricity, others won't. The older the unit, the more likely it is to work. The older units were gravity fed. New units often use electrical pumps and switches. Also the older floor units did not use electrical blowers but rather simply allowed the heat to rise. Be sure to test your unit. Turn it on and the power off and see what happens.

There are free-standing oil stoves that can be retrofitted in homes, much like a wood stove. (Figure 4.12) These can create up to 30,000-BTU output and yet uses less than 1/4 gallon of oil per hour at its highest setting.[3] These are often gravity fed, requiring no power. They cost $1000-2000.

Figure 4.11   Heating oil is stored in large tanks and is often gravity fed to heater.

Figure 4.12   Free-standing oil stoves that can be retrofitted into homes, much like a wood stove. Many require no electricity.

COAL STOVES

In the past coal was a common source of home heating fuel. Coal use in homes has died out in the United States but now there is a new type of coal stove on the market that can be installed in any home just like a wood stove. In fact, it is easier than adding a wood stove in that it only requires a 6" vent that can vent directly out any wall or roof. (Figure 4.13)

These stoves use low-cost anthracite coal that is available in most areas. They are odorless and smokeless. They are very energy-efficient and burn twice as hot as wood. They can heat a three-bedroom house and are easy to operate, many with gravity hopper systems. Many can burn for 24 hours and can be thermostatically controlled.

Figure 4.13 Coal stoves can be added to any home. These newer models burn twice as hot as wood and only need to be refueled every 24 hours.

SOLAR

Solar may definitely be a viable option to heat your water, at times even your home, as well as create electricity in the event of an infrastructure failure. We will not spend much time here on solar, not because we do not feel it is a good way to go, but rather because its expense, lack of availability of solar equipment if the demand gets high, and the brief time left before Y2K make it not feasible for most people. Also solar works in relationship with the amount of available sunlight. Heating or creating electricity with solar in the middle of winter in New Mexico will be quite different than in the Seattle area.

SOLAR WATER HEATERS: Heating your hot water with solar is more affordable than heating your home. (Figure 4.14) Several panels on the roof, for several thousand dollars, will do it in most areas. However, if the water system

Figure 4.14   Solar panels can heat your water but remember it takes water pressure to work.

is not working, you may not have pressurized water, so these will be of little use.

SOLAR SPACE HEATING: Heating a home with solar can cost tens of thousands of dollars and may not be feasible for many retrofits. Some houses are designed to orient toward the winter sun and capture the heat in masonry, adobe, or brick mass walls inside the house that act as heat sinks. These homes are called passive solar, and though adding on a passive solar room is possible, for the most part homes must be designed and built to be passive solar.

An active solar system involves capturing the sun's energy with solar panels, usually on the roof, and then using something like water to bring the sun's heat into mass storage areas. Though this too can be retrofitted on some homes, it is expensive.

PHOTOVOLTAICS (ELECTRICITY FROM SOLAR): Photovoltaic cells can now create electricity from sunlight. (Figure 4.15) These are available and practical, though to install a large enough system to take your entire home off the grid (ah the grid, the poor old maligned grid) can cost thousands of dollars. You can get a small system of cells, inverters and storage batteries for around $1000 that in many areas will create enough electricity to run lights and TVs and radios. This may be a good option as a backup in the event we lose the grid for a period of time. At least you will have lights and can use small appliances.[3]

SOLAR OVENS: Often your heating source can also serve as your stove. There are some very inexpensive solar ovens on the market that can cook a meal in minutes for free just by sitting in the sun. Also your standard two-burner camp stoves

Figure 4.15 Photovoltaic cells such as these can turn sunlight into electricity. You can power a light or an entire house.

can be used but again be sure you have enough fuel. There are gelled ethanol products on the market that come in small cans. These gels light in the can and can be used safely, odorless, and cheaply for cooking (and some heat).

Having said this about solar, we believe that Y2K will steer us back in the direction of renewable, nonpolluting energy sources (solar, wind, wave, hydro, etc.). Once we realize how vulnerable we are with large centralized systems, we will begin to see the wisdom of a smaller decentralized system. If we have a wind or solar system in our houses generating a minimum level of electricity, we will never be prone to system failures again. We would have free, constant non-polluting energy forever. The technology is there but as yet the will is not there to develop these. Y2K may create that will. A picture of the Las Angeles rooftops in the 1930s (notice we did use the "19") shows almost 20% of the homes with solar water panels. They disappeared as the electric an/gas companies paid homeowners to remove them and hook into their centralized systems.

WHERE TO FIND
PRODUCTS LISTED IN CHAPTER

Endnotes

1. Heat-N-Glo of Savage, MN, 1-800-669-4328, www.heatnglo.com and Majestic Fireplaces of Huntington, IN, (1-800-227-8683, www.vermontcastings.com.

2. Riley Stove Company of Townsend, MT, 406-266-5525.

3. Jade Mountain, 1-800-442-1975, www.jademountain.com. (Be sure to mention #241 and get your "Y2K discount or free gift" for readers of this book.) The Survival Center, 1-800-321-2900, http://survivalcenter.com

CHECKLIST FOR HEATING

ALTERNATIVE HEATING

- ❏ Propane heat
- ❏ Generators
- ❏ Wood heat
- ❏ Kerosene heat
- ❏ Oil heat
- ❏ Coal stoves
- ❏ Solar heat

FUEL

- ❏ Propane
- ❏ Kerosene
- ❏ Wood
- ❏ Oil
- ❏ Coal
- ❏ Gasoline (for generator if needed)

OTHER

- ❏ Warm clothes
- ❏ Gloves
- ❏ Wool socks
- ❏ Caps
- ❏ Scarves
- ❏ Blankets
- ❏ Sleeping bags

FOR WOOD HEATING

❑ A chainsaw with fuel

❑ A secure storage area

❑ Kindling and fire starters

❑ A gas jet in your fireplace to start the fire (optional), newspaper

❑ Wooden, waterproof matches

❑ Log carrying bag

❑ A good grate

❑ Fireplace heat deflector (optional, but a good idea with energy-inefficient fireplaces)

❑ Fireplace tools (brush, shovel, bellows, poker, etc.)

SAFETY

❑ Fire extinguisher

❑ Battery-operated or photoelectric smoke detector

❑ Battery-operated or photoelectric carbon monoxide detector

LIGHTING WITHOUT
ELECTRICITY

All the government agencies will not be done on time. There will be some failures,... Right now as a country we do not know where we stand on water, power and telecommunications. If you don't have water, power or telecom, you can't get the job done,

—Joel Willemssen, U.S. General Accounting
Office (GAO)

In the most dramatic warning yet of impending computer crisis in the government, a congressional panel said Wednesday that 37 percent of the most critical computers used by the federal agencies will not be updated in time to handle dates in 2000 and will be subject to widespread failure. The new estimate calls into question assurances by the Clinton administration that it is moving quickly enough to avert serious outages.

—The Wilmington (Delaware) *News Journal,*
March 5, 1998

Any company that neglects this looming problem is simply asking for trouble. If a firm is eventually hit by a Year 2000 breakdown, it will probably be put out of business- not by the authority of any regulator, but by the power of the market itself. And its not just the institutions I'm concerned about. Its the investors who do business with them. A Year 2000

*breakdown could do incalculable damage to investors' fi-
nances, and could undermine their confidence in our entire
financial structure.*

—Arthur Levitt Jr., Chairman, Securities and
Exchange Commission

THE PROBLEM

Should there be a temporary lapse in electrical power, alternative sources of lighting must be provided for in advance. Lighting is essential. If your house is plunged into darkness at 5:30
each afternoon, chances are your mood will follow. Acquiring
emergency lighting before the event, this is relatively inexpensive and easy. After the event, it becomes very difficult, perhaps
impossible (ever try to find a candle or batteries after they have
announced a hurricane is heading your way).

As with cooking, alternative methods of lighting are inexpensive and easily obtainable. However, do not plan as you
would for a three-five day event. This means do not depend on
battery-operated lighting, unless you plan to use batteries
rechargeable by either the sun[1] or by cranking up a generator.
However using your generator to recharge batteries is like cutting butter with a chainsaw and solar rechargers are slow and
depend on available sunlight.

Recommended alternative lighting includes

- Generators
- Solar lantern, flashlights, and electrical systems
- Gas lanterns
- Kerosene lanterns
- Candles
- Battery-operated lanterns and flashlights

GENERATORS

We have listed generators first not because we think everyone should buy one for Y2K (we don't) or that they are the recommended source of alternative lighting (not always), but because many people, when they think about power outages, immediately think about getting a generator. (Figure 5.1) This may be a good idea to power some appliances (lights, TV, washer, fans, blowers for central heating systems or gas hot water heaters, etc.).

Figure 5.1   A small generator can supply all your lighting needs (plus a TV or radio) while using much less fuel than the larger units. Be sure to get extra spark plugs, lubricating oil, and oil filters.

If you can afford it, buying a small generator to provide lighting makes some sense. However, the other methods listed below will also work at a fraction of the cost. If you can afford a generator, you will probably find many uses for it in a Y2K electrically-disrupted world. Small generators can be used to run a video, play music, start your washing machine, charge a battery, run a computer, power a TV, and many other things you would never think of until you were without power. You simply start the generator and plug appliances and lights directly into it, or more likely, since generators should never be run in a living area, into extension cords plugged into the generator. Be sure to use heavy duty extension cords, not the light-weight ones meant for one or two lights. Also never run the generator indoors or in the basement as the fumes are dangerous. If you run it in a garage, be sure to leave a door or window open to the outside for ventilation.

If you are considering buying a generator give it a lot of thought and don't assume bigger is better. The larger the generator the more fuel it will demand. If Y2K disruptions last for months, you would need to store a large amount of fuel. Smaller generator may well serve your needs, cost less and require less fuel than larger units. Also larger units are getting more scarce as we approach the event. By early 1999 already many larger units are taking months to deliver.

You can buy a 1500-1850-watt generator for around $400 at any home center. This will be more than enough to run lighting and small appliances. You can even run your washing machine or gas dryer. It would probably run your refrigerator but when cold foods are available in the stores, your own power is probably not far behind. A $700 Honda generator that has only 650 watts but uses less fuel than the 1500-1850-watt generators, is much quieter and will last much longer.

You can jump up to 5000+ watts and power your whole house but these cost money and take lots of fuel. You can wire them directly into your electrical box but have this done professionally as it is very dangerous. If done incorrectly you can not only ruin your electrical system and generator but also potentially electrocute power company lineman working on the lines. We do not recommend this approach unless money is not a concern and you are determined to live as near as normal life as possible no matter what happens.

In choosing a generator you can also choose from several different fuel sources. Some generators can even run on several different fuels but again these are more expensive. Be sure to check the specs and see how long each generator will run on a gallon of fuel. A 650 kw watt gas generator will run 8 hours on 1 gallon. A 6000-watt gas generator will need 6 gallons for the same hour. You will need six times more fuel for the 6000-watt over the 650-watt—not a good idea unless you need the added wattage. (Figure 5.2)

Propane (as described above) is one possibility. These propane generators cost $3000 and up but are very quiet, fuel-efficient, and dependable. You can store large volumes of propane (LP gas) in below- (500-2500 gallons) and above-ground (5-500 gallons) tanks. Most local propane suppliers will rent you tanks at a nominal yearly fee. Propane generators are expensive but never clog. They are the cleanest and do not smell. A large quantity of the fuel is easy to store and does not age after a year, as will gasoline and diesel. There are even converters that can turn a gas generator into a propane generator for around $300.

Gasoline is the most common and least expensive type of generator. They also require more fuel to create the same wattage as produced by either diesel or propane. Gasoline

Figure 5.2   Plastic sheds like these make excellent storage for fuel. Be sure it is kept a safe distance from the house.

may start to degrade after one year. Gas generators are available from 500 watts upward. They are the most common generators and can be found at any home center or power generator dealer. Some are quite loud, so check the decibel ratings (Honda has some very quiet generators). It is best to buy a generator with "full pressure lubrication." These will last much longer than "splash lubrication." Also try to get a "brushless" unit.

Diesel is more dependable and diesel fuel will last longer than gas but these generators cost more and diesel fuel may be harder to get post-Y2K. Diesel may be noisier but they are very dependable and more efficient than gas. They may be somewhat harder to start in cold weather.

Comparison of Generators (600 KW at 75% power)

Fuel	Gallons Per Hour
Propane	.22/gal.
Diesel	.46/gal.
Gas	.75/gal

If you buy a generator, learn how to work it before the event. You don't want to be sitting in your garage on New Year's Eve at 12:20 AM reading the owner's manual with a flashlight and trying to fill it with gas. Start you generator every two months to keep openings clear. After it has run a few minutes, turn off the gas line from the tank (if there is one) and let the generator run out of gas. This will help the lines from clogging. Always have several extra spark plugs available if your generator uses them. Also keep the fuel tank and all storage tanks topped off so they do not sweat and drip water in the fuel. Shake your generator a little before starting it to mix any water that may have gotten in the tank. You may want to add a gas stabilizer or saver to the tank as well. As always, store your fuel in a safe, dry, secure location but never indoors, in the garage, or attached to the house. Keep a fire extinguisher near by and a battery-operated fire alarm in the storage area.

SOLAR LANTERNS AND FLASHLIGHTS

In the last 20 years solar technology has developed to the point that now solar lanterns, flashlights, radios, water pumps, etc., are all viable alternative emergency equipment. (Figure 5.3) Solar lanterns now cost around $100.[1] (Figure 5.4) These units will provide light for 8 hours on a full charge (full charge is 8 hours in direct sunlight, longer on cloudy or hazy days or wintertime). They have a solar cell that you put in the sun (or toward the sun on cloudy days) and this charges the battery in the unit. After the initial purchase, your lighting is free and non-polluting forever. You do not need batteries or to store dangerous fuel.

Figure 5.3   All of the these lighting devices are solar powered.

There are also solar-powered flashlights, radios, and battery chargers that we recommend. Another thing to consider is to buy several of the solar outdoor pathway lamps. These are rather inexpensive (around $50 at any home center) and several brought inside every night can provide ambient lighting. (Figure 5.5) There are even solar-powered flood lights with cells placed on your roof (be careful though—the noise on the roof may not be a late Santa but a covetous neighbor on Jan. 2, 2000). (Figure 5.6)

Figure 5.4   Solar lanterns are an excellent choice. They will charge even on cloudy days and will burn 8 hours on a full charge.

Figure 5.5   These solar lights are made for outdoor walkways but can be brought inside for ambient lighting.

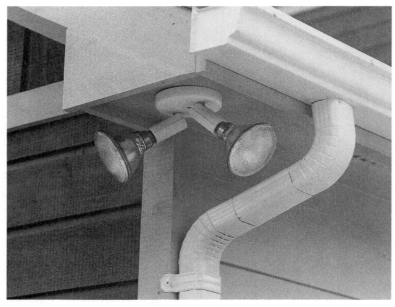

Figure 5.6   Even standard floodlights like these now come in solar units.

You can also now buy small solar electrical systems. These involve solar cells (photovoltaics) usually installed on the roof, toward the sun. These cells create electricity, which is stored in batteries. You can then attach various 12-volt lights and appliances (radios, TVs, videos, fans, water pumps, etc.) to these batteries and presto—free, clean energy. Small systems that will power several lights or appliances cost around $1000-2000. Larger system that can power everything in your home can cost tens of thousands of dollars. Wind generators are also viable if you live where there is a lot of wind.[1]

GAS LANTERNS

Gas lanterns have been the favorite of campers and fisher-men for decades. With these lanterns you must pump up the tank with a built-in plunger for a few pumps to put the fuel under pressure. (Figure 5.7) Recently, a propane and butane model has been introduced but these require that you have a supply of small canisters (unless you can get one that hooks to a larger tank). (Figure 5.8) These lanterns provide a very bright light (the same as a 200-watt bulb) and even give off enough heat to take a chill off the room if the weather is not too cold. They are fairly efficient.

Figure 5.7   These hand-pumped, two-mantle, dual-fuel camp lanterns can burn white or standard gasoline. They give off 200 watts of light but make an annoying hissing sound. There is now a new kerosene version available.

Figure 5.8   These propane gas lanterns work well but require a supply of small propane canisters. Some units can be hooked to larger 5-gallon tanks. Be sure to have a supply of extra mantles. Also cook stoves and small heaters are available.

A two-mantle lantern will burn 40 hours on a gallon of fuel. If you use it for four hours per night you will need 3-4 gallons per month. (A two-burner propane will burn 4.5 hours on a 16 oz canister.) The dual fuel models can burn either white gas or car gas and are recommended for this event. Be sure you have a good supply of extra wicks, as they break often. One major drawback with these lanterns is they make a hissing noise. This is very irritating after an hour reading a book so you may prefer the quiet of kerosene, candles, or solar lighting. You can keep the bright dual-mantle lantern for when you need bright lighting. As always, store your fuel in a safe, dry, secure location but never indoors, in the garage or attached to the house. Keep a fire extinguisher nearby and a battery-operated fire alarm in the storage area.

Two mantle gas lantern fuel consumption

Period	Fuel Consumed per 4 Hours
Day	1/4 Quart
Week	3 Quarts
Month	3 Gallons
Year	36 Gallons

KEROSENE LANTERNS

Kerosene lamps and lanterns of all styles have been popular for centuries. (Figure 5.9) We've seen them in every western we've ever watched. For the most part they are simple devices with wicks, globes, and a container for the kerosene. They come in everything from the railroad swinging lanterns to ornate parlor lamps. (Figure 5.10)

Figure 5.9   Old-fashioned kerosene lamps work well. Keep the wicks trimmed to avoid smoking and be careful—they are a fire hazard. Be sure to get extra wicks.

Given today's technology, a kerosene lantern seems a bit old fashioned and out of place. Kerosene lanterns are an effective and fairly safe lighting source. There are now scented lamp oils which replace kerosene. (Figure 5.11) This lamp oil is generally available in retail stores. Make sure the oil is approved for use in your lamp.

Kerosene lamps and lanterns are a good source of dependable, inexpensive lighting. They give off a slight odor (you can

Figure 5.10   These kerosene "railroad" lanterns work great outside, where wind is an issue.

add scents) and will smoke if the wick is not trimmed periodically. Also, remember to never grab the globe at the top while the lamp is burning. It's hot! We recommend a few kerosene lights and ten gallons of fuel.

There is a kerosene lamp on the market, Aladdin, that works better than all the rest. (Figure 5.12) It burns brighter and with no smell.[2] They are beautiful lamps. However, you will need several extra mantles as they are rather delicate.

There is a difference in lighting quantity and quality, as the kerosene lantern is quite dim when compared to the two-mantle gas lantern (except for the Aladdin). The light output of a kerosene lantern is comparable to a 40- to 60-watt light bulb. The

Figure 5.11   Lamps using scented oils have become popular recently.

gas lantern is equivalent to a 200-watt bulb. However, kerosene lamps burn only about 1/4 the fuel of the gas lanterns.

As a rule of thumb, the typical kerosene lantern burns approximately 1 ounce of fuel per hour. Burning at the rate of 4 hours each day means one lamp would burn 1 gallon per month. A gas lantern needs 3-4 gallons per month. As always, store your fuel in a safe, dry, secure location but never indoors, in the garage, or structure attached to the house. Keep a fire extinguisher near by and a battery-operated fire alarm in the storage area. Remember to add an additive to your to extend their life.

Figure 5.12 Alladin Lamps are kerosene lamps that burn much brighter than standard kerosene lamps. Be sure you have extra mantles—they're fragile.

Kerosene lantern fuel consumption

Period	Fuel Consumed per 4 Hours
Day	4 oz. (1/4 pint)
Week	1 Quart
Month	1 Gallon
Year	12 Gallons

CANDLES

Candles are an obvious option for emergency lighting but don't think the decorative wax candles you have laying around the house are the way to go. (Figure 5.13) Many of these candles will last no more than an hour or so. In fact, these can be a real fire hazard as they tip over easy and drip. They should not be used for emergency purposes.

Figure 5.13 Common household candles like these should be avoided in emergencies. They burn quickly and are a fire hazard.

There are now emergency candles on the market, no bigger than a chicken pot pie, that will burn for 120 hours. The best options are the candles that were designed for emergencies. (Figure 5.14) There are two types of emergency candles available for camping, storage, and emergency purposes. We recommend the type made of hardened wax in a can (Nuwick, $13 for 120 hours) with the capability of utilizing several wicks (usually no more than two is recommended) simultaneously so you can increase the brightness, and even warm food over them.[1] They can boil water in 15 minutes and fry an egg in 5. (Figure 5.15, Figure 5.16)

Figure 5.14   These candles were all made for emergency use. They are long burning and safer when used as directed.

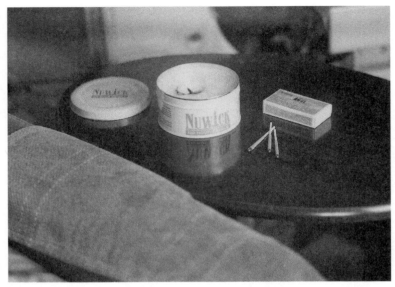

Figure 5.15 These candles will burn for 120 hours and are hard to tip over. You can add an additional wick for more light.

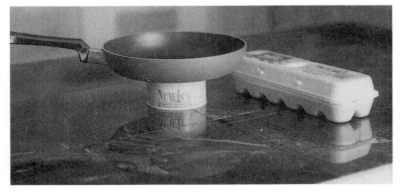

Figure 5.16 This emergency candle can even cook food when two wicks are used.

BATTERY-OPERATED FLASHLIGHTS AND LANTERNS AND MORE

In an emergency, battery-operated lighting is the first thing that comes to mind. (Figure 5.17) In the event of a hurricane or ice storm, where power may be out for only a few days, and then only in one area of the country, these devices would suffice. With Y2K, where power could be out for much longer periods and over a much broader area (relax we'll get the lights turned back on and you can live without electricity for awhile and be happy), these devices should not be relied on as your sole lighting source. Your batteries will soon die and supplies gone. New Conventional "D" cell batteries will power a light 5-8 hours. Older batteries have a shorter life and long-life batteries a longer life than conventional. You can get rechargeable but that assumes electricity to recharge them, in which case why would you need emergency lighting?

Figure 5.17 It is good to have some battery-operated flashlights around but once the batteries are gone they're useless.

You may want to consider solar rechargers, windup Baygen flashlights and radio (you wind a crank and get light or music), or solar lanterns and flashlights.[1] There are even small solar cells that you can place in the sun and will run a radio. (Figure 5.18, Figure 5.19)

Figure 5.18 Windup flashlights and radios are new on the market and require no batteries. You wind for 30 seconds and get 3 minutes of light. Note one on left is also solar powered and has a radio.

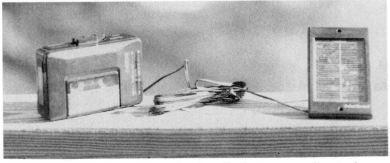

Figure 5.19 There are even small solar cells that you can place in the sun that will run a radio.

There is also a new product on the market called the Porta-Power to Go.(Figure 5.20) It is a portable power backup system that has a variety of usages. It can power DC loads such as lights. Use an inverter (optional) and run typical AC loads such as TVs, computers, radios, powertools, and indoor lighting. The Porta-Power to Go power system can even jump-start your car. Weighing under 20 pounds, its built-in handle makes it easy to tote along. An internal long-life battery is rechargeable with solar (optional), a generator, AC current, or 12-volt DC. Great for emergency backup power.[3]

Figure 5.20 The Porta-Power to Go is a portable power backup system that has a variety of usages. It can power DC loads such as lights, run typical AC loads such as TVs, computers, radios, power tools, and indoor lighting.

Figure 5.21 Wind generation can also be used to create electricity and power several lights or small appliances.

WHERE TO FIND PRODUCTS LISTED IN CHAPTER

Endnotes

1. Jade Mountain at 1-800 442-1972 or www.jademountain.com. The Survival Center, 1-800-321-2900, http://survivalcenter.com

2. Aladdin Industries at 1-800-456-1233.

3. SunSolarSystems at 336-775-0240, www.webaccess.net/~sunsolarsystems.

CHECKLIST FOR LIGHTING

LIGHTING ALTERNATIVES

❏   Generators

❏   Solar lantern, flashlights, and electrical systems

❏   Gas lanterns

❏   Kerosene lanterns

❏   Candles

❏   Battery-operated lanterns and flashlights

FUEL

❏   Kerosene

❏   Gasoline

❏   Batteries

❑   Solar battery recharger

❑   Candles

❑   Lamp oil

OTHER

❑   Extra candle wicks

❑   Extra lantern mantles

❑   Extra kerosene or oil lamp wicks

❑   Extra lightbulbs for flashlights, solar lanterns, etc.

SAFETY

❑   Fire extinguisher

❑   Battery-operated or photoelectric smoke detector

❑   Battery-operated or photoelectric carbon monoxide detector

NONELECTRIC COOKING
APPLIANCES

*I am very, very concerned that even as government and busi-
ness leaders are finally acknowledging the seriousness of this
problem, they are not thinking about the contingency plans
that need to be put into place to minimize the harm from
widespread failures.... I think we're no longer at the point of
asking whether or not there will be any power disruptions, but
we are now forced to ask how severe the disruptions are going
to be.... If the critical industries and government agencies don't
start to pick up the pace of dealing with this problem right
now, Congress and the Clinton Administration are going to
have to...deal with a true national emergency.*

> —Senator Christopher J. Dodd, (D-CT), at the first
> hearings of the Senate Special Committee on the
> Year 2000 Technology Problem, June 12, 1998

*When people say to me, 'Is the world going to come to an end?'
I say, 'I don't know.' I don't know whether this will be a bump
in the road— that's the most optimistic assessment of what
we've got, a fairly serious bump in the road—or whether this
will, in fact, trigger a major worldwide recession with absolutely devastating economic consequences in some parts of the
world... We must coldly, calculatingly divide up the next 18
months to determine what we can do, what we can't do, do*

what we can, and then provide for contingency plans for that which we cannot.
— Senator Robert F. Bennett (R-UT), chair of the Senate Special Committee on the Year 2000 Technology Problem, in a speech June 2, 1998, to the Center for Strategic and International Studies.

I have no proof that the sun is about to rise on the apocalyptic millennium of which chapter 20 of the Book of Revelation speaks. Yet, it is becoming apparent to all of us that a once seemingly innocuous computer glitch relating to how computers recognize dates could wreak worldwide havoc.
— Senator Daniel Patrick Moynihan (D-NY)

THE PROBLEM

As with heating and lighting, most all of our cooking equipment is reliant on central sources of power, either electric or gas. If these sources are interrupted, we're eating cold canned foods and raw pasta—a less than appetizing option. Unlike alternative nonelectric heating options, the cooking options require a small investment in equipment and a much smaller storage of needed fuels. Except for complex baking recipes, these alternative cooking sources will allow us to eat in near normal manner should we lose power and/or gas. Eating as we are accustomed to, has a profound beneficial emotional effect in stressful situations. Therefore, providing a viable cooking alternative is a must.

THE SOLUTIONS

You may feel that providing alternative cooking methods is really not needed. You'll just eat things that don't require cooking. This will work if you are without central utilities for a few days or a week but anything more than that and you'll kick yourself for not having provided for cooking. (Ever try eating raw instant coffee for your caffeine fix?)

Often your heating source can also serve as your stove. You can boil water or cook eggs on top of a kerosene heater but it is a definite safety risk and not advised. If you incapacitate your kerosene heater through misuse in the middle of winter you are up the proverbial creek. You can cook on many wood stoves, even add ovens and water heating devices to them, but this can be an awkward way to go—involving the use of rugged cast iron pots and pans and always the danger of burns. Therefore, it is best to provide for cooking separately from heating.

There are several viable cooking equipment alternatives. These include

- Portable dual-fuel stoves

- Portable kerosene stoves

- Portable propane stoves

- Gelled ethanol products

- Wood stoves and fireplaces

- Solar ovens

Be sure all alternative stoves are approved for inside use. Never use a charcoal barbecue grill inside.

NOTE: COOKING AND HEATING WITH GENERATORS

Many people, when they think about power outages, immediately think about getting a generator. This may be a good idea to power some appliances (lights, TV, washer, fans, blowers for central heating systems, or gas hot water heaters, etc.). However, using a generator to create heat, either for cooking or space heating, requires a large generator and a large supply of fuel. This is a very expensive option, often requiring large storage tanks and expensive generators professionally wired into your electrical system. Even then, it is an inefficient way to heat a home or food. (More on Generators in the Lighting Chapter.)

SAFETY NOTE:

When using these alternate fuels be sure you have three safety devices:

- Fire extinguisher
- Battery-operated or photoelectric smoke detector
- Battery-operated or photoelectric carbon monoxide detector

DUAL FUEL STOVES

The best option by far is to get the standard Coleman (or similar company) pump-up two-burner camp stove. (Figure 6.1) They are cheap, effective, and easy to use. However, do not get the one that only allows the use of white gas. White gas is more expensive and may be hard to find if there is disruption to the refinement or delivery of petroleum products. They now make a dual-fuel model that takes white gas or regular gasoline. You could even siphon gas out of your car to use if necessary. These stoves allow you to cook on two burners at once in a near normal fashion. Avoid the single-burner units made for backpacking. (Figure 6.2) You can even get an oven attachment that you place over the flames for baking (keep those fresh brownies coming when everyone starts to get a little restless without TV).

Figure 6.1   Two-burner, pump-up camp stoves like these make most cooking relatively easy. Be sure to get a dual-fuel one which allows you to use gasoline.

Figure 6.2   Avoid the single-burner units made for backpacking.

Be sure to store enough fuel to be able to cook for as long as you believe disruption may last. Read the specs to determine how much fuel your stove burns per hour and then calculate from there. Store your fuel in a dry, safe, secure place and never indoors, in the garage or in anything attached to the house. Gas, kerosene, and diesel are good for one year or less. After that it could gum up equipment (but often it will not). However, if you plan to store for over several years, you can get a gas or diesel saver chemical and add it to your gas. (Figure 6.3)

Figure 6.3   Be sure to use a fuel saver added to your gas if you plan to store it over one year. Also keep containers full so there is no condensation into your gas. You should also use savers for kerosene and diesel. Add the saver immediately after filling can.

PERIOD	FUEL CONSUMED COOKING 3 MEALS
Day	2 pints
Week	1.25 gallons
Month	5 gallons
Year	60 gallons

KEROSENE COOK STOVES

There are a few cook stoves that use kerosene instead of gasoline. (Figure 6.4) They cost about the same and work just as well and require no periodic hand pumping, as the Coleman camp stoves do. Their only advantage is if you are using a kerosene heating source you only need to purchase one type of fuel. They have several disadvantages including most only have one burner, they need replaceable wicks, and they are harder to locate. These stoves are safe for indoor use.

Figure 6.4   Kerosene stoves are also available but are more cumbersome than gas stoves and most have only one burner.

WOOD STOVES
AND FIREPLACES

People have been cooking on wood stoves and in fireplaces for centuries. If you have either, this is certainly an option (obviously wood stoves are much easier to cook on than fireplaces). Wood stoves can be fitted with water heating units and even ovens that sit on top or are inserted into the flue. You can buy wood cook stoves, with ovens, burners, and water heater and these provide heat as well. If you are planning to use a wood cooking option, you will need to buy a good set of cast iron pots and pans. Normal cookware will not hold up.

GELLED ETHANOL
PRODUCTS

Several products are on the market that use a gelled methanol in a can (similar but better than Sterno—and no you can't drink it if things get too rough). (Figure 6.5) These products come with small stoves and where they are good for basic cooking, like frying eggs, heating coffee, etc., t hey really are not made for cooking full meals for a family. Each can will burn for up to four hours and a case of 24 cans costs about $75.[2] These products are relatively odorless and can be safely used indoors. They also can be used for spot heating if needed.

Figure 6.5　Gelled ethanol fuels are safe to use indoors and will burn for four hours.

PROPANE AND BUTANE CAMP STOVES AND BARBECUES

There are both camp stoves and outside barbecues that can be used with bottled propane. However, barbecues are very inefficient since the flame is far below the pot or pan. (Figure 6.6) These can suffice, but they may be somewhat more awkward to use since they may require being hooked to a 5-gallon propane tank (refillable at most convenience stores—if they're open).

Figure 6.6   Propane or charcoal barbecue grill are inefficient for basic cooking. Never use these grills indoors.

If you decide to go with a propane or butane camp stove try to get one that can use a 5-gallon tank and not just the little propane cylinders used for camping. (Figure 6.7) If you use these little tanks, you will need a lot of them.[3] Also you may want to see if your propane gas supplier can add a propane camp stove hooked directly into your large propane tank.

Figure 6.7   These propane and butane camp stoves require small propane canisters which may be hard to find in emergencies.

STANDARD PROPANE RANGES

A great option would be to use a propane standard kitchen range, the kind installed in many homes. (Figure 6.8) Then you can cook in a normal manner. These are hooked into the large propane underground or above-ground tank that can also supply your heating needs. However, there is one major drawback. Many of these will not work without electricity. They may need electricity for the automatic ignition system. Often the burners will work but not the oven.

Figure 6.8 Propane kitchen ranges are an excellent option—if they work without electricity. Most will allow you to use the burners, but not the oven, if the power is out.

SOLAR OVENS

Solar ovens are good as a secondary source of alternative cooking but not as your primary source. (Figure 6.9) Believe it or not, on a sunny day even a $20 portable solar oven can cook everything from an egg to a pot roast. The best thing about them is that they cook for free and do not pollute or require fossil fuels. We recommend getting an inexpensive solar oven as a viable secondary alternative on sunny days.[1]

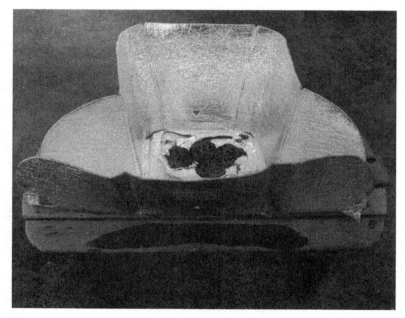

Figure 6.9   Solar ovens, some costing under $20, can cook an entire meal, including chicken, meatloaf, eggs, cookies, etc.

WHERE TO FIND PRODUCTS LISTED IN CHAPTER

Endnotes

1. Jade Mountain, 1-800-442-1972, www.jademountain.com. (Be sure to mention #241 and get your "Y2K discount or free gift" for readers of this book.) The Survival Center, 1-800-321-2900, http://survivalcenter.com

2. Alco-Brite Company, 1-801-874-1025.

3. Glowmaster Corp., 1-800-272-7008, www.glowmaster.com

CHECKLIST FOR COOKING APPLIANCES

APPLIANCE

❏ Portable dual-fuel stoves

❏ Portable kerosene stoves

❏ Portable propane stoves

❏ Gelled ethanol products

❏ Wood stoves and fireplaces

❏ Solar ovens

SAFETY

❏ Fire extinguisher

❏   Battery-operated or photoelectric smoke detector

❏   Battery-operated or photoelectric carbon monoxide detector

FUEL (depending on stove)

❏   Gasoline

❏   Propane (LP bottled gas)

❏   Kerosene

❏   Gelled ethanol

❏   Wood

❏   Fuel saver

STAYING CLEAN, HEALTHY, AND SAFE

The nation's utilities told a Senate panel today [June 12] that they were working to solve expected computer problems when 1999 ends but that they could not guarantee that the lights would not go out on Jan. 1, 2000.

—New York Times, June 13, 1998

Y2K is a "very, very serious problem.... There's no point in sugarcoating the problem... If we don't fix the century-date problem, we will have a situation scarier than the average disaster movie you might see on a Sunday night. Twenty-one months from now, there could be 90 million taxpayers who won't get their refunds, and 95% of the revenue stream of the United States could be jeopardized."

—Charles Rossetti, Commissioner of the U.S. Internal Revenue Service (IRS)

Serious vulnerabilities remain in addressing the federal government's Year 2000 readiness, and... much more action is needed to ensure that federal agencies satisfactorily mitigate Year 2000 risks to avoid debilitating consequences.... As a result of federal agencies' slow progress, the public faces the risk that critical services could be severely disrupted by the Year 2000 computing crisis... Unless progress improves dramatically, a substantial number of mission-critical systems will not be year-2000 compliant in time.

—Joel C. Willemssen in the Government Accounting Office report, June 10, 1998.

THE PROBLEM

As with so many areas of our lives, we do not notice the vast unseen computer systems that allow most of us in the first world to stay relatively clean, healthy, and safe. There is a vast array of computers that allow clean water to be delivered to our homes, drugs to be available at the stores, hospitals to function, police, emergency, and fire teams to respond, etc. If there is a disruption in water supply, disposing of human waste becomes a problem. If this is not handled properly, disease can quickly spread through a community, with devastating effects.

Also there are items like toilet paper often in short supply during emergencies. With a limited ability to keep ourselves and houses clean, disease becomes a greater threat. If the waste treatment plants are not operating properly, then we may be prohibited from flushing our toilets or using other household drains—even if we have water.

Pharmaceutical firms rely totally on computers and if there is a disruption in this industry, prescription drugs could become rare, endangering the health and lives of millions. In talking with a representative of one of the world's largest drug companies, we're told that their suppliers, vendors, and customers that were hooked into the company's mainframe computer would need to be cut off after Dec. 31, 1999 if they could not prove they were compliant, so as not to reinfect the company's mainframe. When asked how many companies were tied to their computer, her answer was 70,000. When asked how could they ever assure that 70,000 companies were Y2K compliant, she said, "We have no idea."

Life-sustaining medical equipment, such as IVs and dialysis machines, must be checked to be sure there are no embedded chips that may make them inoperable or faulty. Medical facilities may become overtaxed if Y2K failures create everything from more traffic accidents due to faulty traffic lights to chainsaw injuries due to the need to provide alternative heating fuel.

Our military, fire, and police forces are totally computerized. Even the local 911 emergency response systems need to be remediated to correct any Y2K related problems. More alarming, as late as December 1998, 13 months before the event, *USA Today* announced that 50% of the counties in the United States, agencies responsible for most 911 systems, had not yet begun the Y2K repairs.

We need to assume that there is a distinct possibility for some period of time (hopefully, days not months) when we may need to provide for our own health and safety needs, perhaps for the first time in our lives.

STAYING CLEAN

Hunger, thirst, being too hot or cold, or just being dirty and in need of a good hot shower, can make most of us irritable. If the conditions continue for weeks or months, it can lead to depression or anger. In earlier chapters we have discussed how to deal with food, water, and heat; now let's take a look at how to stay clean. Though it may not seem as important an area as these others, after a week with no shower, or no toothpaste, or no toilet paper (a telephone book is a very poor substitute for toilet paper, unless you start with computer companies), the importance of cleanliness will come into sharp focus. (Figure 7.1)

Figure 7.1   Store an abundance of toilet paper and other paper products. Each 90-roll box will supply one person for one year.

BATHING: Your ability to bath normally will depend on the availability of water after the event. It may also depend on the availability of electricity, as many water and waste treatment plants cannot continue to operate normally for more than several days on their emergency generators. Allotting 1-gallon per day per person in your water storage plans will give each person the opportunity to sponge bath once a day and that's about it. Showering, tub bathing, even frequent shampooing, is out of the question on 1 gallon per day. However, if you want to provide the normal options, more planning, and somewhat more expense, is required.

Also, realize that if your central sewer system fails, you may not be allowed to use your drains or toilets until it is declared safe. Therefore, you will need plastic or metal containers for washing dishes, washing clothes, and bathing.

If water delivery through your normal sources is disrupted and you want to be able to take a hot bath or shower, you will not only have to store much more water but also create an alternative water heating system and showering system as well. There is one inexpensive alternative that requires little water for a reasonable shower. Solar showers are available at most camping goods stores. These are basically black heavy-duty bags that hold 5-10 gallons of water that you can either hang in the sun to heat or pour preheated water into them. You can probably fashion something similar from things around the house but for $20-30 dollars they are well worth the expense. Then you can just hang it in the shower stall as best you can and go from there. The water pressure is a little low, the shower a little short, the water temperature not quite right, but you feel a lot better afterwards than you did before.

Other than these solar showers, you will have to improvise for your bathing needs. (Figure 7.2) You can always heat water and pour it in the tub but this demands a lot of water, a lot of work, and a lot of fuel. If you are using a wood stove, you may want to consider an add-on water heating device, as these will heat water with no waste of extra fuel.

Be sure to have enough soap and shampoo. We recommend an excellent soap that can be purchased at any health food store, Dr. Bonner's Soap. Dr. Bronner's has been the favorite of environmentalists and back-to-the-landers for decades. Not only is it biodegradable and will not pollute even if poured into a stream, but it can also be used as soap, shampoo, toothpaste, household detergent, dish soap, shaving cream, denture

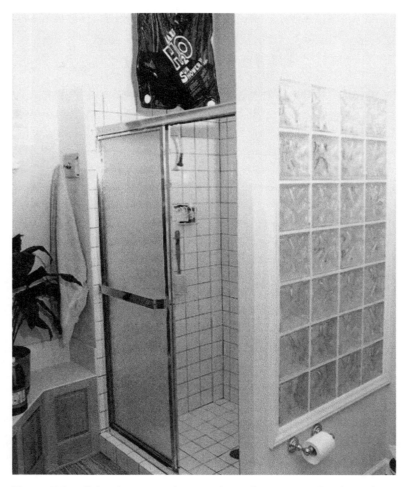

Figure 7.2   Solar showers are inexpensive and easy to use. Just lay or hang the bag in the sun for a few hours and you have a hot shower. This one is hung in a conventional shower for drainage.

cleaner, spray for fruits and plants, diaper soap, and laundry soap. It can be diluted so 2 gallons can last you months. It smells and feels great. (Figure 7.3)

Figure 7.3   Biodegradable soaps like Dr. Bronner's do not pollute the environment. They can be used as soap, shampoo, toothpaste, and laundry and dish soap.

TOILET: You must be prepared if you lose water or your local water and sewer company prohibits anyone from using the drains in their houses. If the waste treatment plant is not working properly, they may need to limit the amount of waste water they can absorb. You may want to consider buying a boat potty for around $50.00. (Figure 7.4) These are small plastic toilets that store a few gallons of water, to which you add a disinfecting scent, that allows you to flush after every use. There is a holding tank that is removable for disposing of the waste water when it is full. Be sure to store enough of its scented liquids to last. Also, most camping stores sell a toilet seat that fits over a 5-gallon bucket, and you fit a plastic bag into the bucket. Primitive, smelly, but it will work. (Figure 7.5)

Figure 7.4   Boat potties like these can work if the sewer system doesn't. Be sure to have enough scented toilet treatment available.

Also, there are more expensive composting toilets ($1000-1500) that do not use water, chemicals, or electricity that can easily be installed in any house.(Figure 7.6) These units are odorless and require a small pipe venting to the outside. The natural heat created by the composting procedure creates a

Figure 7.5   Most camping stores sell a toilet seat that fits over a 5-gallon bucket, and you fit a plastic bag into the bucket.

flow out the vent and a downdraft through the seat hole that eliminates odors. You simply empty a tray full of organic compost once or twice a year.[1]

Figure 7.6   Composting toilets need no water or electricity and only have to be emptied once or twice a year after the waste has turned to compost.

The Packin' Potty™ was designed to bring a bit of civilization to an uncivilized situation, from unexpected disasters to a well-planned camping trip.

The patented design is simple yet very functional. The Packin' Potty is made of lightweight, easy-to-clean plastic, yet is durable enough to hold 400 pounds.

The Packin' Potty starts off about the size of a briefcase, handle and all, has room enough to store toilet paper, sanitary wipes, biodegradable liners with enzyme packets to make it environmentally safe. To use the Packin' Potty, simply lay it on its side, lift the top off, and set it aside. Reach inside the bottom half for the mechanism, stand it up, and spread it out within the bottom half of the potty. Insert the plastic liner and place the top of the potty back on top of the mechanism, and there you go...literally! It can hold up to 400 pounds. The Packin' Potty is priced below $75.[2] Also, if you live downhill from your waste treatment plant, an extended power outage may allow raw sewage to backup into your home. You can install a "backwater valve" in your sewer line or put temporary test plugs in each toilet to prevent this.

It should go without saying that stocking up on toilet paper is a great idea. If you are in charge of the family's preparedness, the last thing you want is to have to explain to your family that you've run out of toilet paper. This can truly test their love for you, while offering them a great opportunity to practice forgiveness. Sixty rolls per year per person is the rule.

DISPOSAL OF HUMAN WASTE: In any emergency, especially ones that continue for weeks or months, nothing is more important than the proper disposal of human waste. If this is not done properly, diseases such as cholera, hepatitis, amoebic dysentery, etc., can quickly appear and devastate a community.

If you are hooked to a private septic system on your property, just keep flushing your waste down the toilet with waste water, as there is nothing in these systems that will be effected by a Y2K disruption. If, however, you are hooked into a central system, and it becomes unusable, you must find an effective way of disposing of all human waste. Local authorities hopefully will notify you quickly what to do if the sewer plant fails. However, if they do not, you must safely dispose of the waste by effective storage, burning, or burying.

If you are burying human waste, bury it so that animals will not get to it. These means at least 2 feet below ground and well covered. Be sure you are at least 50 feet away from any well, spring, creek, lake, or other water source. You can build a "pit privy" if you need to. You need a hole 3.5 x 3.5 feet square and 5 feet deep. Build a 4-foot high wooden riser above it, with a hinged top to keep animals out (and with a hole and a toilet seat in it). Tamp earth around the wooden risers. When the privy fills to within 18 inches of ground level, fill it with dirt (you can add lime as well) and start a new one. Do not build a pit privy on the downslope of a hill. It could leach into the water supply.

HOUSEHOLD GARBAGE: Garbage pickup and disposal may also be interrupted. Even the kitchen sink garbage disposal unit may be useless for awhile. 1999 may be a good time to buy a compost bin. (Figure 7.7) These are simple plastic containers that you set out in your yard. You can dump all your organic food waste (except animal products) into the bin and turn it into usable compost for your garden or ornamental plants. Your paper products can be burned and other waste should be stored in heavy plastic garbage bags until normal garbage pickup and disposal are restored. However, be sure never to put food waste in bags outside as they can attract anything from rabid dogs to disease carrying rodents.

Expect delays in garbage collection and other services. Rodents can be a major health threat where garbage accumulates so make sure you have enough sturdy, lidded containers to hold refuse produced over a two-week period. Be prepared to keep your yard clean if other people's refuse finds its way to you.

Don't allow garbage to accumulate outside your home. In some rural areas, trash can be a particular attraction for a variety of wildlife—some dangerous. Store paper and other flammables away from any heat sources or open flames. If waste builds up, consider burying bags in pits and use lime to cut down on smell and contamination.

WASHING CLOTHES: Washing clothes may become a major issue, especially if any interruption lasts weeks or months. Be sure you go into the New Year with all your clothes washed and ready to go (how about a New Year's Eve

Figure 7.7   Compost bins can be used to turn kitchen waste (except animal products) into usable compost.

wash-the-clothes and fill-the-bathtubs party, if you can stand the excitement). There are small, hand-cranked laundry devices, good for underwear and socks, or even the old non-electric hand washing machines with wringers.[1] (Figure 7.8) Other than these two options, maybe the best bet is a washboard in your bath tub and an outdoor clothesline. (Figure 7.9) If you have a generator, you can probably power your washing machine and, if it's powerful enough, perhaps an electric dryer (or the blower of a gas dryer). You should also look into an indoor clothes line if you do not have one already.

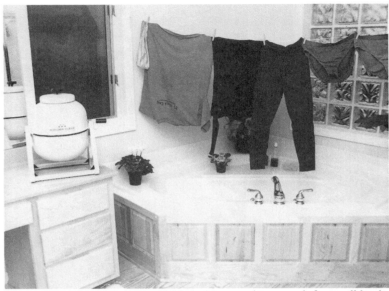

Figure 7.8   Small, hand-cranked washing machines work for small loads. An indoor clothesline can suffice in an emergency.

Figure 7.9   Outdoor clotheslines may blossom in early 2000.

STAYING HEALTHY

Perhaps more than any other area of preparedness, the health and safety issues become quite individualized according to each family's needs. The health needs of each individual must be taken into account to be sure the proper medicines and equipment are available for the duration of any disruption.

In the past decades there has been an explosion in the home health care field. Many people are now effectively cared for at home who in the past would have required hospital care. Because of this there has also been an explosion of medical equipment being used in the home. If anyone in the family uses medical equipment (dialysis machine, IV pump, glucose tester, etc.) be sure that you get a letter from the manufacturer that they will not have any Y2K problems. (Figure 7.10) Even then, if they are wrong, your or your loved ones' health or life may depend on it. If there is any nonelectric, noncomputerized equipment to replace your existing equipment, it may be wise to have it on hand.

Many of us use some type of prescription drugs. If its just a pain killer for an occasional ache, we can do without them. (Figure 7.11) However, if it's a critical drug, say for high blood pressure, asthma, diabetes, etc., where an interruption can cause health problems, even death, I highly recommend going into the event with a 6-12-month supply (why gamble with your health or life). If your doctor will not cooperate, find another one. If your health insurance will not pay for the added months, pay for it yourself. Don't take chances in this area. Pharmaceutical distribution and manufacturing relies heavily on computers.

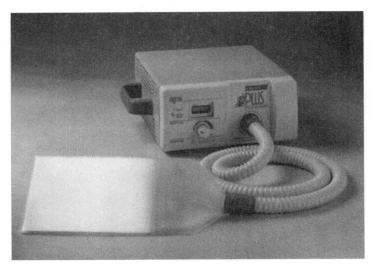

Figure 7.10   Be sure you check with the manufacturers of all medical devices to be sure they will operate properly. Get it in writing.

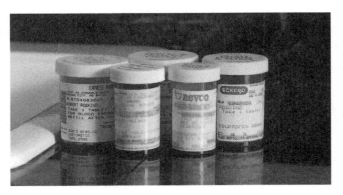

Figure 7.11   Be sure to have adequate stock of needed prescription and off-the-shelf drugs. Your life or health may depend on it.

Also you may want to determine if there are any alternative approaches to whatever conditions presently demand that you take prescription drugs. Often herbs, vitamins, relaxation techniques, teas, etc., may help the condition. Talk to your local health food store or get a good book on alternative practices. If any alternative approaches seem feasible to you, lay in a store of the recommended herbs, vitamins, supplements, teas, etc.

In addition to having all the needed prescription medicines, stock a good supply of over-the-counter drugs. Cold medicines, athlete's foot remedies, calamine lotion, cough medicines, antacids, headache compounds (you might as well expect more headaches and stomach aches in the early part of Y2K) will be much appreciated. Just take a walk through a well-supplied drug department at a discount store and load up.

In addition to the obvious health needs, also consider other, not so obvious health concerns. If any family member has a complex heath issue, it may be a good idea to have a copy of their doctor's records in case they need care and your regular doctor is not available. A supply of vitamins and supplements would be a good idea, in case a balanced diet is not so easily obtainable. Also be sure everyone who wears glasses has an extra pair or two. You may want to get all dental work or planned medical procedures completed by late 1999.

In addition, emergency health situations may become a major issue. The possibility of fires, accidents, falls, heart attacks, strokes, etc., are greatly increased in these situations. At the same time, the normal 911 emergency response teams and hospital services may be not functioning as efficiently. Indeed, you may be called on to be your own emergency team or doctor.

It would be wise to have at least one person in the household trained in CPR and basic first aid. Also have a good emergency first aid and basic health care book available (a book, not a CD). Get a good first aid kit, not a cheap one from a discount store, or even an expensive one that is made for companies to make available for their employees (these are almost worthless except for minor problems). (Figure 7.12) Get a good-quality first aid kit designed for when a doctor is not available for a long time. Many camping stores or catalogs sell these for $100-150. Even some CPR equipment would not be a bad idea if you want to go to that level of preparedness.

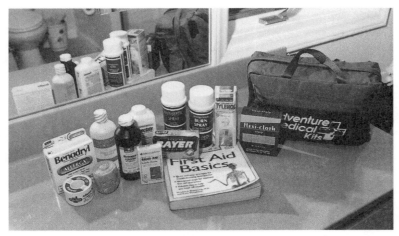

Figure 7.12 Get a good survival first aid kit, not a home first aid kit that assumes medical help is quickly available. Also get a good first aid book and off-the-shelf items.

Make sure your and your child's immunizations are up to date, preferably before the end of 1999 and *make sure* you have a hard copy of every family members' shot records. The frail, elderly people with particular medical problems requiring a caregiver and people with other disabilities must make special plans for their safety in the event that emergency services fail.

Those who have the following conditions may be especially at risk and should take special precautions:

- Acute or chronic respirator illnesses
- Heart aliments
- Unstable or juvenile diabetes
- Dependence on tube feeding
- Epilepsy
- Tracheotomies
- Urinary catheters
- Colostomies
- Dialysis dependence

PAPER PRODUCTS

We seldom realize how reliant we are on paper products until they're gone (ever run out of toilet paper on a camping trip?). It would be an excellent idea to store a generous amount of paper products. In stressful times they will make life much easier. If water is in short supply, washing may be wasteful and paper plates, plastic utensils, and cups may be greatly appreciated.

In addition many of the products will reduce the spread of disease and germs, which is a major concern when infrastructures fail. Sponges and cloth cleaning rags can spread disease as they are reused. Paper products that can be discarded after one use may be wiser when conditions degrade. Most Americans give little thought to diseases such as amoebic dysentery and hepatitis that ravage countries with poor sanitation. Remember that our standards of hygiene can revert immediately to those of the Third World if our infrastructure fails, even for a short time.

Have the following products on hand:

- Toilet paper
- Female paper products
- Paper towels
- Napkins
- Facial tissues
- Paper plates
- Paper bowls
- Paper/ plastic cups
- Plastic eating utensils (Figure 7.13)

Figure 7.13 Paper products are vital not only for convenience but also to reduce the spread of disease in emergency situations. Have an adequate supply on hand.

In doing so, it is important to have a storage area for these products. You want all of these products off the ground and away from heat sources. You can store these items with your food storage on storage shelves. Although paper products aren't that heavy, you may wish to store heavier items with them, so make sure you have sturdy shelves. Some storage shelves require lots of assembly and if you assemble them wrong, you may have structural problems. Know what height and width you need. If you have 8-foot ceilings, you may be disappointed with 60-inch shelves.

STAYING SAFE

In addition to staying healthy, you need to consider staying safe, not only from the usual threats in a normally operating world, but from new or increased threats in a Y2K-disrupted world. A battery-operated or photoelectric smoke detector and carbon monoxide detector are highly recommended, as the ones wired directly into you electrical system may not work if the power goes off unless they have a battery backup. And remember you may be using equipment for lighting, cooking, and heating that increases your fire threat. (Figure 7.14)

You will need a complete list of all emergency phone numbers (police, fire, doctor, Red Cross, FEMA, utility companies, etc.) posted where everyone knows where they are. However, if the phones are down, these will not be much use. Be sure that all cars have a full tank of gas and that you have clear instructions how to get to

- Closest hospital
- Fire station

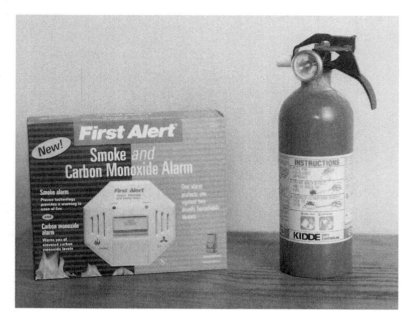

Figure 7.14 Install a battery-operated smoke and carbon monoxide detector and have several fire extinguishers in well-known places.

- Police station
- Doctor's office
- Gas company
- Dentist's office

Be sure you have several fire extinguishers around and test them if they are very old and may have lost their charge. If you rely on a security system, this may be incapacitated, and let's face it, crime may increase if police officers are overloaded and people are in greater need. You may want to add a few locks or deadbolts, steel doors, solar-powered motion detecting devices, floodlights, a battery-operated security system, etc.

Also be sure to store any cash (have enough on hand for however long you feel the problems may last), valuables, gold, or important documents in fire-resistant boxes ($20 at any home center), safes, or the safety deposit box at the bank. (Figure 7.15) A good watch dog will not have any Y2K problems.

Figure 7.15 Fire-resistant safes and boxes are needed if you are storing valuables, important papers, or cash.

If electronic locks rely on electricity, it's likely they either won't open, possibly locking a person in or out, or fail in "safe mode" by releasing the lock. Check to see if there is a manual override; if there is, make sure you have the key or information to use it. If not, you may need to force the door if entry or egress is necessary.

If you need to leave your home, it is a good idea to have many of the items in this chapter readily available in smaller sizes in a kit so that you can move quickly if necessary. You may want to have these and other staple bath products ready in a backpack just in case.

Many people are considering buying a gun for added protection. The reasons for this are obvious: everything from packs of abandoned dogs to criminals feeling less threatened by overloaded police forces. For many of us who do not presently own guns, this decision is complex and I will give no advice here. But whether we own a gun or not, there is one thing we believe to be true.

If Y2K causes major problems within our society, the best way to approach these problem is by pulling together with our neighbors and our communities, not through a bunker mentality of armed individual family units. We understand the emotions of self-protection and we have delved into the bunker mentality in fearful moments. However, to separate from, and perhaps attack, others is not what we are here to learn. If Y2K can open our hearts to each other, allow us to serve each other (even those who laughed at our preparation plans), and treat each other with greater compassion and kindness (Y2Kindness, as my wife is fond of saying). Then the post-Y2K world can be much better. Perhaps we need to shift from "Don't come knocking on my door if you don't prepare" to "I guess I better stock some extra food to help those idiots who just wouldn't listen."

WHERE TO FIND PRODUCTS LISTED IN CHAPTER

Endnotes

1. Jade Mountain, 800 442-1972, www.jademountain.com. (Be sure to mention #241 and get the "Y2K discount or free gift" for readers of this book.) The Survival Center, 1-800-321-2900, http://survivalcenter.com

2. Banyan Industries at 15507 Moorpark St. #101, Encino, CA 91436, Telephone: 818-789-5152, Fax: 818-783-3324.

CHECKLIST FOR HEALTH, SAFETY, AND CLEANLINESS

(Compliments of Y2K Women: www.y2kwomen.com)

❏   Bleach

❏   Dishwashing detergent (antibacterial)

❏   Dishpan

❏   Drying rack

❏   Dishtowels

❏   Hand soap (antibacterial)

❏   Hand soap (waterless)

❏   Sponges

❏   Steel wool pads (Brillo)

- ❏ Rubber gloves
- ❏ Cleanser with bleach
- ❏ Trash bags
    - ❏ Drawstring, white, tall kitchen bags
    - ❏ Black garbage bags
    - ❏ Twisties
- ❏ Baggies (zip lock)
    - ❏ Small
    - ❏ Sandwich size
    - ❏ Large
    - ❏ Thick, freezer bags
- ❏ Aluminum foil (various sizes)
- ❏ Plastic wrap
- ❏ Paper towels
- ❏ Paper napkins
- ❏ Rags
- ❏ Water filters
- ❏ Water purifiers
- ❏ Iodine
- ❏ Manual can opener
- ❏ Knife sharpener
- ❏ Kitchen matches (in waterproof container)
- ❏ Fire extinguisher

- ❑ _____
- ❑ _____
- ❑ Detergent (liquid laundry soap)
- ❑ Bleach
- ❑ Drying rack
- ❑ Clothes line
- ❑ Clothes pins
- ❑ Washtub
- ❑ Buckets
- ❑ Dust cloths
- ❑ Furniture polish
- ❑ Window cleaner
- ❑ Dust cloths
- ❑ Disinfectant (Lysol)
- ❑ Broom
- ❑ Air freshener
- ❑ Toilet bowl cleaner
- ❑ Plunger
- ❑ Drain snake
- ❑ Drain unclogger (like Drano)
- ❑ Sewing kit
  - ❑ Needles
  - ❑ Thread
  - ❑ Scissors
  - ❑ Material

Shower and Tub

❏   Bubble bath (!)

❏   Bath soap

❏   Outdoor solar shower bag

❏   Razor and blades

❏   Shampoo/conditioner

❏   Shaving cream

❏   Tissues

❏   Toilet paper

❏   Moist towelettes or baby wipes

❏   Air freshener

❏   _____

❏   _____

Feminine Hygiene

❏   Maxi Pads

❏   Tampons

❏   Panty liners

❏   Menstrual cup (the keeper)

❏   Washable pads

❏   _____

❏   _____

Hair Care

❑   Hair brushes

❑   Combs

❑   Elastics and ribbons for little girls

❑   Nonelectric curlers (like the little velcro kind)

❑   Curling iron (propane)

❑   Hair cutting scissors

❑   _____

❑   _____

Dental Care

❑   Toothbrushes

❑   Toothpaste

❑   Mouthwash

❑   Dental floss

❑   Denture care products

❑   Adhesive

❑   Cleanser

Eye Care

❑   Extra glasses

  ❑   Extra replacement screws

❑   Extra contacts

  ❑   Saline solution

❑   _____

Makeup

Don't discount this as unimportant! If wearing makeup is part of your lifestyle, make sure that you include enough to last you for awhile. It's important to feel good about how you look! It helps your self-esteem which will help your family.

❑   Cleanser

❑   Toner

❑   Moisturizer

❑   Foundation

❑   Blush

❑   Eyeliner

❑   Eye shadow

❑   Mascara

❑   _____

❑   _____

Personal Grooming

❑   Deodorant

❑   Perfume

❑   Hair spray

❑   Hair color (Ladies, stock up on the L'OREAL now!)

❑   Permanent wave solution (curlers and papers)

❑   Hair relaxer

Checklist Medicine Cabinet

Nonprescription Medications

❑ Activated charcoal (use if indicated for certain poisons)

❑ Advil (Ibuprofen)

❑ Aleve

❑ Antacid (for stomach upset)

❑ Antidiarrhea medication (Kaopectate; Pepto-Bismol)

❑ Aspirin

❑ Benadryl

❑ Cold, flu, and cough remedies

    ❑ Cough drops

    ❑ Nyquil/Dayquil

❑ Hay fever/sinus

❑ Hydrocortisone creme (Cortaid)

❑ Laxatives for constipation

❑ Motrin

❑ Neosporin

❑ Syrup of Ipecac (use to induce vomiting)

❑ Tylenol (Acetaminophen)

❑ Yeast infection medicine

❑ _____

❑ _____

Medical Concerns for Young Children

❑   Band-Aids in lots of sizes

❑   Children's Tylenol

❑   Diaper rash cream

❑   Digital thermometer for young babies

❑   Ear viewer and instructions

❑   Immunizations

❑   Pedialyte (electrolyte fluid)

Specific medicines for your child (check on the shelf life of medications)

❑   _____

❑   _____

Alternative and Natural Health

Note: Although herbal remedies are nonprescription, they can still be dangerous if used improperly. Please read all label for directions and keep out of the reach of children.)

❑   Echinacea with Goldenseal for colds

❑   Cool Cayenne for upper respiratory

❑   L-Lysine for canker sores

❑   Aloe for burns

❑   Melatonin for insomnia

❑   Zinc lozenges for sore throats

❑   _____

❑   _____

Medical Supplies

❑   Ammonia

❑   Glucose

❑   Hydrogen peroxide

❑   Insect bite/sting topical medicine

❑   Insect repellent

❑   Iodine

❑   Petroleum jelly

❑   Rubbing alcohol

❑   _____

❑   _____

Hormones

❑   Hormone replacement medications

❑   Yeast infection medication

❑   Wild yam cream

First Aid Kit
(Recommended FEMA list)

Assemble a first aid kit for your home and one for each car. A first aid kit* should include

❑   Sterile adhesive bandages in assorted sizes

❑   2-inch sterile gauze pads (4-6)

❑   4-inch sterile gauze pads (4-6)

❑   Hypoallergenic adhesive tape

*Contact your local American Red Cross chapter to obtain a basic first aid manual.

- ❏ Triangular bandages (3)
- ❏ 2-inch sterile roller bandages (3 rolls)
- ❏ 3-inch sterile roller bandages (3 rolls)
- ❏ Scissors
- ❏ Tweezers
- ❏ Needle
- ❏ Moistened towelettes
- ❏ Antiseptic
- ❏ Thermometer
- ❏ Tongue blades (2)
- ❏ Tube of petroleum jelly or other lubricant
- ❏ Cleansing agent/soap
- ❏ Latex gloves (2 pair)
- ❏ Sunscreen

Nonprescription Drugs

- ❏ Aspirin or nonaspirin pain reliever
- ❏ Antidiarrhea medication
- ❏ Antacid (for stomach upset)
- ❏ Syrup of Ipecac (use to induce vomiting)
- ❏ Laxative
- ❏ Activated charcoal
- ❏ _____
- ❏ _____

Tools and Supplies
(Recommended FEMA list)

❑   Mess kits, or paper cups, plates, and plastic utensils*

❑   Emergency preparedness manual*

❑   Battery-operated radio and extra batteries*

❑   Flashlight and extra batteries*

❑   Cash or traveler's checks, change*

❑   Nonelectric can opener, utility knife*

❑   Fire extinguisher: small canister, ABC type

❑   Tube tent

❑   Pliers

❑   Tape

❑   Compass

❑   Matches in a waterproof container

❑   Aluminum foil

❑   Plastic storage containers

❑   Signal flare

❑   Paper, pencil

❑   Needles, thread

❑   Medicine dropper

❑   Shut-off wrench to turn off household gas and water

❑   Whistle

❑   Plastic sheeting

❑   Map of the area (for locating shelters)

*Include at least one complete change of clothing and footwear per person.

❏   Clothing and Bedding

❏   _____

❏   Sturdy shoes or work boots*

❏   Hat and gloves

❏   Rain gear*

❏   Thermal underwear

❏   Blankets or sleeping bags*

❏   Sunglasses

For Baby

❏   Formula

❏   Diapers

❏   Bottles

❏   Powdered milk

❏   Medications

For Adults

❏   Heart and high blood pressure medication

❏   Insulin

❏   Prescription drugs

❏   Denture needs

❏   Contact lenses and supplies

❏   Extra eye glasses

*Include at least one complete change of clothing and footwear per person.

CREATE A FAMILY DISASTER PLAN
(Recommended FEMA list)

To get started

Contact your local emergency management or civil defense office and your local American Red Cross chapter.

Find out which disasters are most likely to happen in your community.

Ask how you would be warned.

Find out how to prepare for each.

Meet with your family

Discuss the types of disasters that could occur.

Explain how to prepare and respond.

Discuss what to do if advised to evacuate.

Practice what you have discussed.

Plan how your family will stay in contact if separated by disaster

Pick two meeting places:

1) A location a safe distance from your home in case of fire.

2) A place outside your neighborhood in case you can't return home.

Choose an out-of-state friend as a "check-in contact" for everyone to call.

Complete these steps:

1. Post emergency telephone numbers by every phone.

2. Show responsible family members how and when to shut off water, gas, and electricity at main switches.

3. Install a smoke detector (battery operated) on each level of your home, especially near bedrooms; test monthly and change the batteries two times each year.

4. Contact your local fire department to learn about home fire hazards.

5. Learn first aid and CPR. Contact your local American Red Cross chapter for information and training.

Meet with your neighbors

Plan how the neighborhood could work together after a disaster. Know your neighbors' skills (medical, technical). Consider how you could help neighbors who have special needs, such as elderly or disabled persons. Make plans for child care in case parents can't get home.

Remember to practice and maintain your plan.

The Federal Emergency Management Agency's Community and Family Preparedness Program and the American Red Cross Disaster Education Program are nationwide efforts to help people prepare for disasters of all types. For more information, please contact your local or state office of Emergency Management, and your local American Red Cross chapter. Ask for "Your Family Disaster Plan" and the "Emergency Preparedness Checklist."

Or write to FEMA, P.O. Box 70274 Washington, DC 20024 FEMA L, 189 ARC 4463.

COMMUNICATIONS AND TRANSPORTATION

The millennium bug is one of the most serious problems facing not only British business but the global economy today. The impact cannot be underestimated.

—British Prime Minister Tony Blair,
USA Today, April 13, 1998

Michael Harden, President and CEO of Century Technology Services, Inc. and author of two Y2K books, compared Y2K to the great Yellow Fever epidemic that struck the Mississippi Valley in 1878. The deadly disease, carried by mosquitoes, broke out on the Gulf Coast and slowly worked its way up the river to Memphis, Tennessee. The people in that city knew in advance that the epidemic was on its way. They knew approximately when it would arrive. They knew it would kill them. The government and the media said, "Don't panic. Everything will be all right." Relieved by these assurances, most stayed in the city.

Fifty-five percent of the population died. Many Catholic nuns chose to remain to give aid and comfort to those afflicted with the disease. Most of them perished and today they are known as the 'Martyrs of Memphis.' The city was disestablished as a political entity and was not rechartered for fourteen years.

—Jim Lord, World Future Society Holds Y2K
Conference, January 4, 1999

185

Joel Willemssen of the U.S. General Accounting Office doesn't sugarcoat his answer. "All the government agencies will not be done on time. There will be some failures," he says...

Air travel? The Federal Aviation Administration concedes it remains at least three months behind where it should be on Y2K preparedness.

Defense? The Pentagon received a "D-minus" in the last congressional Y2K report card, but plans war games in June 1999 to demonstrate its preparedness.

The Department of Energy got an "F" in the same report, placing in doubt what it can do in 1999 to ensure electrical power is available on January 1, 2000.

And the Internal Revenue Service is so far behind that the GAO says U.S. citizens could receive erroneous tax bills in 2000 or, on a brighter note, refund checks they aren't entitled to.

—"Fed Agencies among Serious Stragglers in Y2K Preparations," CNN Online, December 29, 1998

THE PROBLEM

There is a distinct possibility that the normal communication systems (phone, Internet, telegraph, postal delivery, FedEx, UPS, etc.) may experience disruptions early in 2000. Though many of the large companies say they plan to be ready (but no guarantees), remember there are thousands of small phone companies that must deliver you a dial tone before you can even access the large long-distance carriers. There are concerns that many of these smaller companies may experience problems.

In addition, if you rely on the phone, TV, and radios for your contact with emergency services, there is the possibility you may be unable to get information if you are not prepared. The Internet may also be at risk. If you rely on this for your business or personal needs, it would be wise to make alternative plans. Most of the Internet equipment does not have Y2K problems (or so we are told), but if power or phone service is lost in some areas, this could effect the Net.

THE SOLUTION

There is little you can do to assure phone service, other than hope the telephone companies, large and small, fix it in time. (Figure 8.1)You may want to consider having a cellular phone as well as conventional service. The cellular system may work when the conventional system does not, and visa versa. If you get a cell phone, it may be best to get service from a large provider. (Figure 8.2)

While scanners, copiers, and printers may contain embedded chips, they generally don't have calendar functions and should not have Y2K problems. However, if you've added transaction-logging components with date-stamping capabilities to such equipment, check with the equipment's manufacturer to learn whether the added component will cause Y2K problems.

Fax machines have calendar functions. (Figure 8.3) According to manufacturers, most current models won't have Y2K problems. Some older models, while they'll continue to function, may date stamp incoming and outgoing faxes with the wrong dates. Contact the manufacturer for more information.

Figure 8.1 Hopefully both your local service provider and long-distance provider will be ready in time.

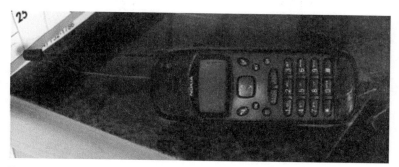

Figure 8.2 Cell phones may work when other phones don't—and vice versa.

Figure 8.3 Fax machines have calendar functions. According to manufacturers, most current models won't have Y2K problems

Getting news from the outside world after the power goes off is as easy as using a battery-powered radio or TV. You can even get radios that you wind up for 3 minutes and then play for 30 minutes or solar-powered units so you never need batteries. However, a small radio can go a very long time on one set of batteries. You may want to get a radio that also offers shortwave so that you can pick up news from other states and countries.

Short of carrier pigeons, almost all forms of two-way communications rely heavily on computerized systems to work effectively. If electrical power is down in your area, but your phone company has alternative power or is in an area where electricity is working, your phone may still work if you have a phone that doesn't require an external AC power supply. Many cordless phones don't work if the power is out. Also some of the integrated phone/answering machine devices need power. If your phone plugs into a 110-V electric socket in addition to the phone jack, check and see if it works when unplugged from the electrical socket. If not, go buy a cheap phone that works on just the phone jack alone without the need of external power supply. This way you might be able to use your phone in an electrical outage.

The option to the average homeowner to be able to effectively communicate with others should these systems fail are few and expensive. They include handheld walkie talkies, CB radios, ham radios, shortwave radios, an short-range tele-mobile and satellite telephone systems. All of these systems have severe drawbacks in regard to how many people can be contacted, how far the reach, and/or how much they cost. Because of this, most of us will just stay incommunicado until normal systems are restored.

Handheld Walkie Talkie: There is a new generation of battery-operated handheld walkie talkies recently available at most electronic stores or large discount stores. Though they claim ranges of a mile, this depends greatly on the terrain. Any hills or trees greatly reduce their range. They cost around $100 per unit and require batteries (which must be replaced often). Marine VHF radios are good for 50-100 miles.

CB Radios: CB (Citizens Band) radios have been around for years and are used so that a base (i.e., a dispatcher) can talk to many subunits (i.e., company trucks). It also allows the subunits to all talk to each other. These units cost approximately $40-200 each and can be used either with AC or battery-operated (any car battery will work).Their range is between 1 to 10 miles (longer if conditions are right). The reason for this broad range is that conditions such as terrain, weather, sunspots, etc., will all make a difference. This may be a viable option if you want to remain in constant contact with friends or loved ones in your immediate area.

Ham Radios: Across the world there is a system of ham radios (or amateur radios), a noncommercial system of personal communication. There are over 2,000,000 ham operators in the world, with over 600,000 in the United States. There is no age restriction for operators and though this is mostly a hobby, in emergencies ham operators are of great value. Though the range varies, by subscribing to a local repeater service, ham radio operators are able to talk with other ham operators all over the world (something to consider in a worldwide emergency). They cost around $200 and require an operator's license (easily obtainable with a little study of the rules and regulations).

Ham radio equipment can operate on electricity, batteries, or solar units. With batteries and portable solar units, the transmitters and receivers can be carried from place to place, so that ham operators can be "stationed" in various locales during an emergency. Handheld devices are also available.

For more information on amateur radio see Beginner's Guide to Ham Radio, on-line at http://www.irony.com/ham-howto.html.

Amateur Radio

Relay League, Colorado Public Information Coordinator, Erik Dyce, Phone: (303) 751-4605.

Portable Satellite Phone Systems: Though there are private satellite phones that will allow you to talk to another person who has the same system, these are very expensive ($3000-5000 plus $1.50 per minute) and still rely on a satellite operating correctly. If you can afford it and staying in touch with a few people is vital or important to you, this may be an option. They can be battery operated and are the size of a briefcase and include their own small antennae.[1]

TRANSPORTATION

THE PROBLEM

Transportation, of all types, may be problematic after Y2K. On the personal level, the family car should operate as before. (Figure 8.4) Earlier in this unfolding crisis, there was talk that cars may stop, or air bags inflate, because of chips in the cars. However, this seems to not be the case. Ask you local dealer if there are problems with your car, as the recent information regarding Y2K and cars is still not as definitive as we would like.

Figure 8.4 Ask you local dealer if there are problems with your car, as the recent information regarding Y2K and cars is still not as definitive as we would like.

However, even if you car operates perfectly, you may not be able to get gas and oil as easily as before. Much of our crude oil (37%) comes from other countries in South America and the Mid East. These countries are very far behind in their Y2K remediation. Also in August 1999, the Global Positioning Satellite (GPS) will give bad data to any ship or plane that has not updated its GPS equipment. With millions of ships and planes relying on the GPS, this could upset the flow of oil. (Figure 8.5)

Also refineries, oil rigs, offshore oil rigs, pipelines, etc., are all computer controlled. There are over 10,000 chips in a offshore platform. Failures in this system could make gas, heating fuel, oil, etc., scarce. In addition, the train system in this country is now fully computerized, from one central location.

Figure 8.5   It takes many computers, in many countries, to get gas to this pump. Will they all work in 2000?

Trains are used extensively to transport gas, oil, coal, etc. A normal coal-fired electrical generation plant needs a one-mile long train load of coal per day. A failure in the train system can not only interrupt passenger service but fuel deliveries and electrical production as well.

Air service is also at risk. The FAA (Federal Aviation Administration) was running far behind on their Y2K repairs in early 1998. By late 1998 they said they had caught up and there would be little or no disruption in air service in the United States in early January 2000. However, keeping air service in tact is not as easy as just the FAA getting their act together. Airports, airlines, ticketing services, fuel companies, insurance companies, radar systems, planes, parts companies, etc. must be ready as well. The president of a major U.S. airlines said that his company deals with 17,000 companies to keep their planes flying. Insurance companies have said that they will not insure airlines until they are sure everything is ready. No insurance, no flights.

THE SOLUTIONS

Obviously there is little you can do if their is an interruption in plane, train, or bus service. If you are planing any vacations or visits to loved ones, you may want to make them in 1999. If there are people you want with you in case there are Y2K problems, tell them to get there by late December. If you rely on planes or trains for your business, you must ask yourself if there anything you can do if these are not available in early 2000.

As far as the car goes, be sure to have a full tank of gas on New Year's Eve. You may want to store gas, but follow these safety precautions:

1. Use only clean, marked, and approved gasoline containers;

2. Store gas away from the house, and not in garages, basements, or sheds attached to the house;

3. Keep containers full to keep water from condensing inside;

4. Gas is good for one year or less. Use a fuel saver if storing for longer;

5. Have a fire extinguisher and a battery-operated smoke detector nearby;

6. Keep gas in locked, dry area away from any fire threats or children.

Check with your local dealer to see if your car has any chips that may fail in 2000. Get it in writing. Some people are buying vehicles built in the 1950, 1960s, etc., before there were chips put in cars. However, manufacturers are saying cars will be OK. Be sure to get any needed work done on your car before the rollover. Afterwards, this may be much more difficult. If you are thinking about getting a new car, consider gas mileage. Gas rationing could be a reality post-Y2K.

There are always low-tech alternative forms of transportation available. Bicycles would be a great idea. (Figure 8.6) Be sure they are in good operating condition. Have several spare tires and tire repair kits and tubes available. Get a good pump and repair manual. Mopeds and motorcycles are a possibility as they use little gas. And be sure everyone has some good walking shoes.

Figure 8.6   Bicycles could be handy in early 2000. Have extra tires and tubes on hand.

PREPARING OTHER EQUIPMENT

In addition to your heating system, several other pieces of equipment should be checked for Y2K compliance. (Figure 8.7) Unlike other emergencies, even if the power stays on some of your vital equipment may not work. Some equipment may have microchips or microprocessors (embedded systems) built into them that could cause the equipment to fail after December 31, 1999. Even if the equipment does not need to keep track of the date, the designer may have used some of its memory to do just that. Be sure to check

Figure 8.7   Be sure there are no Y2K problems with thermostats or heating systems. Ask the manufacturer to confirm it for you in writing.

with the manufacturer to be sure that will not be a problem for you. You can expect a runaround, vague answers, avoidance, refusal to put it in writing, etc., when dealing with many manufacturers regarding their Y2K compliance. Keep pressing until your satisfied.

Equipment that may need to be checked for possible embedded systems problems, includes

- Heating thermostats
- Heating and air conditioning systems
- Medical equipment
- Well pumps
- Generators
- Cars
- Farm equipment
- VCRs
- Coffee makers
- Garage door openers

Figure 8.8   A well-stocked cabinet full of games, toys, cards, etc. will help keep everyone entertained if the power goes out. Don't overlook this. People can get stressed without their TV. Don't forget lots of books, especially uplifting ones.

Figure 8.9   A good collection of hand tools would be a good idea. Be sure to have tools to shut off gas and water lines.

Endnote

1. Jade Mountain, 800 442-1972, www.jademountain.com. (Be sure to mention #241 and get the "Y2K discount or free gift" for readers of this book.) The Survival Center, 1-800-321-2900, http://survivalcenter.com

9

MONEY, FINANCES, AND IMPORTANT PAPERS

Federal Reserve Chairman Alan Greenspan said Wednesday that the Year 2000 computer bug is already hurting the economy and has warned of bigger damage ahead. "Inevitable difficulties are going to emerge." He said. "You could end up with...a very large problem."

"Some people with technological expertise think the whole 'millennium bug' issue is overblown. Don't you believe it", said Kelley. "Comments that doubt the seriousness of the problem are dead wrong," he said.

—Edward Kelly, Federal Reserve Board member,
Miami Herald, March 1, 1998

Some of the nation's largest banks, already racing to upgrade their own computer systems to meet the Year 2000 deadline, are acknowledging another worry! Problem loans may well rise if some borrowers fail to upgrade their computers in time.

—*Wall Street Journal*, March 18, 1998

THE PROBLEM

Although the Year 2000 is a good reason to be prepared, many of the ideas in this chapter should be accomplished anyway. So if you prepare yourself for the Year 2000, you probably will feel a lot more comfortable about your affairs in general.

After all, you really should know where your will is, where your insurance is, how much is in your 401K, and more. Having them ready, up-to-date, and ready to go is always a good idea.

THE SOLUTION

It would be a good idea to have copies of important papers in case you need them and access to them is interrupted. If you keep these papers in a safety deposit box, you may want to move them home (in a fireproof security box) for the New Year's weekend in case the bank loses power, cannot reopen, or the vault door has problems.

It is also essential that as close to the event as possible you get good records of all your assets and loans. Before New Year's Eve 1999, get your bank, broker, mortgage company, credit card companies, auto loan company, etc., to give you your status as of December 31,1999, if possible. If their computers garble your account, at least you have a starting point to argue from.

It is especially important to make sure you have your bank statements, your 401K, IRA, retirement account, stock, bond, and other financial instruments. Also insurance policy records as this information is computerized and its loss could mean that you have no way of proving your ownership. If you trade stocks via the Internet, you want hard proof that your transactions have occurred. Keep your checkbooks and your credit card statements handy. Use credit cards that give you the best documentation of your purchases. Any proof of ownership, whether it be your car, or your boat, or your house, should also be available to you. Since the Y2K hits right after the holidays, make sure your receipts for returns are handy too.

If you find that you have to leave your residence for whatever reason, you may want to be able to take all or part of your documentation with you. So be prepared to be able to pick it up and run. Have it well organized and totally up-to-date. Remember that the year will have just ended and that your taxes are also an issue, so make sure you have your last pay stub and any other tax-related documentation.

Also be sure you have duplicates of any medical or dental records that may be needed and not available through the normal channels. Birth certificates, marriage records, passports, citizenship papers, deeds, car registration, promissory notes, and other important papers should be kept at home in a fireproof box ($20 at any home center) in case you cannot access your safe deposit box or normal records. Remember if there is a bank holiday declared, safe deposit boxes may be inaccessible as well.

Important Papers to Have Available

- Birth certificates for each member of your family
- Marriage licenses or certificates
- Baptismal, confirmation, ordination, and other religious records
- Social Security cards and financial information
- Deeds, titles, and other proofs of ownership
- Mortgages and other loan agreements
- Passports
- Citizenship papers
- Car titles
- Promissory notes
- Wills
- Power of attorney

- Living wills
- Loan statements showing exactly what you owe
- Credit card statements
- Insurance policies and proof of premium payment
- Tax returns
- Membership papers
- Contracts and other legal documents
- Diplomas and academic transcripts
- Medical, dental, and pharmaceutical records
- Bank statements
- 401K, IRA, retirement account
- Stock, bond, and other financial instruments
- Insurance policies

To get a copy of Social Security cards, you can apply at the local Social Security Administration (SSA) office. Submit a Personal Earnings and Benefit Estimate Statement (PEBES) from the SSA (can also download a printable copy of the form at the SSA's Web site at www.ssa.gov/online/ssa-7004.html. Complete the form and mail it in. This document lists your earnings and all the taxes you paid to Social Security and Medicare for every year of your working career.

Send a copy of PEBES form SSA-7004 to
Social Security Administration
Wilkes Barre Data Operations Center
P.O. Box 7004
Wilkes Barre, PA 18767-7004

If you do not have copies of your taxes from the last few years, you can get copies from the IRS. Their toll-free number is 800-829-1040. The automated phone system will work you through the options and request Form 4506. It will take two to three months to get a response from the IRS so start early.

MONEY AND FINANCES

Both the Red Cross and FEMA recommend that every family have several weeks' money put aside in case ATM machines, credit cards, banks, credit unions, brokerage houses, etc., are not functioning fully after the event. Having a few weeks' extra cash makes sense so that you can purchase necessary items needed to live normally. However, this does not address the broader issues of what happens if you cannot access your checking or savings account to pay monthly bills, or what happens if your assets are tied up or lost in cyberspace, or what happens if you lose your job or your bank goes under.

CASH: Many people are considering withdrawing much of their assets and converting them into tangible products like cash, U.S. bonds, and precious metals. There is also concern about long-term investments in IRAs, retirement funds, etc., where there can be tax consequences for liquidation. This area of financial planning is past the realm of this book and the expertise of the authors.

That the Y2K bug is a problem for the banks can be understood by looking at what they are spending to try to fix it. The SEC requires quarterly reports to show Y2K expenditures. Below is a list of what some large banks are planning to spend on Y2K remediation.

Estimate ($millions)

Bank	Current	Previous
Bank One	350	315
BankAmerica	550	500
Chase Manhattan	363	300
Wells Fargo	300	273
J.P. Morgan	300	250
National City	65	40
Wachovia	80	55

Banks hold only 1.5-3% or so of the deposits in actual cash in reserve. The rest is invested and loaned to companies and individuals. If more than this reserve is withdrawn, the FDIC (Federal Deposit Insurance Corporation) guarantees all deposits up to $100,000. There is a concern that if enough were withdrawn, even the FDIC could not handle the problem. The FDIC announced in 1998 that they are printing $50 billion extra dollars to increase their reserves to $200 billion. The government has even stopped burning the old money in order to have yet a larger reserve available. Should the public lose faith in the banking system and begin to withdraw their funds in large numbers, we can create a run on the banks that could collapse our economic structure, and thereby our society. The U.S. government will probably do whatever is needed to be sure the banks do not fail. Again we offer no advice in this area other than to explain the issue and its ramifications.

The ABA (American Banking Association) suggests that customers should read the Year 2000 information that banks will be sending out and, if they have any questions, they should ask their banker. Furthermore, the ABA advises keeping your monthly bank statements and paper records of your transactions, especially for the months preceding January 2000. According to the

ABA, if customers bank on-line, then they should ensure their PC is Year 2000 compliant. Most computer and software makers have Web sites detailing their products' readiness for the date change, the association says. On-line customers should also make records of their bank accounts on a backup disk.

The ABA also advises customers to "avoid scam artists who offer to "hold" your money for you through Jan. 1, 2000."

"The safest place for it is in the bank," the association notes, adding that, for the New Year's weekend of 1999-2000, "take out only as much cash as you would for any holiday weekend....If you should feel you need more, your bank will be ready," it says.

If you do wish to keep money or other valuables at home, make sure you take precautions to secure any cash against theft and fire. You can put your money in a safe deposit box (and hope it is accessible after Jan. 1, 2000). If you keep it at home, buy a good fire-resistant box or safe and hide it wherever you think is best (if you were smart enough to earn it, you're smart enough to hide it).

THE STOCK MARKET: It is very unclear what the impact of the Y2K will be on the stock market. However, there are some companies that stand to gain from the year 2000 and there are those that stand to lose. Certainly, if you are thinking about investing in a company, you should find out about their level of Y2K exposure as it may impact the stock as the year rolls around. Again, make sure your transactions are well documented, as you want to be able to prove that your transactions have occurred.

PRECIOUS METALS: Precious metal, especially gold, is being heavily considered by many as an alternative. Gold has always been considered a safe haven in unstable times. Gold, silver, and platinum coins and bullion can be purchased from some banks and any reputable gold dealer. You can take possession of the metal or store it in the dealer's vault (and hope their computers do not lose your account info and their vault doors can open). You can even open a gold IRA, and keep the gold stored at the broker's vault. You can also buy gold options. Options allow you to buy 100 oz. of gold on or before a certain date. For instance, you could buy a June 2000 $360 gold option for $150-$250. This allows you to purchase 100 oz. of gold for $360 anytime before May 12, 2000. No matter what the price of gold goes to, all you can lose is the $150-$250. If gold goes to $660, you make $30,000 (100 oz. x $300 profit).

Gold is preferred because you need 75 times more weight in silver to create the same value of gold. $10,000.00 in silver can be a heavy, cumbersome asset. Not so with gold. However, if things were to get too unstable, the U.S. government has the right to call in all gold minted after 1933 for $50.00 per ounce. This is why the American gold coins say $50 on them though they trade for much more.

Coins minted before 1933 are considered collector's pieces (numismatic or seminumismatic) and trade for considerable more than coins minted after 1933. Also, you need to understand the market to know what the numismatic and seminumismatic coins are worth. The government may not seize the records of your gold dealer and send someone to your house to buy your gold stash at $50/oz. However, once they declare that every U.S. citizen must turn in their gold at that price, it immediately becomes illegal to have gold, the price is dropped to $50/oz, and the value of your gold crumbles. Be aware that gold may not be as liquid as you would like in an emergency. If you plan to buy precious metals, you should also consider having some cash on hand.

GETTING YOUR PC READY FOR Y2K

Several times in my career, I have seen IT disasters. These are rare Peak experiences. We're all about to see something that's never happened before: A coordinated, world wide, information technology failure. Lots of systems will survive but lots will fail too. The failures will be odd, spectacular, unlike anything we can imagine now.

"What flows from that? This is what I don't know. Everyday, I try to see past the wall but the curtain remains drawn.

—Cory Hamasaki, DC Y2K Weather Report,
January 7, 1999

Y2K is "a crisis without precedent in human history."

—Edmund X. DeJesus, "Year 2000 Survival Guide,"
BYTE (July 1998)

If we could turn back the clock, I'd like to go back to 1970 when Cobol guru/grandfather Bob Bemer had gathered together 86 professional organizations—including the AMA—and submitted a proposal to President Nixon asking him to declare a National Year of the Computer. 1970 or 71 would have been a year during which all computer users; nation wide (and by default, world-wide)—would concentrate

209

on upgrading their date fields from 2 to 4 digits. President
Nixon refused to sign the proposal and it fell by the wayside.

—Rev. Dacia Reid, citing an unpublished paper, "Y2K for
Scoffers" by Kal Gronvall of Investments Rarities,
Incorporated, Minneapolis, MN

DOES YOUR PC NEED TO BE FIXED?

As if getting your home ready for Y2K isn't enough, you
may need to get your desktop PC ready as well. Many of you
may have heard that if you have newer PC, or a MAC, then
you are ready for the Year 2000 and there is nothing that you
need to do. This is usually not true. In some newer PCs and
all MACs the clock in your computer—the hardware
clock—will properly rollover into 2000. (Figure 10.1) However, you probably still have problems in other areas of your
system—in the software, the stored data, and transfer of
data. These problems must be fixed or they could cause serious errors in some applications.

The good news for most people is preparing your computer
for the Year 2000 rollover will not be that difficult. In fact if
you use your computer only for simple things like accessing
the Internet, word processing, playing games, and perhaps a
simple personal accounting program, then you may have no
trouble at all. You might decide to wait till 2000 and see what
your PC does. You can pass this chapter over if your use of
your PC is as outlined above. In any case, your fixes will be
simple.

However, getting your PC ready for Y2K may be more difficult if

Figure 10.1 The MAC is Y2K-compliant but software, stored data, and the sharing of data may not be.

1. You use large databases or spreadsheets, corporate financial software, financial planning software, or homemade applications;

2. Your PC is tied into a network, or a mainframe at the office, it will be more difficult;

3. You track dates and appointments into the future with a calendar program;

4. You track tax data or a stock or investment portfolio;

5. You bank on-line and your bank says you must be Y2K compliant;

6. You are using licensed software or dated passwords these may expire and wipe out your program or make it inaccessible.

7. You use the Internet with a noncompliant system after January 1, 2000, you could lose passwords and other info stored in the "cookie" files created to let users access site features.

In the cases listed above, fixing any Y2K bugs in your system before the roll over may be best. You can easily test to see how your computer will rollover. You simply advance the date to December 31, 1999 at 11:58 PM and see if it rolls over to 2000. If it does, your "hardware" is Y2K ready. If it rolls to 1900 (or 1980 or 1984 in some units), it must be fixed. However, advancing the clock can be potentially dangerous and, unless your are ready to lose your data, is a bad idea. There are a number of books that suggest good testing methods, but regardless of the method, backing up the system is a must. If you perform the test in a multitask environment, like Windows, another function could be running that does something unpleasant when the date is advanced. So, always do this from a pure-DOS prompt. Also if you use any dated passwords or licensed software, advancing the date may cause these to expire. When you roll the clock back, you will have permanently deleted the passwords or licensed software.

This simple test will just determine if your "hardware" (the computer box) is Y2K compliant, not the entire system. There still may be problems in your software, stored data, and any data sharing between programs or computers. Again, make sure you back up or you may find that your Y2K problem may arrive early.

A BRIEF HISTORY OF THE Y2K/PC PROBLEM

In 1983, IBM and Motorola got together and came up with the specification for a chip. The chip became known as the NC 1468RTA. This chip was installed in the PC AT by IBM in1984. When you booted it up in the morning, you didn't have to type date and time when the machine started. This chip had its own real time clock function already built in, a little bit like a wristwatch that you wear. It has a battery, and it just keeps ticking along. It keeps telling the time. Then it tells the time to the rest of the computer system.

Unfortunately, the NC 1468RTA specification only counted in years. It didn't count in centuries. So when it gets to the year 99, it rolls over to the year 00. As far as the clock's concerned, there's nothing happening. It's just ticking along the year 00. The problem is that to save space, programmers used two-digits, and most of the operating systems, and computer software, and everything that we're using that's a calculator in our lives requires a four-digit year. So we have a situation with a fundamental component of the computer only counting in two-digit years.

But, luckily, we've got something in the middle, called the Basic Input Output System, or BIOS. This is a computer software program that runs in every single PC that tells the PC how to behave. It takes this two-digit year from the real time clock chip and translates it into a four-digit year, which it passes on to the operating system. The bad news is most of the

BIOSs get it wrong. They roll from 1999 to 1900. The good news is we can fix it, relatively easily. It takes about a minute to diagnose a faulty machine and two minutes to correct it. It's not a very large part of the problem. However this only corrects the problem at the hardware and operating-system levels. The greater problems occur in the software, stored date data, and transfer of data levels.

FIXING YOUR PC

The first thing that you need to do is to realize that it's your own problem. Nobody cares more about your computer system than you. Certainly not the people that sold it to you; they have your money. It's not an issue that you can just call up someone and get them to come in and fix it, unless you're prepared to pay for it. You need to understand what this problem actually means to you depending on your PC system and what you use it for.

If you call your hardware manufacturer (Apple, IBM, Dell, Compaq, Gateway, etc.), they may tell you, "Your computer is Y2K ready" or "Just download this fix and you're ready." Technically this may be true. Your computer, the actual box sitting on your desk, is ready but they do not address the entire system. Are your software programs and applications ready? Is your operating system ready? Even Windows 98 was diagnosed with a Y2K bug. Does your stored data, most with two-digit year dates, need to be reworked into four-digit year dates? Will the data transfer correctly between different programs or different computers after the rollover? These are questions you must answer yourself.

Most (but not all) PCs built since 1997 are Y2K ready. All MACs are Y2k ready. However, just the hardware is ready.

Your software and data will have all the problems of those stored or running on older, Y2K noncompliant PCs.

We wish this chapter could tell you everything that you need to know about preparing your computer for the year 2000 but no one could do that. If anyone says they could, they would be deceiving either you or themselves. There are just too many combinations of hardware, operating systems, software, and stored data for any one book to tell you everything you need to know. Each computer, with its unique software and data, must be understood and approached—*uniquely*. However, this chapter will point you in the right direction, tell you when you will need to get more information, and advise you of the most common mistakes to avoid. The key misunderstanding is that people think that computers are going to stop. They're actually not. They're going to carry on, right through 2000. It's just that you won't be able to trust the result of what's coming out of them.

THE FIVE LEVELS OF YOUR PC

There are actually five areas or levels in your computer where date-sensitive data is used. Each level can cause century-date-related problems after January 1, 2000, or even before. The first level is the hardware level, or the problems within the equipment itself. Fixing your hardware problem, that is the little clock inside your computer's motherboard that keeps the time and date, is relatively simple. The process of fixing it is clear and defined. The second level is the operating system that runs between your programs and your hardware. As with the hardware, fixing Y2K problems at this level is simple.

The third level is the software level or problems occurring in your applications or programs. The fourth level is your stored data—all the information you have been entering and storing into your computer for years. And the final, and perhaps most complex area, is the transfer and exchange of these data between programs or between computers. In the last three levels, you will no longer have a well-defined path to determine your own.

In these areas you must develop a clear awareness of how your system processes year dates—both two and four digit. You will need help from your hardware and software manufacturers. If your computers are networked to computers from other enterprises or individuals, you will need to cooperate with them as well to be sure your fixes will allow for a continuous flow of data between them and you after the millennium. However, this chapter will point you in the right direction and tell you where to get road maps from your hardware and software manufacturers and other professionals if needed. *Remember an important rule: Always, always backup your data before working wih your PC to fix Y2K problems!*

LEVEL 1:
HARDWARE

Let's go through each of the five levels and look at how to correct each. Lets begin at the first level and perhaps the simplest to fix, the hardware level. (Figure 10.2) This level is the smallest part of your overall problem and the easiest to solve. Almost every computer will be fixable at this level though a small percentage may need to be replaced.

In your hardware, built into every computer, is a clock or counter—actually it's a chip with a battery that serves to keep the time and date. Its called the Real Time Clock or RTC. This real time clock may or may not roll over properly

Figure 10.2   Y2K problems may be built into your hardware, the computer box itself where the computer is storing the data.

from 1999 to 2000. It must be tested and fixed if necessary. (Figure 10.3)

You can call your manufacturer to see if the real time clock will roll over to 2000 (see list of hardware and software manufacturers in Reference section in the back of the book). If it will not, they will instruct you on what to do. Usually you can go to an Internet site and download a fix or they will send you a disc. Also in your hardware is something called the BIOS which is short for Basic Input Output System. This BIOS is another chip running a small program that takes the two-digit year from the real time clock and translates this two-digit year, say 99, into a four-digit year, 1999. The BIOS then feeds that

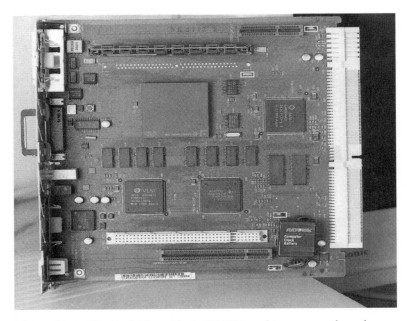

Figure 10.3 The Real Time Clock (RTC) is a chip connected to a battery that tells the computer the date and time. Many RTCs will not roll over properly to 2000.

four-digit year up to your operating system and software applications. The problem is that some BIOSs and real time clocks may not roll over properly to the year 2000.

However, the best recommendation for many PC users is to buy an off-the-shelf PC Y2K diagnostic software. For $25-50 you can purchase Y2K remediation software at your computer store that will fix this problem and any problems with the operating system, as well as identify (but not fix) any software programs that may have problems. (Figure 10.4) Some new Y2K PC fixes claim to not only identify but also fix any Y2K problems in any software you are running on your PC. However, many Y2K/PC experts doubt these claims and these products are too new to evaluate.

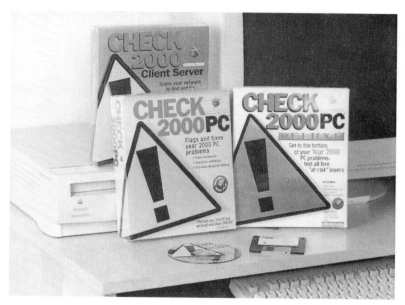

Figure 10.4 Y2K diagnostic software will correct the date in the BIOS and identify any Y2K-problematic software you might be running.

LEVEL 2:
OPERATING SYSTEM

As you can see, the hardware level is not difficult to correct. Our next level is the operating system, also called the OS. The operating system is a software program that initializes the functions of your computer and allows the hardware to interact with your programs. In most desktops the operating systems are either Windows (90% of all PCs), UNIX, DOS, or

MAC. You need to be aware of how your operating system handles dates and in some situations you may need to adjust the preferences, protocols, and settings features to handle four-digit year dates. If you are using Windows or MAC operating systems, these should roll over without any major problems.

Year 2000 problems at the operating system level again are relatively easy to fix. Usually the same software that you bought and used to fix the hardware problems will automatically fix the operating system problems. You may want to contact the company that created your operating system, like Microsoft or Apple, to see if they have a free upgrade they can send you or that you can download from the Internet.

Most PCs are running a classic operating system such as Windows, MAC, etc. With the MAC you go to the "Control Panels" under the apple and then click on "Date & Time." Then click on "Date Formats" and then select the "Show Century" option.

With Windows you can open the "Control Panel" and go to the "regional settings" part of the control panel. Check to see if the "regional settings" part has the short two-digit date-style year (MM-DD-YY-month-date-year, i.e., 12-31-99). The normal way of installing the PC with either Windows or Windows 95 is to use the MM-DD-YY setting. In fact, that is the way it sets it up automatically for you. However, a number of programs take their understanding of how to display dates or how to accept the input of dates from whatever it says in that screen.

So, if you change MM-DD-YY (12-31-99) to MM-DD-YYYY (12-31-1999) so you're using a four-digit year, then some of the programs will behave differently. They will start to ask you for four-digit years, and will come to expect that you will always type in a four-digit year.

Changing the "regional settings" to MM-DD-YYYY will correct most of the problems with common software packages. However, if you're running some home-grown packages, things you've written yourself, it's possible that they may not fix the proper effects, it may make the problem worse. Try this, but don't be surprised if something peculiar happens. And always, always, always, back up before you try anything like this.

LEVEL 3:
SOFTWARE AND APPLICATIONS

The third level is all your software and applications. These are the programs that you see everyday advertised on television. You see them in the retail stores—bookkeeping programs, accounts systems, even word processors and spreadsheets. They all have potential Year 2000 problems. And the issue here, very different from the hardware issue, is that it's not black and white. It's not yes and no. It's not compliant or noncompliant. It's not just whether the software is or is not compliant. More importantly, you need to be aware of the way to use that program in a compliant manner. You may have to change the way you use the program, not necessarily change the program.

With software Y2K problems, things get a little trickier and the corrections are not so simple. You must determine for each piece of software that you run whether it is ready for the Year 2000 or not. This is usually done by contacting its manufacturer through their 800 number or Web site (see list of hardware and software manufacturers in Reference section). They will often tell you need to buy the upgrade or download a fix or patch from their Web site or from a disc they will send you.

In some cases you will be required to purchase an upgraded version, adding insult to injury.

However, even following the software manufacturer's instruction this may not be as simple as it seems. In fact even the term "Year 2000-ready" or "Year 2000 compliant" is really hard to define. Often you may use a program one way and it will perform with no Year 2000 problems and someone else can use the exact program another way and it will have problems on their system. Or two programs can both be considered Year 2000 compliant, but because the process dates differently, they cannot talk to each other.

The other thing is that people don't believe this problem. However the problems are real. Some programs simply don't work in the next century. Some programs take dates from the operating system and don't seem to qualify that date. If your operating system thinks it's 1980, then the program thinks it's 1980, even if the program "knows" that yesterday is 1999. A program may take dates from the OS, so if your invoicing program gets told that today is 1980 and yesterday is 1999, it says "okay" and prints your invoices with 1980 across the top. There are problems with date manipulation, where the dates are changed behind the scenes. You can't actually see what's going on, but dates are changed and corrupted without your knowledge.

That is why, in the end, this is your problem to solve. No matter what your software and hardware manufacturers tell you, you must understand how each of your software programs handles the century date rollover and determine if that will work for you and, if necessary, whether different programs will be able to talk to each other. However, if you are only using one program, say an accounting program to pay bills or run a small business, this will not be that difficult.

Some of the software Year 2000 fixes you can purchase that correct your hardware and BIOS problems will also identify which of your software programs have problems. (Figure 10.5) Even though they tell you which of your software programs have Year 2000 problems, you still must fix them. These tools only identify Y2K problematic software. They do not make the software Y2K-compliant. And most importantly you must understand how your applications convert two-digit year dates to four-digit year dates. However, you just need to go to this level of understanding if you are running sophisticated software involving financial projections, important bookkeeping, or if you are transferring data between programs or computers, etc. The average user does not need to read any further for this third level.

Figure 10.5 Diagnostic tools will tell you which of your software programs have Year 2000 problems but you still must remediate the software.

However, if you are running sophisticated software or trans-ferring data between programs or computers, as with the data level, in this area it is essential that you understand how your year dates are used and stored in your software programs and operating system. Some programs use a method called "win-dowing." They may take any two-digit year date over 50, called the pivot date, and make the century 19 and take any date under 50 and make the century 2000. So 67 is 1967 but 12 is 2012. Others may use a different pivot date, say 20 or 29, instead of 50. Some software will add or delete 28 years to the date. This is called encapsulation. However the year dates are handled, it is essential that you understand this for each application and the system in general so that you can adjust your system to work after the rollover. This can be a very com-plex task—but one that must be done. And remember always back up your data—verify the backup and backup again!

If you want to actually test some of your programs, this can be quite an involved task. You need to put in dates over the date-rollover point and put in dates in the next century; then you move your application and the operating system date up to the end of the century and see what happens in your pro-grams to dates before, during, and after. This is a straightfor-ward way of doing testing. But you can completely and utterly wipe out your programs if you do this. Quite a lot of programs have a little licensing utility in there that detects whether or not you're moving the date around unnecessarily. And that can lock you out of the system if you move it too far in the future. Equally, if your PC runs backwards, some of these licensing programs will detect that time has gone backwards, and lock you out.

Also, you could corrupt your own data. You need to be extremely careful when you're doing this testing. Of course, most of the tools that are available in the retail stores that do this type of testing don't do it on your live system. They do a comparison. They do a very safe analysis of what is actually there, and how it performs in the laboratory when it was tested under lab conditions. They don't muck around with your own system. It's actually safer to use those types of systems than to try and do all the testing yourself. Of course, if you developed your own programs yourself, then there is a good chance that you need to test those programs.

LEVEL 4:
STORED DATA

Again, if you are not using sophisticated software involving projections, future invoicing, etc., and are not transferring data between programs or computers, problems in the data and data transfer area are of little concern. In this section we will be looking at problems and solutions at the date-data and transfer of data levels. Though for some situations this area can be a simple fix, for many it can be by far the most complex levels of the Year 2000 problem. There are no easy solutions at this level. You must have a complete and accurate awareness of how your two- and four-digit year dates are stored and used. This is a challenging task, but doable.

There are basically two ways dates are handled in your computers: explicitly and implicitly. By explicitly we mean that dates are stored as four-digit years, 1998 is stored as 1998, not the two digit 98. This fully expanded year date eliminates all date ambiguity and if all our dates had been handled that way, you wouldn't need this book. But we didn't store our dates this way. Instead we usually stored them with only the two-year digit with implicit century. So 1998 was 98—and the computer must use logic in a program to make the date value accurate.

You have to be aware of how your dates are being used and stored. Once you have determined that your software programs are ready for the Year 2000 rollover, you must be sure that your old data that were stored as two-digit year dates will work with them. You will need to contact the software manufacturer to find out and hopefully they will tell you what you need to do for each program you run. Some upgraded programs will work fine with the old data. With other programs you may need to make a few adjustments. And with yet others you may need to reenter all your old data with four-digit year dates.

The year 2000 is a very good excuse to go through that and recatalog what you've got on your system. There are some very cheap ways of doing this now. You can buy a ZIP drive and store your data on discs. (Figure 10.6) You can buy a CD-ROM drive that will actually fit into your machine. You just write CDs on your own. A good "spring cleaning" may be wise in late 1999.

Figure 10.6 ZIP drives are a very good way to store pre-Y2K data.

LEVEL 5:
TRANSFER OR SHARING OF DATA

The fifth and final level, and perhaps the most complex, is data transfer. This is the transfer of your data within your computer between various software programs or, the more complicated transfer of data between different computers, say your home computer and your company's mainframe at their headquarters. If you are transferring your data between two software applications in the same machine, you must understand how date data are stored in each and how they flow between the programs. If they both handle the dates in the same manner, transferring data between two programs should be no problem.

However, if they don't, there can be. For example, even two different versions of the same software program, say version 3 and version 4 spreadsheets, may handle the dates differently and therefore their exchange of data may be incompatible. In this case, the only way to exchange data between the two versions may be to manually go in and convert the two-digit year dates to four-digit year dates. You must determine if both programs convert two-digit year dates to four-digit year dates in the same manner. If they don't, you will need to adjust the way you use the programs. Again you will need information from your software manufacturer here.

If you're using your PC to do four or five different things, it's quite possible, to outline the potential problems, to draw a little graph on your spreadsheet program and put it into a word processing document so that you can then print it out and present it as a report. And that's fairly straightforward, although there may be some year 2000 issues in the way the data are shared between those two different programs. If you're running a small business, you may be having network PCs that are sharing central information, in which case, the way the information is stored on the central machine could well be very different from the way the programs handle it on the different individual PCs. You then need to analyze the differences between the two.

If you're running in a large computer environment where you're a user at home, it's quite possible that your corporate information is sitting on a mainframe or some very big servers back in head office. In that case, you really need to talk to the IS/IT manager about how he's dealing with the different ways that data are exchanged in your organization. This isn't something that you should be really diving into yourself. This is where you might want to sit down in some sort of committee meeting and discuss how are you going to process these data. In large corporations, most people don't even know how many PCs they have, let alone what those PCs are doing. When it comes down to sharing the data information, very few seem to know how it happens, and who does what. It is a matter of sitting down centrally and analyzing the problem.

As we mentioned earlier, in the PC world there are two common methods: expansion and windowing. Let's take a look at each. Expansion is where you expand all year dates to four digits so they always show the proper century. Expansion solves the problem once and for all, where windowing, a program of adding the correct century to a two-digit date, only puts the problem off (the program might ad "19" to "67" to make "1967"). It is essential to understand that there can be no transfer of data between programs that have stored the year dates differently unless you provide for translation into the same date data language.

If you are dealing with small spreadsheets, for instance, you may decide to manually expand all your year dates to four digits.

For larger databases you may want to create a program that will translate for you, both for dates within a single program, as well as transfers. To make better decisions, you must understand the limitations of the software as well as your information processing needs.

AND THEN THERE'S THE LEAP YEAR Y2K PROBLEM

As if the problem didn't need to be any worse, it certainly got worse because the year 2000 is a leap year. Pope Gregory XIII, in 1582, declared the year 2000 a leap year. However, the rule, generally, is that the leap year is every fourth year, unless it's the century, and unless it's divisible by 400. So, 1900 was not a leap year because it was a century *not* divisible by 400. 1600 was a leap year, 2000 is a leap year.

Remember we were saying the PCs actually go back to the year 1900. Well, if your PC goes back to 1900, 1900 wasn't a leap year, but the year 2000 is. 1900 had no February 29. 2000 will. So, there are different versions of different spreadsheet packages. Some of them think 1900 was a leap year, and some of them think it wasn't. It's a classic case between Lotus 1-2-3 and Excel. There is some incompatibility there between what they do and what the reality is. So, again we need to just be aware of what the issues are in regard to the programs.

IN CONCLUSION

As you can see there may be a lot of information you may have to gather from others. The Year 2000 is approaching. If you do not get your computer ready in time three different problems may occur. You equipment may totally cease to function or what is called "abend," or gross noticeable errors may occur that are easily detected or finally, the most insidious—unnoticeable errors may occur that you may not be aware of initially. So as you can see, it would be wise to get your system ready before the event so there is plenty of time for testing.

If, after seeing what is involved in preparing your desktop for the Year 2000 you feel that you cannot fix it yourself, you have several options:

1. You can take it to a computer repair shop or computer consultant to remediate;

2. You can wait for the January 1, 2000 rollover and see how badly your system has been affected and fix it after the event

3. You can live with the corrupted data and calculations;

4. Or you can fix all Y2K problems and be sure that your hardware, operating system, software, and data are century date ready and that you can use them in the appropriate manner.

One final, and somewhat disturbing, thought. Before the Year 2000 we have been pretty much able to trust what our computers were doing, after all the glitches were worked out, was correct and reliable. Well beginning in 2000, and actually for many of us in 1999, we can no longer make this assumptions. We need to start distrusting our computers and examine their assumptions and calculations given the extent of the Year 2000 problems involved. This is a profound change in the way we view and use our computers.

AND NOW FOR SOME GOOD NEWS

Y2K can be seen as anything from a random computer blunder to a punishment meted out by a punitive God on His immoral or defiant children. But perhaps, just perhaps, it is a gift in disguise.

Y2K AS A GIFT

The first lesson Y2K can teach is that we must use our technology with greater wisdom. The power of our technology now threatens our existence. Our technology, as of 50 years ago, has vastly outstripped our wisdom. In this one fact lies the threat to the entire species. The threat of this spread between our technology and our wisdom to use it has created nuclear waste and weapons, germ and biological threats, El Nino, the hole in the ozone level, global warming, and now Y2K.

All of these threaten our very life on the planet and we are not addressing them effectively. Our technology has outgrown our wisdom and we must catch up.

Albert Einstein made two great quotes that sum up this issue. He stated that the day we exploded the first atomic bomb, everything in the world changed—except human consciousness. And because of this, he said, we drift toward the abyss. With or without Y2K, we are steadily drifting toward that abyss.

The second quote was in response to a question regarding what weapons he thought might be used in a third world war. After some thought, he responded that he did not know what weapons would be used in a third world war, but in the fourth we would use sticks and stones.

Our technology has brought us to the point that if it is not infused with greater wisdom, we will destroy ourselves. Y2K will be our first global technological crisis. If we learn from it, we may take our other technological threats seriously and pull back from the abyss.

The second great lesson of Y2K is that we must cooperate, as individuals, as businesses, as countries, as a world. The bold competitive, enemy-thinking paradigm that has existed on this planet for generations must diminish and give way to a more compassionate one or the above threats will catch us. Y2K demands cooperation for our computer-based infrastructure to be repaired, both before and after January 1, 2000.

To survive, every large company must cooperate with the smaller companies that they do business with. Every country must help other countries that are their trading partners. Every person must help their neighbor or else the overall problems will spill over and affect whatever well-thoughtout preparations we have made. The only way to effectively reduce the effect of Y2K before and after the event is through cooperation: individually, nationally, corporately, and globally.

If, no matter how great the impact, Y2K can teach us these two lessons, its legacy to the planet may be as important as the lessons taught by our greatest spiritual teachings and teachers. It may serve to remind us that we are all interconnected and interdependent.

Given my thinking above, I have expanded this to what I believe may be Y2K's hidden code below.

THE HIDDEN CODE OF Y2K

Only two things threaten our existence:
A breakdown of society as we know it;
The continuation of society as we know it.

—Jan Blum, Seeds Blum Company

Many lessons that mankind must learn to continue life on this planet, with the present power of our technology, can be taught within one seemingly random computer event, Y2K.

These lessons include

1. Our competitive, power-driven instincts must quickly evolve into cooperative ones. As Martin Luther King, Jr., said: "The choice is no longer between violence or nonviolence but rather between nonviolence or nonexistence."

2. We must deal with our nuclear weapons, plants, and waste rationally as they pose a continuing threat to the entire species, now and for many generations yet unborn.

3. We must stop polluting at our present level. Most pollution comes from the first world. One person in the United States pollutes more than 500 people from Nepal.

4. We must return our value system to one more centered in people and relationship, as opposed to the present one centered on ownership and things.

5. We must further develop, and eventually convert to, our decentralized, nonpolluting sources of energy (wind, solar, wave, hydro, etc.) There are less than 50 years of fossil fuels left and their use is destroying the environment.

6. We must address our other technological threats and evaluate and deal with their impact: global warming, biological, nuclear, and chemical weapons, El Nino, ozone level, pollution, etc. Like Y2K they are threatening, but unlike Y2K their deadline is not known.

7. We must become more self-reliant, depending more on ourselves, our communities, and each other as opposed to relying solely on our leaders and government, who often do not have our best interests at heart.

8. The large corporations must adjust, or be made to adjust, priorities to include not only profit but concern for the environment and people as well.

9. There must be a renewal of the use of nonhybrid seeds. At the present rate that seed companies are promoting and selling hybrid seeds (seeds that are only good for one season), in 20 years there will be almost no nonhybrid seeds available. We would have genetically engineered all food seeds on the planet to be non-renewable.

10. The unabated barrage of sexuality, vulgarity and commercialism in our media cannot continue on its course. It undermines real values and stable family structures.

11. Just as American Indian leaders planned seven generations ahead, so must we consider and plan for the generations that will follow us.

12. Technology and material growth must cease to be an end in itself. We must ask, "What is it for?"

Almost every lesson we must learn to continue on this planet with the power of our existing technology is listed above. Failure to learn any one of them continues to put our species at risk. Y2K has the ability to teach us every lesson.

This is absolutely necessary if we are to continue on this planet much longer, given the existing level and power of our technology. These lessons will not be learned easily. As with all other human lessons, they will be learned through our pain. But they can be learned.

As individuals asking what we can do to usher in this new paradigm, the answer is clear: in addition to whatever actions and work we feel called to do,

Love ourselves and each other as much as we can.

—Robert Roskind, March 1999

REFERENCES AND RESOURCES

GENERAL Y2K INFORMATION

- Reference #1) Y2K BOOKS

- Reference #2) Y2K VIDEOS

- Reference #3) Y2K WEBSITES

  — Family Preparedness

  — Community Groups

  — General Y2K Sites

  — Federal

  — State

  — International

  — Business

  — Academic

  — Electronic and Print Media

  — Y2K Services and Vendors

- Reference #4) SAMPLE LETTERS
  - Banks
  - Local Government
  - Law Enforcement
  - Electrical Utilities
  - General Institutions
  - Health Care
  - Telecommunications

- Reference #5) COMPUTER HARDWARE AND SOFTWARE CONTACT INFO
  - Y2K COMMUNITY RESOURCES

- Reference #6) Y2K COMMUNITY GROUPS

- Reference #7) Y2K COMMUNITY RESOURCE GROUPS
  (Courtesy of Y2K Community Project— www.y2kcommunity.org)

- Reference #8) COMMUNITY ORGANIZING TECH- NIQUES AND TOOLS
  (Courtesy of Y2K Community Project— www.y2kcommunity.org)
  - STATE Y2K RESOURCES

- Reference #9) STATE Y2K WEBSITES
  - FEDERAL GOVERNMENT RESOURCES

- Reference #10) U.S. SENATORS AND REPRESENTA- TIVES CONTACT INFO

- Reference #11) U.S. GOVERNMENT'S Y2K FREE HOTLINE

- Reference #12) Y2K For Kids
  (Courtesy U.S. Government's Y2K Site)

- Reference #13) CONSUMER ALERTS

  — Preparing Your Personal Finances for the Year 2000

  — Electronic Products

  — What Do Consumers Need to Know about Insurance?

  — Questions for Investors to Ask about the Year 2000

  — SEC? September 1997

  — Information-Technology and Home-Office Products

- Reference #14) The Red Cross and Y2K

- Reference #15) FEMA (Federal Emergency Management Agency) and Y2K

- Reference #16) Y2K and People with Disabilities

- Reference #17) Principles and Objectives for Nuclear Nonproliferation and Disarmament

REFERENCE #1
Y2K BOOKS

Time Bomb 2000: What The Year 2000 Computer Crisis Means To You!
Edward and Jennifer Yourdon
$19.95; Paperback—420 pages
Prentice Hall PTR; ISBN: 0-13-095284-2

Making the Best of Basics: Family Preparedness Handbook
James Talmage Stevens
$19.95; Paperback—320 pages
Gold Leaf Press, ISBN: 1-882723-25-2

Don't Get Caught with Your Pantry Down! How to Find Preparedness Resources for the Unexpected and Expected!
$29.95; Paperback—520 pages
Historical Publications, Inc., ISBN: 1-881825-19-1

The Year 2000 Problem: Strategies and Solutions from the Fortune 100
Dr. Leon Kappelman
$44.95
International Thomson Computer Press; ISBN: 1-85032-9133

Y2K: What You Must Know to Protect Yourself, Your Family, Your Assets and Your Community When the Lights Go Out on January 1, 2000
Victor W. Porlier
$10.95; Paperback—144 pages
Harper Collins; ISBN: 0062736752

Y2K for Women: how to Protect your Home and Family in the Coming Crisis
Karen Anderson
$19.95; 224 pages
Sovereign Press; ISBN 0965-4974-1-0

Whatcha Gonna Do If the Grid Goes Down? Preparing Your Household for the Year 2000
Susan E. Robinson, Mark Stansell (Illustrator), Stephany Evans (Editor)
$22.95; Spiral-bound—136 pages, 1st edition
Virtual Sage; ISBN: 0966762509

How to Survive Y2k Chaos in the City—A Preparedness and Self-Reliance Handbook
Ken; Eirich, Nancy Eirich
$15.95; Paperback—112 pages, 1st edition
Infoage Consulting and Publishing; ISBN: 0968429300

Awakening: The Upside of Y2K
Judy Laddon (Editor), Tom Atlee (Editor), Larry Shook (Editor)
$10.00; Paperback—188 pages, 1st edition
Judy Laddon; ISBN: 0-9667030-06

Countdown Y2K: Business Survival Planning for the Year 2000
Peter De Jager, Richard Bergeon
$29.99; Paperback—352 pages, 2nd edition
John Wiley & Sons; ISBN: 0471327344

Got Beans? Get Ready for the Year 2000 Computer Crisis
Ingrid Harding
$7.95; Paperback—96 pages
Porch Publishing; ISBN: 0966789121

Panic Now! The Y2K Millennium Bug Will Effect You!
Philip Steinman, Charles Bethancourt (Editors)
$17.95; Mass Market Paperback—150 pages, 1st edition
Wisdom Publishing, Inc.; ISBN: 0966586808

*Quandary 2000: The How To Guide for Developing and
  Implementing a Plan to Address the Y2K Computer Issues*
William H. Dudley
$29.95; Unknown binding
JC Consulting; ISBN: 0966985702

Spiritual Survival During the Y2K Crisis
Steve Farrar
$12.99; Paperback—252 pages
Nelson-Hall Company; ISBN: 0785273093

What Will Become of Us?: Counting Down to Y2K
Julian Gregori (Editor)
$14.95; Paperback—240 pages
Academic Freedom Foundation; ISBN: 1892709007

Y2K: It's Already Too Late
Jason Kelly
$17.95; Paperback—375 pages, 1st edition
ISBN: 0966438701

Y2K: The Millennium Bug
Shaunti Christine Feldhahn
$12.99; Paperback
Multnomah Publishers Inc.; ISBN: 1576734706;

Y2K Book of Resource Lists: What You Need to Prepare
$10.95; Spiral-bound—35 pages
Practical Preparedness; ISBN: 096691290X

Y2K Citizen's Action Guide
Eric Utne
$4.95; Paperback—120 pages
Utne Reader Books; ISBN: 0965381625

Y2K Equals 666 (Revised)
David Hutchins
$9.95; Hardcover, 1998
Hearthstone Pub.; ISBN: 1575580349

The Y2K Survival Guide; Getting To, Getting Through, and Getting Past the Year 2000 Problem
Bruce F. Webster
$19.99; Paperback—300 pages, 1999
Prentice Hall; ISBN: 0130214965

Y2K Survival Handbook for the Urban Family
Allen M. Mullins, O. Dwayne Price and C. Diane Palmer
$19.95; Paperback—115 pages, 1998
Cimarron Press; ISBN: 0966845803

The Y2K Workbook For Small Business
Donald G. Petersen
$199.95; Spiral-bound—130 pages
Petersen Consulting Group; ISBN: 0966753003

Y2K, the Day the World Shut Down
George E. Grant, Michael S. Hyatt
$12.99; Paperback—320 pages
Word Books; ISBN: 084991387X

Y2K: How to Protect Your Family in the Quiet Crisis
Todd H. Phillips, Darren R. McMaster
$14.95; Paperback—128 pages
Safe 2000, Inc.; ISBN: 0966779703

Year 2000: Best Practices for Y2K Millennium Computing
Dick Lefkon (Editor)
$39.95; Paperback, 1998
Prentice Hall PTR; ISBN: 0136465064

Year 2000: The International Directory of Y2K Conversion
Resources
Bohdan Szuprowicz
$195.00; Paperback, 1998
Computer Technology Research Corporation; ISBN: 1566070619

Year 2000 Best Practices Manual
COG Information Technology Subcommittee
$45.00; Ring-bound—354 pages, 2 Volume Set ,Vol. 1-2
Metropolitan Washington; ISBN: 1583530002

Year 2000 Manual
Deirdre Mueller, Marc Korody (Editor), and Jeremiah Hall
(Editor)
$29.95; Spiral-bound—70 pages, 1st edition
IntelliSource; ISBN: 0966620909

The Year 2000 Survival Guide
Kenneth E. Koller
$9.95; Perfect—64 pages
In Line Publishing, Inc.; ISBN: 0966857003

Year 2000: Mom and Pop's Small Business Guide
Diana Driscoll, Rich Driscoll
$89.95; Spiral-bound—75 pages, 1st edition
Priority Consultants, Inc.; ISBN: 0966772725

You and the Year 2000: A Practical Guide for Things That Matter
Jeffrey M. Shepard
$19.95; Paperback—181 pages
Indigo Ink Publishing; ISBN: 0966808401

Your Y2K Workbook
Joe L. Miller
$29.95; Spiral-bound—153 pages
Your Y2K; ISBN: 0966932307

Action for Y2K:A GrassRoots' Guide to the Year 2000
Richard T. Wright, Cathryn Wellner
$12.95; Paperback—152 pages
Winter Quarters Press; ISBN: 0969688725

After the Fireworks: Business and Technology Strategies for Surviving Y2K Hits (Advanced and Emerging Communications Technologies Series: A Desk Reference
Unhelkar Bhuvan
$59.95; Hardcover
CRC Press; ISBN: 0849395992

Bits and Bytes Y2K and Beyond
Timothy V. Kelly
$20.00; Mass Market; Paperback—235 pages, 1st edition
Network Technology Services; ISBN: 0966649109

Deadline Y2K
Mark Joseph
$24.95; Hardcover—320 pages
St. Martins Press (Trade); ISBN: 0312202024

Does Y2K Equal 666
Noah W. Hutchings
$9.95; Paperback
Hearthstone Pub.; ISBN: 1575580284

Earthpulse Flashpoints; Y2K—A Special Report
Nick Begich (Editor), William Thomas
$4.95; Paperback, 1998
Earthpulse Press, Inc.; ISBN: 1890693170

Electric Utilities and Y2K
$35.00; Paperback—153, pages 1st edition, 1998
Rick Cowles; ISBN: 0966340213

Emergency Procedures for Urban and Suburban Living Applies to Y2K
Ralph W. Ritchie
$24.95; Unknown Binding—236 pages Revised edition, Vol. 1
Ritchie Unlimited Publications; ISBN: 0939656302

Glitch—The Y2K Conspiracy
David Kedson
$18.95; Paperback—365 pages, 1998

How to Move Your AS/400 beyond Y2K: The Complete Story
Julie A. Ransom (Editor)
$69.00; Mass Market Paperback—262 pages, 1998
AS/400 Press; ISBN: 0966337506

How to Profit from the Y2K Recession: By Converting the Year 2000 Crisis into an Opportunity for Your Investments and Business
John Mauldin
$24.95; Hardcover—256 pages

St. Martins Press (Trade); ISBN: 0312207069

Millennium Information—The Y2K Computer Problem Solutions and Options
Millennium Info Group
Paperback, 1st edition, 1998
Sun Pub Co.; ISBN: 0895404184

Mongo's Y2K Survival Plan for the Complete Idiot!
Garry Brooks, Ben Herr
$14.95; Hardcover—160 pages, 1st edition
First Light Publications; ISBN: 1889553131

Soul Tsunami: Sink or Swim in Y2K Culture
Leonard I. Sweet
$19.99; Hardcover, 1999
Zondervan Publishing House; ISBN: 0310227623

The Y2K Computer Crash Scenario: What to Expect and How to Protect Your Assets, Your Credit, and Your Way of Life
John Mrozek
$15.00; Paperback, 1998
Paladin Press; ISBN: 1581600062

Y2K, Crying Wolf or World Crisis
James F. Gauss
$12.99; Paperback—360 pages
Bridge-Logos Publishers; ISBN: 0882707604

Your Essential Y2K Manual
James F. Gauss
$2.99; Paperback—28 pages, Manual edition
Bridge-Logos Publishers; ISBN: 0882707647

Y2K MAGAZINES

Y2k News
www.y2knews.com
20 Our Way
Crossville, TN 38555

Y2K Solutions
www.y2k-solutions.net
9121 E. Tanque Verde Road, #105-313
Tucson, AZ 85749

REFERENCE #2
Y2K VIDEOS

Y2K CONSUMER VIDEOS

Ed Yourdon's Year 2000 Home Preparation Guide
featuring Ed and Jennifer Yourdon and James Talmage Stevens
This video shows you how to prepare your home and family for Y2K. Includes food storage, water storage and treatment, heat, light, cooking, safety, health, and more.
50 minutes; $19.95
Y2K Solutions Group, Inc.: 888-Y2K-4YOU,
www.readyfory2k.com

Preparing Your PC for the Year 2000
featuring Dr. Leon Kappelman, Karl Feilder, and Tom Becker
This video is for anyone who owns or operates a computer. It assumes no particular level of "computer expertise." It explains, in

everyday terms, what you will need to do to prepare your computer, its software, and stored data for the year 2000 rollover.
30 Minutes; $19.95
UPC: 051679028017; ISBN: 156522-000-5
Y2K Solutions Group, Inc.: 888-Y2K-4YOU, www.readyy2k.com

Y2K Consumer Awareness Video
featuring Dr. Leon Kappelman
In this video, Dr. Leon Kappelman, an internationally recognized expert on the Year 2000 problem, addresses its origin, its scope, its risks, and solutions. Punctuated by quotes and articles from other credible sources, the video presents the problem clearly and honestly, allowing the viewer to draw their own conclusions.
20 Minutes; $19.95
UPC: 015679028079; ISBN: 1-56522-008-0
Y2K Solutions Group, Inc.:888-Y2K-4YOU,
www.readyfory2k.com

Y2K the Clock Is Ticking (1998)
List Price: $24.95
$20.99
Edition Details:
• NTSC format (for use in United States and Canada only)
• Color, NTSC
• Number of tapes: 1
• ASIN: 1888147407

Y2K Family Survival Guide (1998)
$14.95; Rated: NR
Starring: Leonard Nimoy et al.
Edition Details:
• NTSC format (for use in United States and Canada only)
• Color, NTSC
• Number of tapes: 1
• ASIN: 6305300224

Y2k Millennium Meltdown: The Silent Bomb (1998)
$22.95; Release Date: February 16, 1999; Rated: NR
Edition Details:
• Color, NTSC
• Number of tapes: 1
• ASIN: 6305298874

BUSINESS AND PROFESSIONAL VIDEOS

#502:Y2K Awareness Video
featuring Dr. Leon Kappelman
In this video, Dr. Leon Kappelman, an internationally recognized
expert on the Year 2000 problem, addresses its origin, its scope, its
risks, and solutions. Punctuated by quotes and articles from other
credible sources, the video presents the problem clearly and honestly, allowing the viewer to draw their own conclusions.
25 Minutes; $49.95
UPC: 015679028079; ISBN: 1-56522-008-0
Y2K Solutions Group, Inc.: 888-Y2K-4YOU, www.y2kvideos.com

#201 PC NETWORK REMEDIATION SERIES
featuring Dr. Leon Kappelman, Karl Feilder, & Tom Becker
This series is designed to train business owners, managers, computer
field engineers, and help desk personnel to prepare a network of
desktops for the year 2000. It includes three videos: hardware solutions, software solutions, and date data solutions.
3 Videos (30 minutes each)
UPC: 015679028062; ISBN:1-56522-006-4
Y2K Solutions Group, Inc.: 888-Y2K-4YOU, www.y2kvideos.com

#301 YEAR 2000 MANAGEMENT SERIES
featuring Dr. Leon Kappelman
This series is designed for managers, executives, supervisors, and
business owners who are responsible for preparing their enterprise

for the Year 2000 rollover. It includes two videos: Video #1: What Every Manager and Executive Needs To Know About the Year 2000 and Video #2: Strategies and Solutions For the Year 2000.

2 Videos (1 hour each); $199.95/set including Leon Kappelman's book and CD

UPC: 051679028000; ISBN: 1-56522-005-6

Y2K Solutions Group, Inc.: 888-Y2K-4YOU, www.y2kvideos.com

#702: Solutions to Year 2000 Problems with Infrastructure and Embedded Systems

featuring Dave Hall

Time: 4 one hour videos; $399.00

Learn to evaluate best practices for successfully dealing with embedded systems projects. Explains problems already recognized, development of checklist of areas to investigate, and an exploration of alternative solution strategies.

4 Hours; $399.00

UPC: 05J1679028123; ISBN: 1-56522-010-2

Y2K Solutions Group, Inc.: 888-Y2K-4YOU, www.y2kvideos.com

#703: Management Strategies for Dealing with Y2K Disclosure Obligations and Contingent Legal Exposures

featuring Richard Williams

This series will provide you with the information about the nature and scope of corporate disclosure obligations. Find out where and how to place responsibility for fact finding and disclosure duties, and who should be part of the team, what to report, and how to report it.

4 Hours; $399.00

UPC: 051679028130; ISBN: 1-56522-011-0

Y2K Solutions Group, Inc.: 888-Y2K-4YOU, www.y2kvideos.com

#704: AS/400: GETTING THROUGH THE YEAR 2000
featuring Glenn Ericson

Learn how to beat the clock and survive your AS/400 Year 2000 Project. Explains how to determine the scope of the problem, what options exist and which method(s) are best, where to start, tool selection, pitfalls to avoid, and alternative steps.

4 Hours; $399.00

UPC: 051679028147; ISBN: 1-56522-012-9

Y2K Solutions Group, Inc.: 888-Y2K-4YOU, www.y2kvideos.com

#705: Testing in the AS/400 Midrange Environment: A Panel Discussion
featuring Glenn Ericson, Brian Bennett, and Gary Peskin

Presenters in this video outline the pros and cons of a variety of test tool methodologies and solution aids for the AS/400. Experts highlight the differences with mid-range Year 2000 testing, talk about risk-based test planning, the role of users, and give suggestions on building your test team.

Length: 2 hours; $199.00

#710: The Seven Parallel Paths of Risk Management
featuring Andrew Pegalis

Detailed information to help you structure an effective corporate Year 2000 risk management program. In this series you will learn the importance of simultaneous analysis of internal I/S systems, embedded chips, EDI exposures, legal/auditing issues, vendor compliance, external business dependencies, insurance considerations, and disaster recovery.

1 Hour; $99.00

UPC: 051679028154; ISBN: 1-56522-013-7

Y2K Solutions Group, Inc.: 888-Y2K-4YOU, www.y2kvideos.com

#711: Data Issues in a Year 2000 Project
featuring Miro Medek

Learn how to minimize the impact of Year 2000 renovation on your production database environment. Explains how to assess your databases, the differences between client/server database applications and typical legacy application projects, and data issues and solutions that are important in database management systems.
1 Hour; $99.00
UPC: 051679028161; ISBN: 156522-014-5
Y2K Solutions Group, Inc.: 888-Y2K-4YOU, www.y2kvideos.com

#712: Year 2000 Insurance Issues
featuring Richard Williams and Kirk Pasich

Find out how, when, and why you need to prepare and submit insurance claims. This series covers the availability of coverage under liability policies, director and officer policies, errors and omissions policies, and defending your Year 2000 claims. Perfect for I/T personnel, financial officers, corporate legal counsel, business owners, etc.
1 Hour; $99.00
UPC: 051679028178; ISBN: 156522-015-3
Y2K Solutions Group, Inc.: 888-Y2K-4YOU, www.y2kvideos.com

#714 An Enterprise Risk/Contingency Planning Checklist
featuring Edward Yourdon

This video discusses the need to stress risk management, contingency planning, and disaster planning and recovery.
Length: 60 minutes; $99.00

#715: Managing External Vendors
featuring Jennifer McNeill

This video addresses how to overcome and avoid problems with external vendors that hinder Year 2000 projects.
Length: 60 minutes; $99.00

#716: Safe Harbor Testing: How Much Testing Is Enough?
featuring Don Estes

This video addresses how to achieve a safe level of risk from Y2K testing at a price you can afford.
Length: 60 minutes; $99.00

#717 Year 2000: The Transition from System to Business Triage
featuring Dr. Howard Rubin

This video discusses the need to stress risk management, contingency planning and disaster planning and recovery. Mr. Rubin provides information that will be valuable in helping you to assess the risk inherent in your organization's business transition network and with individual business partners. The "state" of the problem and the "state" of the solution developed from his analysis are quite clear: The technology problem itself keeps shifting and growing as companies dig deeper into the issues.
Length: 60 minutes; $99.00

#718 Cost Recovery
featuring Laurence Eisenstein

This video explains assessment methods, contingency planning, and triage strategies for dealing with your business networks. It addresses how to review and assess opportunities to recover costs from third parties. You will review contractual claims, breach of warranties, negligence and misrepresentation claims, statutory remedies, and insurance claims.
Length: 60 minutes; $99.00

#719: Fidelity Investment's Methodology and Tools for a Client/Server Year 2000 Conversion
featuring Stuart Greenberg

This video presents how a client/server Year 2000 conversion varies significantly from the conversion of mainframe applications. You

will learn what the requirements are for methodology and tools for a client/server conversion and the planning, inventory, analysis, and testing needed.
Length: 60 minutes; $99.00

#720: Distributed Systems for the Year 2000
featuring Christopher Jesse
This video presents information to develop a methodology for addressing Year 2000 problems across the distributed enterprise. In this video, you will outline the issues, the common-sense considerations, and a practical methodology to solve the Year 2000 distributed enterprise dilemma. You will focus on examples and critical factors that are often unseen and, if not addressed, may prove to be fatal.
Length: 60 minutes; $99.00

#721: Year 2000 Litigation: The Defenses
featuring Vito Peraino.
This video discusses three primary legal issues: directors' and officers' litigation, litigation based on tort (both negligence and strict products liability), and litigation based on contract.
Length: 60 minutes; $99.00

REFERENCE #3
Y2K INTERNET LINKS

FAMILY PREPAREDNESS

http://readyfory2k.com
> *Yourdon, Stevens, Y2K Solutions Group, Inc. site*

http://www.yourdon.com
http://millennia-bcs.com/CASFRAME.HTM
http://members.home.net/shadow-scout/
> *Conniry's Wilderness School*

http://www.prepareyourself.com/	*Complete Y2K Survival Site*
http://www.josephproject2000.org	*Joseph Project*
http://www.prepareyourself.com	*Prepareyourself.com*
http://www.prepare4y2k.com	*Preparing for the Year 2000 Crash*

COMMUNITY GROUPS

http://www.resilientcommunities.org/	*Resilient Communities*
http://mypage.goplay.com/tfhouse	*Kingdom Crossroads*
http://year2000-discuss@year2000.com	
	year2000-discuss@year2000.com

Y2K SITES

http://www.coolpages.net/2000/	*2000 and You*
http://www.cairns.net.au/~sharefin/Markets/Alternative.htm	
	Alternative Survival Information
http://bug2000.to	*Bug 2000*
http://www.gmt-2000.com	*Greenwich Mean Time*
http://www.itaa.org/year2000.htm	*ITAA*
http://www.unt.edu/bcis/faculty/kappelma	*Leon Kappelman*
http://www.admin.ch/dff/f/aktuell/2000/index.htm	
	Official Year 2000
http://www.cix.co.uk/~parkside/y2kweb.htm	
	Pocket Guide to Year 2000
http://www.ocweb.com/y2k/Practical.htm	*Practical Preparation*
http://prepare4y2k.com/stages.htm	*Preparefory2k*
http://www.RighTime.com	*RighTime Company*
http://www.safehaven.co.nz	*Safehaven*
http://www.y2kreview.com	*Sanger's Review of Y2K*
http://www.utne.com/y2k/	*Y2K Citizen's Action Guide*
http://year2000.com	*Year2000.com*
http://www.cairns.net.au/~sharefin/Markets/Y2k.htm	
	Year 2000 Information
http://y2krun.com	*Y2KRun.com*
http://www.y2kanswers.com	*Y2kanswers.com*

http://y2kwatch.com   *y2kwatch.com*
http://www.y2k.com   *www.y2k.com*

FEDERAL GOVERNMENT

http://tecnet0.jcte.jcs.mil:9000/htdocs/teinfo/index.html
                                                Department of Defense
http://www.disa.mil   *Defense Information Systems Agency*
http://www.doncio.navy.mil/y2k/year2000.htm
                                                Department of the Navy
http://www.faay2k.com   *Federal Aviation Administration*
http://www.fdic.gov/about/y2k
                                Federal Deposit Insurance Corporation
http://www.itpolicy.gsa.gov/mks/yr2000/y2khome.htm
                        Federal Government Year 2000 Information Directory
http://www.fda.gov/cdrh/yr2000/ipyr2000.html
                                        Food and Drug Administration
http://www.gao.gov/special.pubs/publist.htm
                                        General Accounting Office
http://www.irs.ustreas.gov/prod/news/y2k/index.html
                                        Internal Revenue Service
http://www.army.mil/army-y2k   *U.S. Army*
http://www.gsa.gov   *U.S. General Services Administration*
http://www.itpolicy.gsa.gov/mks/yr2000/y201toc1.htm
                                Year 2000 Information Directories

STATE GOVERNMENT

http://alaweb.asc.edu   *Alabama*
http://www.state.akfi.us/local/akpages/ADMIN/info/yr2000.htm
                                                          Alaska:
http://www.gita.state.az.us/y2k.htm   *Arizona Year 2000*
http://www.dis.state.ar.us/y2k/y2kintro.htm   *Arkansas Project 2000*
http://www.year2000.ca.gov   *California 2000 Homepage*
http://www.state.co.us/gov_dir/gss/imc/imcy2kproj.html
    Colorado Commission on Information Management (IMC)Year 2000

Project Office http://www.doit.state.ct.us/y2k
Connecticut Year 2000 Program Office
http://www.state.de.us/ois/y2000/welcom1.htm
Delaware Year 2000 Now and Beyond
http://y2k.state.fl.us   *Florida: State of Florida Year 2000 Taskforce*
http://www.year2000.state.ga.us
Georgia: State of Georgia Year 2000 Project Office
http://www.state.il.us/ps2000/
Illinois: Prairie State 2000 Authority
http://www.ai.org/dpoc/
Indiana: Data Processing Oversight Commission
Year 2000 Assessment RFP
http://www.state.ia.us/government/its/century
Iowa: Century Date Change Year 2000 (Under Construction)
http://www.state.ks.us   *Kansas*
http://www.state.ky.us/year2000/index.htm
Kentucky Year 2000 Resources
http://www.state.la.us   *Louisiana*
http://www.state.me.us/   *Maine*
http://idf.mitretek.org:8080/mdy2k
Maryland Year 2000 Program Management Office
http://www.state.ma.us/dls/year2k.htm
Massachusetts: Preparations and Plans for the
YEAR 2000 Date Change
http://www.state.mi.us/dmb/year2000
Michigan Year 2000 Project Office
http://www.state.mn.us/ebranch/admin/ipo/2000/2000.html
Minnesota: Year 2000 Information Clearinghouse
http://www.its.state.ms.us/yr2000
Mississippi—Project Information Resource Center
http://www.state.mo.us/oit/efforts/y2k/index.shtml
Missouri's Year 2000 Effort
http://www.mt.gov/isd/year2000/index.htm
Montana Year 2000, It's closer than you think

http://www.das.state.ne.us/das_cdp/rfp/rfp.htm
Nebraska: Century Date Change Documents
http://www.state.nv.us/doit/y2k   *Nevada Year 2000 Project*
http://www.state.nh.us/das/ditm
New Hampshire Information Technology Management
http://www.state.nm.us   *New Mexico*
http://www.irm.state.ny.us/yr2000/yr2000.htm
New York Year 2000 Coordination and Resources
http://year2000.state.nc.us/index.html
North Carolina: Statewide Year 2000 Project
http://www.state.nd.us/isd/y2k   *North Dakota: Year 2000*
http://www.state.oh.us/y2k   *Ohio Year 2000 Projects*
http://www.state.ok.us/index.html   *Oklahoma*
http://www.state.or.us/IRMD/y2k/year2k.htm
Oregon: Year 2000, Don't Let It Happen To You
http://www.state.pa.us/Technology_Initiatives/year2000
Pennsylvania's Responses to the Year 2000
http://www.doa.state.ri.us/year2000/index.html
Rhode Island: Year 2000 Transitional Information
http://www.state.sc.us/y2000
South Carolina 2000 Error! The Year 2000 problem
http://www.state.tn.us/finance/oir/y2k/webindex.html
Tennessee Year 2000 Index
http://www.dir.state.tx.us/y2k   *Texas Year 2000 Project Office*
http://www.gvnfo.state.ut.us/sitc/YEAR2000/y2k-itcom.htm
Utah Year 2000 Presentation to the Information Technology
Commission 10/10/96
http://www.state.vt.us   *Vermont*
http://www.cns.state.va.us/y2000/index.htm
Virginia DIT Year 2000 Project
http://www.wa.gov/dis/2000/y2000.htm
Washington Year 2000 Project Information Program
http://www.state.wv.us/stac/1998plan/index.htm
West Virginia Governor's Office of Technology
http://badger.state.wi.us/y2k   *Wisconsin Year 2000 Challenge*

http://www-cio.state.wy.us/y2000
Wyoming Year 2000 Information Page

INTERNATIONAL

http://www.y2k.gov.au/	*Australia—New South Wales*
http://www.ogit.gov.au/year2000/index.html	
	Australian National Government
http://www.aiia.com.au/Year2000.html	
	Australian Industry Information
http://www.bankofengland.co.uk/y2t0298.htm	*Bank of England*
http://strategis.ic.gc.ca/year2000	*Canada #1*
http://www.info2000.gc.ca	*Canada #2*
http://www.info2000.gc.ca/Home.asp	*Canadian Year 2000*
http://www.y2kegypt.com	*Egypt*
http://www.homeoffice.gov.uk/index.htm	
	England and Wales—Internal Affairs
http://www.iki.fi/~jpatokal/y2k	*Finland*
http://www.themis-rd.com	*France #1*
http://www.mygale.org/~haeken/2000.htm	*France #2*
http://ourworld.compuserve.com/Homepages/Jahr2000	*Germany*
http://www.year2000.gov.hk/	*Hong Kong*
http://www.meh.hu	*Hungary*
http://www.tempo.co.id	*Indonesia*
http://www.irlgov.ie/	*Ireland*
http://www.zenginkyo.or.jp/en/link04.htm	*Japan Banking*
http://www.cpttm.org.mo/y2k/english/index.htm	*Macau*
http://ncb.intnet.mu/y2k/main00.htm	*Mauritius*
http://www.mp2000.nl/millen/Millen.nsf/frames/	
frameset?OpenDocument	*Netherlands*
http://www.year2000.co.nz	*New Zealand*
http://www.nim.com.au/year2000/ye02009.htm	
	New Zealand Year 2000
http://www.y2k.govt.nz/index.html	
	New Zealand Readiness Commission

http://www.sommersoft.no   *Norway*
http://odin.dep.no/html/nofovalt/depter/nhd/publ/y2k/
  e-index.html   *Norwegian Government Y2K Follow-Up Plan*
http://www.y2k.gov.ph   *Philippines—Manila*
http://www.EUnet.pt/ano2000   *Portugal*
http://www.y2k.qld.gov.au/news/viewreport   *Queensland*
http://www.map.es/csi/2000.htm   *Spain*
http://www.ncb.gov.sg/ncb/yr2000/y2k   *Singapore*
http://www.ctv.es/USERS/estrella/2000.htm   *Spain*
http://www.an2000.tn/   *Tunesia*
http://www.homeoffice.gov.uk/y2k.htm   *UK Police*
http://www.un.org/members/yr2000   *United Nations*
http://www.worldbank.org/y2k/pages/english/emain.htm
                                                        World Bank
http://www.ispo.cec.be/y2keuro   *Y2kEuro*

BUSINESS

http://www.cio.com/forums/y2k/index.html   *CIO Forum*
http://www.jks.co.uk/y2ki/confer/notices/smerpt1.htm
          Helping the Small Business Tackle the Year 2000
http://www.jks.co.uk/y2ki/aware/download/index.htm
=   *Interactive Guide to Year*
http://www.lawsight.com/x2kb.htm   *LawSight*
http://www.jpmorgan.com/MarketDataInd/Research/Year2000/
index.html   *JP Morgan*
http://www.jks.co.uk/y2ki/guide/gmed.htm
                  Medium Organization Year 2000 Guide
http://www.prudential.com/corporate/techatpru/cotzz1004.html
          Prudential's Year 2000 Kit for Small Business
http://www.frbsf.org/fiservices/cdc/bulletins.html
     Small Business and The Year 2000 by the Federal Reserve
http://www.jks.co.uk/y2ki/guide/gsmall.htm
                   Small Organization Year 2000 Guide
http://www.usplastic.com   *United States Plastic Corp*

http://www.support2000.com/sme.htm   *Year 2000 Support Center*

ACADEMIC

http://www.cwru.edu/president/audit/y2k/y2k.htm
Case Western Reserve University
http://www.gatech.edu/year2000   *Georgia Tech*
http://www.ttuhsc.edu/pages/year2000/ttuy2k.htm
Texas Tech University
http://ag.arizona.edu/agnet/y2k.html
University of Arizona, College of Agriculture
http://csn.uneb.edu/year2000   *University of Nebraska*
http://admin5.hsc.uth.tmc.edu/ishome/2000/2000.htm
University of Texas, Houston

ELECTRONIC AND PRINT MEDIA

http://azstarnet.com/~nuu/Y2K/index.htm
Arizona Daily Star Online
http://www.currents.net/advisor/y2k/index.html
Computer Currents
http://www.computerworld.com/home/features.nsf/all/980608y2k
Computer World
http://www.infoworld.com   *InfoWorld Media Group Inc.*
http://www.y2knews.com   *Y2Knews*

Y2K SERVICES AND VENDORS

http://www.acty.com/year_2000.html   *ACTY*
http://www.ains-inc.com/y2k.html
Advanced Information Network Systems, Inc.
http://year2000.caci.com   *CACI*
http://www.speedc.com   *Managing Y2K*

http://www.magmacom.com/~reynolds   *Marco Software*

http://www.microbanker.com/year2000.html   *Microbanker Inc.*

http://www.mitre.org/research/y2k   *MITRE*

http://www.ncs.com/ncscorp/top/prodserv/y2k-b.htm
National Computer Systems

http://www.pya.ca/seminar/y2k.html   *Ptack, Young & Associates*

http://www.tyler.net/tyr7020/y2k.htm   *Year 2000 PC BIOS Testing*

http://www.storefrontmall.com/mall/solutions/pc-y2k/y2k.htm
Solution Services

http://www.strangehappenings.com   *StrangeHappenings.com*

http://www.transcend2000.com
Transcend 2000 Project Management

http://www.watchhill.com/year2000.htm   *Watch Hill Consulting*

http://www.y2knews.com   *Y2K News Magazine*

MISCELLANEOUS

http://www.bytewise.com/atlyear2000/html/contact.html
Atlanta Year 2000 Users Group

http://www.co-intelligence.org/Y2K.html
The Co-Intelligence Institute

http://www.EPRI.COM   *Electric Power Research Institute*

http://www.euy2k.com   *Electric Utilities and Year*

http://www.yourdon.com/articles/y2kfunprofit.html
Y2K for Fun and Profit

http://www.isgnet.com/y2k
Y2K Bug Spray, A Humorous Solution to the Y2K problem

http://www.dfiy2k.org/y2kkids.html   *Impact of Year 2000 on Kids*

REFERENCE #4
SAMPLE LETTERS

COURTESY OF THE CASSANDRA PROJECT
(www.cassandraproject.org)

Resources: Sample Letters: Bank Letters

[To]

[Title]

[Institution name]

[Dept.]

[street]

[city, state, zip]

[date]

Dear [],

I am greatly concerned about the Year 2000 problem, and its possible impact on the reliability, accuracy, and continuity of the services you provide.

Specifically I have the following questions:

1. Does [institution] have a Year 2000 mitigation project?

2. What is the status of its mitigation activities?

3. What assurances can you give that [institution] will be able to provide timely and accurate service in the event of power, communication, and/or equipment, etc., failures?

4. Will [institution] have sufficient funds available should several customers make substantial withdrawals?

5. Will ATMs and debit cards function, and correctly?

6. Will customer records and accounts continue to accurately reflect any activity regardless of possible Y2K interruptions?

7. Will automatic payments and deposits be processed, and on time and accurately?

8. Has [institution] developed contingency plans to ensure continued operation should third-party (suppliers, vendors) failures occur?

9. Will you publicly inform your customers of your Y2K efforts and progress? If so, when, and by what means?

I would appreciate a written response to my questions and concerns, as well as assurance that your services will continue before and after December 31, 1999. I look forward to receiving your reply soon. Thank you for your time and attention.

Sincerely,

[your name]

[street]

[city, state, zip]

[phone]

Resources: Sample Letters: Local Government

[To]

[Title]

[Dept. Name]

[address]

[city, state, zip]

[Date]

Dear [],

I am greatly concerned about the Year 2000 problem, and its possible impact on the reliability and continuity of the services you provide. Specifically I have the following questions:

1. Does [city, county] have a Year 2000 mitigation project?

2. What is the status of your mitigation activities?

3. Has [city, county] developed contingency plans to ensure continuity of services to residents in your jurisdiction in the event Y2K failures occur?

4. Has [city, county] developed contingency plans to ensure continued operation should third-party (suppliers, vendors) failures occur?

5. What steps are being taken to ensure the public's health and safety should critical infrastructure {e.g., power, water, traffic systems, etc.} fail?

6. Will you publicly inform residents of your Y2K efforts and their progress? If so, when, and by what means? I would appreciate a written response to my concerns, as well as assurance that your services will continue after December 31, 1999.

I look forward to receiving your reply soon. Thank you for your time and attention.

Sincerely,

[your name]

[address]

[city, state, zip]

[phone]

Resources: Sample Letters: Law Enforcement

[To]

[Title]

[department]

[street]

[city, state, zip]

[date]

Dear [],

I am greatly concerned about the Year 2000 problem's possible impact on the reliability and continuity of the services the [city] Police Department provides. Specifically I have the following questions:

1. Does the Department have a Year 2000 mitigation project?

2. What is the status of its mitigation activities?

3. What assurances can you give that the department will be able to provide timely and effective service in the event of power, communication, and/or equipment failures?

4. What steps are being taken to ensure the public safety should traffic systems, security systems, etc., fail?

5. Has [org] developed contingency plans to ensure it will be able to continue to provide basic/essential/emergency services in the likelihood Y2K failures occur?

6. Will you publicly inform residents of your Y2K efforts and progress? If so, when, and by what means? I would appreciate a written response to my questions and concerns, as well as assurance that your services will continue before and after December 31, 1999.

I look forward to receiving your reply shortly. Thank you for your time and attention.

Sincerely,

[your name]

[street]

[city, state, zip]

[phone]

Resources: Sample Letters: Electric Utility

[To]

[Title]

[Dept.]

[street]

[city, state, zip]

[date]

Dear [],

I am greatly concerned about the Year 2000 problem's possible impact on the reliability and continuity of the services your company provides.

Specifically I have the following questions:

1. Does [company] have a Year 2000 mitigation project?

2. What is the status of its mitigation activities?

3. Are embedded systems and controls being reviewed as an integral part of (company's) Y2K effort?

4. What assurances can you give that you will be able to provide timely, safe, and effective service in the event of equipment and/or communication, etc., failures?

5. What steps are being taken to ensure the public health and safety with regards to maintaining heat and light in the middle of winter?

6. Have contingency plans been created to ensure you will be able to continue to provide basic/essential emergency services in the likelihood Y2K failures occur?

7. Will you inform your customers and the public of your Y2K efforts and progress? If so, when, and by what means?

I would appreciate a written response to my concerns, and look forward to receiving your reply shortly. Thank you for your time and attention.

Sincerely,

[your name]

[street]

[city, state, zip]

[phone]

Resources: Sample Letters: General Institution

[To]

[Title]

[Co/Org Name]

[address]

[city, state, zip]

[date]

Dear [],

I am greatly concerned about the Year 2000 problem, and its possible impact on the reliability and continuity of the services you provide. Specifically, I have the following questions:

1. Does your organization have a Year 2000 mitigation project?

2. What is the status of your mitigation activities?

3. Have you developed contingency plans to ensure you will be able to continue to provide service in the likelihood Y2K failures occur?

4. Has [institution] developed contingency plans to ensure continued service should third party (suppliers, vendors) failures occur?

5. Will you publicly inform your customers of your Y2K efforts and their progress? If so, when, and by what method?

I would appreciate a written response to my concerns, as well as assurance that your services will continue after December 31, 1999.

I look forward to receiving your reply very soon. Thank you for your time and attention.

Sincerely,

[your name]

[address]

[city, state, zip]

[phone]

Resources: Sample Letters: Health Care

[To]

[Hospital/clinic name]

[Dept.]

[street]

[city, state, zip]

[date]

Dear [],

I am greatly concerned about the Year 2000 problem's possible impact on the reliability, safety and continuity of the services you provide. Specifically, I have the following questions:

1. Does [org] have a Year 2000 mitigation project?

2. What is the status of your mitigation activities?

3. What assurances can you give that you will be able to provide timely, safe, and effective service in the event of power, communication, and/or equipment failures? Will your backup systems function?

4. What assurances can you give that the medical devices (e.g., X-ray equipment, heart monitors, defibrilators, infusion pumps, etc.} will function safely and correctly?

5. What steps are being taken to ensure patient safety and the accuracy and availability of patient records, prescriptions, etc.

6. Have contingency plans been created to ensure [org] will be able to continue to provide basic essential emergency services in the likelihood Y2K failures occur?

7. Has [institution] developed contingency plans to ensure continued operation should third-party supplier and vendor disruptions occur? {Specifically with regards to ambulance services, blood bank, paramedic services, etc.}

8. Will you inform your clients and the public of your Y2K efforts and progress? If so, when, and by what means? I would appreciate a written response to my questions and concerns, as well as assurance that your services will continue before and after December 31, 1999.

I look forward to receiving your reply soon. Thank you for your time and attention.

Sincerely,

[your name]

[street]

[city, state, zip]

[phone]

Resources: Sample Letters: Telecom

[To]

[title]

[company]

[dept.]

[street]

[city, state, zip]

[date]

Dear [name],

I am greatly concerned about the Year 2000 problem's possible impact on the reliability and continuity of the services your company provides. Specifically, I have the following questions:

1. Does your company have a Year 2000 mitigation project?

2. What is the status of its mitigation activities?

3. What assurances can you give that you will be able to provide timely and effective service in the event of power, and/or equipment, etc., failures?

4. Will cell phones, pagers, etc., continue to function?

5. Have contingency plans been created to ensure you will be able to continue to provide basic and emergency services in the likelihood Y2K failures occur?

6. Will you inform your customers and the public of your Y2K efforts and progress? If so, when, and by what means? I would appreciate a written response to my questions and concerns, as well as assurance that your services will continue before and after December 31, 1999.

I look forward to receiving your reply soon. Thank you for your time and attention.

Sincerely,

[your name]

[street]

[city, state, zip]

[phone]

REFERENCE #5
COMPUTER HARDWARE
AND SOFTWARE
MANUFACTURERS

Software Manufacturers

http://www.adaptec.com/tools/compatibility/y2k_form.html
Adaptec Inc.; (800) 442-7274

http://www.adobe.com/supportservice/custsupport/main.html
Adobe Systems Inc.; (800) 833-6687

http://www.adobe.com/supportservice/custsupport
Aldus Corp.; see Adobe Systems

http://home.alphasoftware.com/tech/index.htm
Alpha Software (800) 225-3766

http://www.altera.com
Altera Corp. (800) 443-7610

http://www.megatrends.com
American Megatrends Inc. (800) 828-9264

http://www.amsoftware.com/Countdown/index.html
American Software Inc. (800) SCM-2WIN

http://www.apple.com/macos/info/2000.html
Apple Computer Inc. (800) 767-2775

http://www.applix.com/products/y2k.htm
Applix Inc. (800) 8AP-PLIX

http://www.artisoft.com
Artisoft (Lantastic) (800) 293-3936

http://www.ascend.com
Ascend Communications Inc. (800) 621-9578

http://www.autodesk.com
Autodesk Inc. (800) 879-4233

http://www.banyan.com
Banyan Systems Inc. (800) 222-6926

http://support.baynetworks.com/index.html
                              Bay Networks Inc. (800) 822-9638
http://www.bentley.com/services
                              Bentley Systems Inc. (800) 236-8539
http://www.bmc.com
                              BMC Software Inc. (800) 841-2031
http://www.boole.com
                              Boole and Babbage Inc. (800) 544-2152
http://www.inprise.com
                              Borland International Inc. (800) 233-2444
http://www.ctron.com/manuals
                              Cabletron Systems Inc. (603) 332-9400
http://www.caci.com/2000.html
                              CACI International Inc. (703) 841-7800
http://www.candle.com
                              Candle Corp. (800) 843-3970
http://www.centurasoft.com
                              Centura Software Corp. (650) 596-3400
http://www.cincom.com
                              Cincom Systems Inc. (800) 224-6266
http://www.cisco.com/warp/public/752/2000/index.html
                              Cisco Systems Inc. (800) 553-6387
http://www.claris.com/support
                              Claris Corp. (800) 544-8554
http://www.compuserve.com   CompuServe Inc. (800) 848-8990
http://www.cai.com
       Computer Associates International Inc. (800) 753-4321
http://www.compuware.com   Compuware Corp. (800) 535-8707
http://www.seagate.com   Conner Peripherals Inc. (408) 456-4500
http://www.corel.ca/support/support.htm
                              Corel Corp. (888) 772-6735
http://www.dell.com/year2000/exec/business.htm
                              Dell Computer Corp. (800) 289-3355
http://www.delrina.com/techsupp/techsupp.htm
                              Delrina (U.S.) Corp.; see Symantec

http://ww1.digital.com/year2000/status.html
                    Digital Equipment Corp. (800) 344-4825
http://www.kodak.com   Eastman Kodak Co. (800) 242-2424
http://www.esri.com
Environmental Systems Research Institute Inc. (800) GIS-XPRT
http://www.farallon.com/support/year2000/index.html
                    Farallon Communications Inc. (800) 463-1956
http://www.hp.com   Hewlett-Packard Co. (800) 752-0900
http://www.horizons.com
                    Horizons Technology Inc. (800) 828-3808
http://www.ibi.com/index.html
                    Information Builders Inc. (800) 969-4636
http://www.informix.com   Informix Corp. (800) 331-1763
http://www.interbase.com   InterBase Div. (888) 345-2015
http://www.intergraph.com   Intergraph Corp. (800) 345-4856
http://www.software.ibm.com/year2000
       International Business Machines Corp. (800) 426-3333
http://www.intersolv.com   INTERSOLV Inc. (800) 547-4000
http://www.intuit.com/quickbooks/technical_support/index.html
                            Intuit Inc. (800) 446-8848
http://www.jdedwards.com/technology/y2000.asp
                       J.D. Edwards and Co. (800) 225-5224.
http://www.lawson.com   Lawson Software (800) 477-1357
http://www.support.lotus.com
                    Lotus Development Corp. (800) 343-5414
http://www.support.lotus.com   Macromedia Inc. (800) 326-2128
http://www.marcam.com/corp/pressrel/961022b.htm
                            Marcam Corp. (800) 962-7226
http://www.merc-int.com/year2000
                    Mercury Interactive Corp. (800) 837-8911
http://www.microcom.com   Microcom Inc.; see Compaq
http://www.micrografx.com/support/shome.html
                         Micrografx Inc. (800) 733-3729
http://www.microsoft.com/year2000
                       Microsoft Corp. (800) 426-9400

http://www.mot.com/General/year2000
                    Motorola Inc. (800) 551-1016
http://www.netmanage.com/products/year2000
                    NetManage Inc. (408) 973-7171
http://help.netscape.com/index.html
                    Netscape Communications Corp. (800) 638-7483
http://www.nai.com/services/support/2000/year2000.asp
                    Network Associates Inc. (800) 671-9272
http://www.novell.com/p2000/product.html
                    Novell Inc. (800) 453-1267
http://www.on.com   ON Technology Corp. (800) 767-6638
http://oracle.com/year2000   Oracle Corp. (800) 633-0596
http://www.platinum.com/products/year2k/y2k.htm
                    PLATINUM technology inc. (800) 442-6861
http://www.progress.com   Progress Software Corp. (800) 477-6473
http://www.qms.com   QMS Inc. (800) 523-2696
http://www.quark.com/ts001.htm   Quark Inc. (800) 788-7835
http://arachnid.qdeck.com/qdeck/support
                    Quarterdeck Corp. (310) 309-3210
http://www.radius.com/support/support.html
                    Radius Retail Inc. (650) 404-6400
http://www.rational.com   Rational Software (800) 720-1616
http://www.sco.com/technology/y2k
                    Santa Cruz Operation Inc. (800) 726-8649
http://www.sas.com/ts   SAS Institute Inc. (919) 677-8008
http://www.scantron.com   Scantron Corp. (800) 722-6876
http://www.shiva.com/remote/yr2000.html
                    Shiva Corp. (800) 977-4482
http://www.sgi.com/features/1998/jan/y2k/index.html
                    Silicon Graphics Inc. (800) 800-7441
http://www.sagafyi.com
                    SOFTWARE AG Americas Inc. (800) 843-9534
http://www.stercomm.com
                    Sterling Commerce Inc. (800) 299-4031
http://www.sterling.com   Sterling Software Inc. (800) 889-0226

http://www.stratus.com   Stratus Computer Inc. (800) STR-ATUS
http://www.sungard.com
                SunGard Data Systems Inc. (800) 758-5804
http://www.sybase.com/services   Sybase Inc. (800) 879-2273
http://www.symantec.com/y2k/y2k.html
                        Symantec Corp. (800) 441-7234
http://www.ssax.com/y2k
            System Software Associates Inc. (312) 258-6000
http://www.unisys.com   Unisys Corp. (800) 448-1424
http://www.visio.com/yr2000.html   Visio Corp. (800) 446-3335
http://www.wonderware.com   Wonderware Corp. (714) 727-3200
http://www.wordperfect.com   WordPerfect Corp.; see Corel

Hardware Manufacturers

http://www.acer.com/aac/support/year2000/index.htm
                    Acer America Corp (800)733-2237
http://www.alr.com/alr_corporate_information/year2000
                Advanced Logic Research Inc. (800) 257-1230
http://www.alphamicro.com/y2k
                    Alpha Microsystems (800) 777-7406
http://www.amd.com   AMD (800) 538-8450
http://www.info.apple.com   Apple Computer Inc. (800) 767-2775
http://www.ast.com   AST Research Inc. (800) 876- 278
http://www.att.com/year2000   AT&T Corp.; see NCR Corp
http://www.award.com
            Award Software International Inc. (800) 800-2467
http://www.europe.canon.com
                Canon Computer Systems Inc. (800) 848-4123
http://www.cardtech.com/support/cy2k.htm
                Cardinal Technologies Inc. (800) 775-0899
http://www.compaq.com/year2000
                Compaq Computer Corp (800) 652-6672
http://www.cdc.com   Control Data Systems Inc. (800) 257-6736
http://www.convex.com   Convex Div.; see Hewlett-Packard

http://www.creaf.com   Creative Labs Inc. (800) 998-1000
http://www.cyrix.com   Cyrix (800) 848-2979
http://www.dg.com/products/html/year_2000_compliance.html
                      Data General Corp (800) 328-2436
http://www.us.dell.com/year2000/exec/y2kprob.htm
                      Dell Computer Corp (888) 560-8324
http://www.dfiusa.com/support.asp
                      Diamond Flower (916) 568-1234
http://ww1.digital.com/year2000/status.html
                      Digital Equipment Corp (800) 344-4825
http://www.encore.com   Encore Computer Corp (800) 327-8581
http://www.epson.com/legal/index.html
                      Epson America Inc. (800) 289-3776
http://www.everex.com   Everex Systems Inc. (800) 821-0806
http://www.fujitsu.com   Fujitsu America Inc. (800) 626-4686
http://www.gateway.com   Gateway 2000 Inc. (800) 846-2301
http://www.harris.com   Harris Corp (800) 4-HARRIS
http://www.hp.com/go/year2000
                      Hewlett-Packard Co (800) 752-0900
http://www.hitachi.com   Hitachi America Ltd. (800) 241-6558
http://www.hea.com Hyundai Electronics America (800) 568-0060
http://www.software.ibm.com/year2000
                      IBM Personal Computer Co (800) 426-4968
http://support.intel.com/support/year2000/assess.htmvz
                      Intel Corp (800) 628-8686
http://www.maximuspc.com/tech/bios.html
                      Maximus Computers Inc. (800) 899-0142
http://www.mei.micron.com/Services
                      Micron Electronics Inc. (800) 209-9686
http://www.micronpc.com/about/year2000/index.html
                      Micron Technology Inc. (208) 368-4400
http://www.microtouch.com/custinfo.htm
                      MicroTouch Systems Inc. (800) 642-7686
http://www.mela-itg.com   Mitsubishi (800) 843-2515
http://www.modcomp.com   MODCOMP Inc. (800) 322-3287

http://www.mot.com/General/year2000/
  Motorola Microcomputer Div. (800) 551-1016
http://www.ncr.com/support/   NCR Corp. (800) 262-7782
http://www.nec.com/support5.html
  NEC Technologies Inc. (978) 264-8000
http://www.ocean-usa.com/ocean/b_tech.htm
  Ocean Information Systems Inc. (800) 325-2496
http://support.packardbell.com/year2000/
  Packard Bell NEC Inc. (800) 733-5858
http://www.panasonic.com/host/support
  Panasonic Personal Computer Co. (800) 211-7262
http://www.ptltd.com/techsupp/techsupp.html
  Phoenix Technologies Ltd. (800) 677-7305
http://www.samsung.com   Samsung (800) 767-4675
http://mazda.genauto.com/Year2000
  Sequoia Systems Inc. (800) 562-0011
http://www.sharp-usa.com   Sharp (800) 237-4277
http://www.supercom.com   Supercom (408) 456-8888
http://www.tandy.com   Tandy (817) 390-3700
http://www.tatung.com   Tatung (800) 767-4440
http://www.ti.com/corp/docs/year2000/index.htm
  Texas Instruments Inc. (214) 575-3686
http://www.texmicro.com/techsupport/techservice.html
  Texas Microcomputers Inc. (972) 699-3100
http://www.toshiba.com/tais/csd/support
  Toshiba America Information Systems Inc. (800) 457-7777
http://www.tbeach.com   Turtle Beach Systems; no 800 listing
http://www.twinhead.com   Twinhead Corp. (800) 995-8946
http://www.unisys.com   Unisys Corp. (800) 448-1424
http://www.winbook.com
  WinBook Computer Corp. (800) 725-3468
http://www.wyse.com   Wyse (800) 800-9973
http://www.zds.com   Zenith Data Systems Corp. (800) 227-3360
http://www.mcs.net/~djtech
  ZEOS International Ltd. (800) 228-5390

REFERENCE #6
Y2K COMMUNITY GROUPS

Kellie Andrews
naycag@egroups.com
North Alabama Y2k Community Action Group
Huntsville, AL
AKY2K Ready
Anchorage, AK

H.A. "Red" Boucher
(907) 349-2192 Voice
(907) 349-7031 Fax
email redbou@alaska.net
Alaska Y2K Ready
P.O. Box 111038
Anchorage, AK 99511-1038

David La Chapelle
P.O. Box 21592; Juneau, Ak 99802
dlachape@ptialaska.net
The Tides of Change
Juneau, AK

Chris Dolmar/Jeff Long
dolmar@ptialaska.net
Alaskans for Y2K Awareness
Douglas island, AK

Lisa Zach
903-792-7448; lzach1@gte.net
Y2K—Texarkana In Action
AR

Steve Haag
shaag7@aol.com
Timberline
Flagstaff AZ

Tucson Year 2000 Center
PO Box 42663
Tucson, AZ

Will Hepburn or Erin Mitchell
520-778-4000; y2kcoalition@hotmail.com
Y2K Coalition
Prescott, AZ

David Bradshaw
877-492-5277; ideaman@y2knet.com
Y2KNET
Phoenix, AZ

Greg Wiatt
520-541-9727; gwiatt@northlink.com
Concerned Christians for Christ Preparedness Group
Prescott, AZ

David Sunfellow
sedonay2k@wild2k.com
The Sedona Y2K Task Force
Sedona, AZ

Tom Greco
CIRC@azstarnet.com
Y2K Community Preparedness Group
Tucson, AZ

Jim
520-204-2837; Jimreese@kacina.net
Arizona R.V y2k community
Sedona, AZ

Soleil Tranquilli
SoleilPaz@aol.com
Sacramento Valley Y2K Prep
Sacramento, CA

Margaret Janssen
janssm@aol.com
Sacramento Valley Y2K Prep
Sacramento, CA

Shelley Evans
650-726-0999; MarionHMB@aol.com
Coastside Citizens' Emergency Preparedness/Y2K Group
P.O. Box 567
Half Moon Bay, CA

Bob Banner
805 544 9663; hopedance@aol.com
San Luis Obisp County Y2K Action Alliance
San Luis Obispo, CA

Martin Jones
www.sandiegoy2k.com; mjones3@home.com
San Diego Y2K
San Diego, CA

Rebecca Kaplan
510-595-5505; oak2001-org@anamorph.com
Oakland 2001: Y2K network for community preparedness & advocacy
Oakland, CA

Mark Snyder
619-748-4612; mark@marksnyderelectric.com
San Diego Regional Y2K Action Group
San Diego, CA

Diann Powell
310-313-1007 Hotline
Westside Y2K Preparedness Task Force
Los Angeles, CA

Elizabeth Ward
831-464-5344; tsginc@cruzio.com
Santa Cruz Y2K Community Task Force
Santa Cruz, CA

Robert Orenstein
510.748.0600; rlo@perforce.com
Alameda Island Y2K Preparedness Group
Alameda, CA

Carol Tatsumi
makatepa@wonderlan.com
South Bay Y2K Awareness and Preparedness
Los Angeles, CA

Sheri Nakken
530-478-1242; wncy2k@nccn.net
Western Nevada County Y2k Preparedness Network
Nevada City, CA

Carol Sutton
jvsutton@aol.com
Inland Empire Y2K
Riverside, CA

Donna or Gary Conover

530-755-3330; djc@clear-cxn.net
The Conover Y2K Group
Yuba City, CA

Jason and Annie Corbett

408-984-6461; jasonc@aimnet.com
Silicon Valley Y2K Community Action Group
San Jose, CA

Theresa Mitchell

LoneXan@aol.com
Sonoma County Y2k Group
www.sonic.net/y2k
Santa Rosa, CA
& Winterhaven. MO

Dan Leahy

danleahy@primenet.com
East Bay Y2k Prep Group
Concord, CA

Mark Phillips

(805) 961-2095; info@sby2k.org
www.sby2k.org
Santa Barbara Y2K (SB Y2K)
Santa Barbara, CA

Monica McGuire

MonicaTMcG@aol.com
Santa Cruz Y2K Task Force
Santa Cruz, CA

Metro Y2K Task Force

REX@LOSTHORIZON.COM
Metro Church Y2K Task Force
Santa Monica, CA

Wendy Tanowitz
415-460-0925; wendyt@jps.net
Marin Y2K Action
San Anselmo, CA

John O'Brien
P.O.Box 1591; Chico, CA 95927-1591
www.Buttecounty.com
Year 2000 Action Group
Chico, CA

David L. Goodwill
DGoodwill@hotmail.com
DavidinIrvine
Irvine, CA

Mick Winter
707-257-2737; mick@westsong.com
www.y2knapa.com
Napa Valley Y2K
Napa Valley, CA

Bill Seavey
805-938-1396; P.O. Box 2916; Orcutt, CA 93457
wlseavey@hotmail.com
North Santa Barbara County Y2K Preparedness Group
Orcutt, CA

Bill Crane
303-421-9114; y2kb@uswest.net
You2KanB Y2K Prepared
North Jeffco area, CO

Mark Burrows
970-704-9778; y2k@geekspeak.net
www.geekspeak.net/y2k
Carbondale Community Preparedness Group
Aspen-Rifle, CO

Jim Fischer
y2k@gobuffs.com
Broomfield 2000
Broomfield, CO

John N Miller
jnmiller@uswest.net
Roxborough 2000 Community Action Group
Roxborough, CO

Cindy Brown
www.forklift-specialists.com
Franktown Community Preparedness Group
Franktown, CO

George Sullivan
taur696@aol.com
The Volunteer Citizens of Arapahoe County for Y2K Preparedness
Arapahoe County, CO

Ira Kalfus
303-743-7708; k4wou@aol.com
The Emergency Preparedness Group
P.O. Box 18914
Denver, CO

Steve Teichner, Director
Loveland2K@aol.com; www.creativespots.com
Loveland 2000, A Community Task Force
Loveland, CO

John Steiner and Margo King
steiner_king@earthlink.net
BCY2K, Boulder County Y2K Community Preparedness Group
Boulder, CO

Jeff Hogan
970-484-9179; jeffhogan@juno.com
Fort Collins Year 2000 Support
Fort Collins, CO

Dave Hartman
302-398-9751; detlef7777@aol.com
Emergency Preparedness Eastern Shore
Houston, DE

Gordon Davidson
202-237-2800; cvldc@visionarylead.org
The Center for Visionary Leadership
Washington Area Y2K Community Alliance
Washington, DC

Stephen Balkam
sbalkam@rsac.org
Northwest DC Year 2000 Group
Washington, DC

Dr. Jerome D. Harold
305-754-3595; Jeremy305@aol.com
Dade-Broward Community Preparedness Group
Miami, FL

Doug
ocalay2k@hotmail.com
Central Florida Y2K
Ocala, FL

Blane Land
850-484-9940; blane@aloha.net
Community Y2K Planning Guide
Pensacola, FL

Cyndi Florio
954-721-5014; tojam4c@aol.com
In One Accord
Tamarac, FL

Sharon Joy Kleitsch
727-550-9660; kleitsch@gte.net
Tampa Bay Y2K: Preparing for the Future
Tampa Bay, FL

Lolita
transetcet@aol.com
West Broward County
(Sunrise/Plantation/Davie/Weston/Tamarac/Coral Springs)
Plantation, FL

Ken Griesbach
tentmaking@juno.com
First Baptist Church of SouthWest Broward
Hollywood, FL

Arthur Bouchard
abouchar@gte.net
Pinellas County Grassroot Effort
Pinellas County, FL

Joose Hadley
727-447-2147; citstacom@earthlink.net
Citizens for a Stable Community:
Providing Y2K Solutions for our Community
Pinellas and TampaBay Area, FL

Susan Mills
newtoncoy2k-subscribe@egroups.com
Y2K Contingency and Awareness Group—Newton County Georgia
Covington, GA

Tom or Sharon Miller

P.O. Box 1901; Cedartown, Georgia PC/30125
rdsupply@bellsouth.net
Rainy Day Supply
Cedartown, GA

Sheila Lewis Busby

770-333-0448; sheila@lookup.org
Douglasville Community Y2K
Douglasville, GA

Daniel and Mary Kochan

mkochan@mindspring.com
Douglasville Community Y2K
Douglasville, GA

Jim Greer

770-992-9709; jmgreer@accessatlanta.com
Atlanta, GA

Bill Lynes

912-897-5153; wlynes@g-net.net
Omega Group
Savannah, GA

Sybil Spencer

sybhi5@webtv.net
The Big Island Y2K Prep Team
Hilo, Hawaii County, HI

Mark Miyashiro

808-236-1372; Alohamin@aol.com
P.O. Box 5344; Kaneohe, HI 96744
Spirit of Truth Ministry
Kaneohe, HI

Jo B'
808-246-6085; greydog@aloha.net
Share a Rainbow
Lihue, Kauai, HI

Karlos deTreaux
808-826-4211; y2k@aloha.net
www.hawaiiy2k.com
CSRC, Box 33
Hanalei, HI

Roger Henry
rogerbhenry@juno.com
Marcus Emergency Preparedness Group
Marcus, IA

Steven Ellson
515-261-0070; n0uxv@worldnet.att.net
Delaware 2000
Delaware Township, IA

Ann Kendrot
basann@micron.net
Sandpoint Y2KForum
Sandpoint, ID

Wayne Matulis
surveyor1@iolusa.com
Alliance of Concerned Citizens
Joliet, IL

Antoine Denerome
312-719-4366; ThohT@yahoo.com
2000 NOW
Chicago, IL

Bob
630-645-0809
Noah's Ark for 2000
Villa Park, IL

Ron Dunning
618-949-3798; tronone@shawneelink.com
Y2K & Beyond
Pope, CO

Karla D.
4GIVN@aol.com
Community Care
Rockford, IL

Antoine Denerome
ThohT@yahoo.com
Children of Liberty
Chicago, IL

Kent Morgan
317-897-1320; smorgan@on-net.net
Y2K Indianapolis
Indianapolis, IN

Mark Magers
magers@gateway.net
Indianapolis Y2K Awareness Project
Indianapolis, IN

Richard Lauby
(913) 541-0151; RLauby@aol.com
Kansas City Aware
Overland Park, KS

Scott Plauche
318-332-6854; plauchs@mindspring.com
Breaux Bridge Y2K Prep Group
Breaux Bridge, LA

Ronnie Free
freesinc@softdisk.com
Shreveport-Bossier Y2K Awareness Group
Shreveport, LA

David Carmical
Shreveport/Bossier "Y2K" Preparedness
Shreveport, LA

David M. Goodwyn
318-981-8393; dgoodwyn@acadianay2k.org
Acadiana Y2K Awareness Group
Lafayette, LA

Carol Baroudi
617-747-4045; carol@baroudi.com
Y2K Arlington
Arlington, MA

Marc
1-617-926-0404 x3240; pelletier@gte.com
InChristWeAre
Andover, Ma

Brice Wilson
413-256-1084; y2k@siriuscommunity.org
Valley Year 2000 Center at Sirius
Pioneer Valley, MA

Ian Wells
978-446-0114; ianwells@bigfoot.com
Belividere Neighborhood Association Year 2000 Project
Lowell, MA

Kimichelle Boseman
eternalselfbeing@yahoo.com
Lee Avenue Civic Association
Takoma Park, MD

RG Steinman
301-565-2025
Silver Spring Y2K Community Preparedness Group
Silver Spring, MD

Dorothy Lam
301-797-5269; lamdm@geocities.com
Why Care about Y2K Community Initiative
Hagerstown, MD

Steve Kane
301-441-3809; srkane@earthlink.net
Greenbelt Y2K Community Preparedness Group
Greenbelt, MD

Jim Brewster
301-203-2591; jkbrew@erols.com
Accokeek Y2K Community
Prince Georges/Charles County, MD

Eileen or Patti
y2kwise@bigfoot.com
Y2K Wise
Anne Arundel County, MD

James Crawford
301-274-4747; smmac@us2000.org
Southern Maryland Millennium Action Committee (SMMAC)
Charles, Calvert, St. Mary's Counties, MD

Ruby Roberts
517-484-8240; Y2Kcatlansing@worldnet.att.net
Y2K Community Awareness Team
Lansing, MI

Donald A. Higby
517-832-5887; casino_man21@hotmail.com
Central Michigan Y2K Preparedness Association
Midland, MI

Andrew McFarlane
616-256-2829; l2k@leelanau.com
L2K
Leland, MI

Lee Knudsen
P.O. Box 82027; Rochester Mich. 48308
Featheredhook@msn.com; 1-248-650-0441
Paint Creek Reserves
Rochester, MI

Bob Mangus
248-625-5887 ; 248-912-8729 pager; rmangus@netquest.com
Year 2000 Citizen Action Group
Oakland County, MI

Nate Rein
nateo1@concentric.net
www.angelfire.com/mn/plan4y2k/
Mpls/St. Paul Y2K preparedness group
Minneapolis, St. Paul, MN

f. Williams
fwilliams@trib.net
mid-missouri y2k project
MO

Chris Baker
ckbaker@fidnet.com
Salt & Light in 2000
New Haven, MO

Pastor Dennis Flach
601-445-8574
ntzncepc@iamerica.net
Natchez New Covenant Presbyterian Church
Natchez, MS

Walter McGill
601-462-7552; crmin@ix.netcom.com
The Heavenly Way Adventistry
Rienzi, MS

Teresa Gaul
htgaul@rockymountnc.com
Jilco 4 y2k Preparedness
Nashville, NC

Wendy Booth
336-229-0820; weeboo16@hotmail.com
Y2K Information Exchange
Graham/Burlington, NC

Dan & Nora Waltman
704-545-8780; CNDETECT@AOL.COM
The Old Ways
Charlotte, NC

Carolyn Deal
cwdeal@aol.com; 336-854-4555
Earthgarden sustainable living community
Asheville, Greensboro, NC

Margo & David Stebbing
505-466-1332; Articular1@aol.com
Eldorado Y2K Information & Action Group
Eldorado, NM

Valentine Riddell
505-466-0791; orenda@orenda-arts.org
y2ksantafe@egroups.com
Galisteo Y2K Citizen Preparedness Committee
Galisteo, NM

Noah Gordon
505-989-5751; noah.gordon@cwix.com
Y2K Information Hotline for Santa Fe
Santa Fe, NM

Tyler Hannigan
505-758-8945; silverhawk@silverhawk.com
Taos Y2K Community Preparedness Group
Taos, NM

John Zoltai
(505) 672-3177; jtz@lanl.gov
Northern New Mexico Y2K
Los Alamos, NM

E. Tom Behr
908-647-6489; ethomasb@aol.com
Friends of Long Hill Township
Long Hill Township, NJ 07946

James Ranish
732-417-7308; y2kok@aol.com
Central NJ Y2K Community Preparedness Group
East Brunswick, NJ

Glenn L. Klotz, Director
Lee00@earthlink.net; http://home.earthlink.net/~lee00/index.html
Atlantic County Y2k Action!
Margate, NJ

Chris King
cnyy2kgroup@scctel.com
The Central New York Y2K Survival Group
Syracuse, NY

Rev. Kevin L. Baker
716-759-0648; vineyard@vcfbuffalo.org
Vineyard Christian Fellowship: Y2K Seminar/Joseph Project
Clarence-Akron, NY

Douglas E. Renz
y2kfuture@juno.com
Future Generations Y2k Preparedness Group
Wolcott, NY

Amanda Walker
702-392-1877; www.y2k-lasvegas.com
Y2K Community Solutions Group
Las Vegas, NV

Linda Weber
914-624-8488; Natasha400@aol.com
Rockland County Y2K Community Readiness Group

Joyce Jagger
607-936-4389; jaguar244@aol.com
Corning Care Givers
Steuben County, Corning, NY

Gene Ira Katz and/or Hope Bitzer
PO Box 6601; Ithaca NY 14851; geneirakatz@yahoo.com
Ad-Hoc Emergency Preparedness(y2K) Group, Tompkins County
Ithaca, NY

Brian Donnelly
914-753-9039; docveneer@yahoo.com
Millennium Awareness Group
Sloatsburg, NY 10974

Eric Schmidt
eschm@be.bricker.com
Greater Columbus Year 2000 Information Council
Columbus, OH

Andy Ingraham Dwyer
614- 447-1586; adwyer@io.com
Columbus Y2k Community & Individual Prep
Columbus, OH

Phil Marcischak
440-205-2333; phil.marcischak@pccmentor.com
Chardon Christian Fellowship Y2K Task Force
Chardon, OH

Jeff Keim, Regional Director
-419-877-0081; wakecall@aol.com
The Joseph Project 2000/Toledo
6632 Providence St.
Whitehouse, OH 43571
P O Box 2369 (mail)
Whitehouse, OH 43571-0369

Stan Gleeson
513-874-4943 (day); stangleeson@hotmail.com
Tri-State Joseph Project
Serving greater Ohio, Kentucky and Indiana

Phillip W. Bullington
440-949-7859; pwb@en.com
Unite Now
Sheffield Lake, OH

Rick McKinney
812-637-1918; JwalkerRMc@aol.com
The Trib Force
Harrison, OH

Mark & Debbie Peters
937-927-5684; judah7@bright.net
Christ is our Sufficiency
6090 Church Lane
Sugar Tree Ridge, OH 45133

Andy
zeaal@webzone.net
Y2KOK Email Discussion Group
OK

Charles Buck
charlesbuck2000@www.hotmail.com
Portlands Y2K Preparations Task Force
Portland, OR

Christopher Frankonis
y2kinfo@y2k.millennium-cafe.com
Inner SE Portland Y2K Preparedness
Portland, OR

Ron Johnson
503-873-1484; rondjohn@gte.net
Silverton Y2K Task Force
Silverton, OR

Steve Bennett
polky2k@navicom.com
Polk Y2K Taskforce
Dallas, OR

RV-Y2K Task Force
541-608-9265
countdown@rv-y2k.org
Rogue Valley Year 2000 (RV-Y2K) Task Force
Medford, OR

Kathy
prepare4y2k@earthling.net
Daniel Boone Y2K Group
Douglassville, Berks County, PA

Robb Ware
Y2KROBB@AOL.COM
DelCo Y2K Awareness
Aston, Delaware County, PA

Carolyn
HealthAndWellness@msn.com
Health & Wellness
Green Lane, PA

Susan K. Minarik
724-847-9575; sminarik@ccia.com
Beaver County Y2K Community Preparedness Group
Beaver County, PA

David Floyd
401-294-3974; dantien@worldnet.att.net
www.visioning.com
Y2K Prepared Rhode Island
PO Box 1654
North Kingstown, RI 02852

James Westbury
843-462-7910; Jwestbury@Infoave.net
Harleyville Chapter of Y2K
Harleyville, SC

Michael S. Morrison
615-898-1175; dpmusic@hotmail.com
Nashville Now
Nashville, TN

Jerry Walkoviak
signsofthetime@compuserve.com
Y2K and Beyond
Franklin, TN

Julianne Wiley
423-434-2172; jlw@planetc.com
Tri-Cities 2000
Johnson City, TN

Craig Waller
615-356-7624; buznethel@mindspring.co
The Waller Group
Nashville, TN

Lily Harvey
lilyharvey@webtv.net
Surviving Y2K
Gallatin, TN

Jeri
mycpc@mycpc.com
Mid-Cities Y2K Community Preparedness Co-op (MYCPC)
Hurst/Euless/Bedford, TX

Dave Moore
409-986-7769; DMCMFA@aol.com
Galveston County Y2K Group
Hitchcock, TX

Jean Staffen
512-835-8802; jstaffen@flash.net
Y2K Preparedness Group
Austin, TX

Ruenette C. Bolden
409-982-7922; encore@ih2000.net
Southeast Texas Y2K Preparedness Work Group
Port Arthur, TX

Reynolds Griffith
409-468-1883; rgriffith@sfasu.edu
Nacogdoches Y2K Group
Nacogdoches, TX

Rev. Michael Rothman
903-791-1246; acts14@juno.com
Kingsland Community Fellowship
Northeast TX

Lisa Zach, Project Director
903-792-7448; lzach1@gte.ne
Year 2000—Texarkana In Action
Texarkana, TX

Sam Loy
512-282-60537; sloy@iphase.com
Austin Community Emergency Preparedness Group
Austin, TX

Richard Lanoue
512-833-9198; idrive4free@yahoo.com
Y2K Alert Group
Austin, TX

Lamesia A.Holiday
PEOPLEAGLOWMINISTRY@prodigy.net
People Aglow Ministry
Houston, TX

Tom White
915-367-4446; tom.w@usa.net
Permian Basin Community Preparedness
Midland-Odessa, TX

Adrian D. Heath
281-292 4889; adrianheath@yahoo.net
http://home.swbell.net/adheath
Montgomery County Project 2000
Montgomery County and other counties, TX

John Horton
801-240-2341; hortonjl@ldschurch.org
Utah Year 2000 Users' Group
Salt Lake City, UT

Russell Peterson
ProvoY2K@yahoo.com
Provo/Orem Y2K Preparedness Group
Provo, UT

Jennifer Mueser Bunker
Jen@bunkergroup.com; www.bunkergroup.com/y2k
Northern Utah Y2K Community Preparedness Group
Ogden, UT 84403-0096

J.V.Davenport
y2kinblack@fcmail.com
The Year 2000 in Black
Newport News, VA

Bill Truitt
540-745-5319; warrior@swva.net
Y2K Preparedness Group
Floyd, VA

Tony McKenna
free@naxs.com
Simple Abundance
Abingdon, VA

Mark
800-416-2879; ymmarket@inna.net
Middle Peninsula Y2K Preparedness Network
Gloucester, VA

Tonja Bento, President/Jay Golter, Coordinator
703-971-8641; 202-898-3924 (days); JGolter@aol.com
info@novay2k.org; www.novay2k.org
Northern Virginia Year 2000 Community Action Group
(NOVA Y2K)
Springfield, VA

concomm@usa.net
N.H.-Vt. Committees of Correspondence
Bradford, VT

S. Jones, founder
253-631-4129; sjones@nm-software.com
www.nm-software.com
Kent/Covington/Maple Valley Y2k
Covington Wa, 98042

Keith Mayeaux
509-465-4021; kmayeaux@integrityonline4.com
Suncrest Year 2000 Community Preparedness Group
Nine Mile Falls, WA

Fredrica or Werner Kundig
clouds@rockisland.com Or

Kiko Harrison
Orcasy2k@rockisland.com
Orcas Y2K Ready
Eastsound, WA

Pamela
P.O. Box 2737; Everett, WA 98203
seamaids@gte.net; http://www.selfreliant.com
PJR Solutions "Don't get scared....Get Prepared!"
Everett, WA

Anita Kulp
Year2KPrep@aol.com
Year 2000 Preparedness Council
Seattle, WA

Jeff Martin
Shadetree1@hotmail.com
Y2K REMNANT
Buffalo, WY

UK

Cae Gests
0161 226 6979
cae.gests@redbricks.org.uk; oobentley@redbricks.org.uk
www.redbricks.org.uk
00Bentley
Hulme, Manchester, UK

Australia

Michael Pulsford
tafkam@mailexcite.com
y2k adelaide
Adelaide, South Australia

Matt Bolton
m3it@technologist.com
Aussie Y2k Group
Victoria, Australia

Canada

Karen N. Spanier, Director
403-247-5259; (403) 247-8616 Fax
info@c-f.net; www.c-f.net
Calgary Y2K Community Preparedness Project
Calgary, AB Canada

Richard T. Wright
hjttp://grassrootsgroup.com
Millennium Cafe
Williams Lake, B.C. Canada

New Zealand

Helen Jansen
0064 3 44 11446; yhaqutn@yha.org.nz
yk2NZ
Queenstown, New Zealand

REFERNCE #7
Y2K COMMUNITY RESOURCE
GROUPS

(Courtesy of Y2K Community Project—
www.y2kcommunity.org)

National/International Community Support Initiatives

Many organizers have recognized the opportunity to amplify the
effectiveness of local communities by providing resources, guidance,
and/or coordination projects of national or international scope.
Here are some examples.

Resilient Communities

www.resilientcommunities.org

From their Web site: "Resilient Communities was initiated by Robert Theobald and Northwest Regional Facilitators (NRF) to promote connection, conversation, research, action and learning
among people who believe we each have an opportunity create a
better future. It comes amidst the tailwinds of concern and controversy of Y2K or the millennium bug...Something's afoot in the
United States, and Canada, and Australia, and Europe, and Asia and
Africa — all over the world. Increasing numbers of people are saying
they want a different life than that being offered by industrial-era
society...The developers of this project believe that a forum is
needed which focuses attention, brings people together, provides
opportunity for dialogue, and engenders a commitment for action
at many different levels. We believe that the theme of resilience is
the basis for creation of that forum. Robert Theobald argues that
"resilience is the ability of systems to cope with shocks and to
bounce back." Enduring ecological systems are inevitably resilient,
coping with climatic and other shocks. One core issue today is that
personal, family, community and socioeconomic systems have

become more brittle during the industrial era: restoring this resiliency is therefore a critical challenge."

Coalition 2000

http://www.coalition2000.org/

From their Web site: "Coalition 2000 will help communities prepare for the Year 2000 by developing useful tools and providing reliable information through a collaborative process involving community, government, and private sector groups...Coalition 2000 is a network of community preparedness resources, acting as a clearinghouse, to provide the public with credible awareness information, preparedness tools, and community action plans. A collaborative process, involving many organizations and experts working on year 2000 issues, will produce efficiencies and create beneficial synergies. The Coalition will mobilize Public/Private/Community partnerships that are inclusive and diverse, evoking the collective wisdom of leaders, experts, and the public-at-large."

National Y2K Civic Leadership Initiative

Washington, DC

Lois Saboe, Executive Director

703-641-8787; 703-641-9853 fax; bdfutures@aol.com

From E-mail: their goals include to "galvanize a National Network for Community Resilience and synchronize the efforts of those dedicated to Community Y2K Contingency Planning...[to] create the collaborative communities attitude and national infrastructure for sharing practices and lessons learned that are vital to the success of far more communities in 1999 and beyond. We must focus on maintaining a robust infrastructure and intact supply chains for as long as possible. Many communities are latecomers to the social implications of Y2K. Early adaptors make a tremendous difference by getting to know each other and sharing lessons learned. By working together, we pave the way for others."

Arlington Institute: Project Y2K
Washington, DC
http://www.arlinst.org/
From their Web site: "The Institute was founded by John L. Petersen in 1990...A policy and research institute...[w]e seek to give perspective to the shapes and patterns that emerge from the confluence of the many interdependent forces that are now redefining the global strategic environment...We attempt to be change agents — effectively moving new concepts into the policy arena and creating intellectual frameworks for understanding them...The Y2K event is the first event of its kind in modern history that is, at the same time, global in scope, potentially disastrous, and intrinsically out-of-control...We must invent a new mindset and methodology that reflects the interdependent networked character of this new era and implement it, fast...The Arlington Institute has obtained a major grant to develop and manage a large-scale effort to enable people at all levels to intelligently respond to this issue. We intend to respond to the burgeoning need for credible information and strategies, a service that is now sorely lacking. Our interest is less in the technological implications of the problem and much more in the social and economic possibilities that might evolve from this situation...The way we can positively influence the social sector is by pumping large amounts of knowledge into the system so that it can self-organize and reconfigure itself to most effectively conform to the new situation. By inserting information into the system and providing the forum where people can convert it to knowledge, we will in essence, be stimulating the immune system of the social system."

The Cassandra Project
http://cassandraproject.org/home.html
Cassandra was a character in Greek mythology whose curse was "to always speak the truth and never be believed." This pioneering site was founded and named by organizer Paloma O'Reilly at a time when public understanding of Y2K was only beginning to develop, in the face of even greater denial than is evident today. The site has

evolved into a tremendously useful compendium of news, communication facilities, articles, and links, and now has major sections in Spanish as well. Focus is on individual and community preparedness, with an emphasis on understanding Y2K's expected impact in a variety of areas.

DFIY2K.org:
http://www.dfiy2k.org/
DFIY2K.org is focused on enterprise and community Y2K contingency-planning and preparation. From their Web site:"DFIY2K.org is the web-based volunteer organization behind the critical initiative, spurring appropriate contingency-planning and community preparation for the Year 2000 (Y2K) millennium computer bug problem.
Organizers include Co-Founding Directors, members, and alliances of the Data Fitness Initiative & Coalition (DFIc) and online leaders such as the Ziff Davis Y2K Supersite at www.ZDY2K.COM. They also include leading information technology and Y2K technical, business and legal-risk experts such as William Ulrich, Steve Hock and Ian Hayes, Triaxsys Research, various government agencies, enterprises, and concerned citizens everywhere." The organization is co-host of national roundtables on community contingency planning and preparation for the Year 2000 computer problem, held on December 3rd in Seattle, WA and December 8th in Washington, DC.

Center for Year 2000 Community Action Plans (CYTCAP)
Newport Beach, CA
Steve Tartaglini, Managing Director
949-475-6810; 949-475-6811 fax; director@center4y2k.com
The Center for Year 2000 Community Action Plans (CYTCAP) is a nonprofit 501 (c) 3 organization; co-host of national roundtables on community contingency planning and preparation for the Year 2000 computer problem, held on December 3rd in Seattle, WA and December 8th in Washington, DC.

The Joseph Project
http://www.josephproject2000.org/
From their Web site: "The Joseph Project 2000, a Christian-led nonprofit, desires to prevent and respond to the potential impacts of the Year 2000 computer problem in a professional and balanced manner—engaging Christians in pro-active personal and professional awareness, preparedness and service, so that they might be ready to bless their neighbors during any potential time of difficulty." The project is focused on activating and supporting local church groups.

Mainstream Media Project
Arcata, CA
Mark Sommer, Director
707-826-9111; 707-826-9112 fax; mmp@humboldt1.com
A public education initiative using radio to expand public awareness of the Year 2000 computer problem; guest speakers are predominantly community organizers and Y2K experts.

REFERENCE #8
ORGANIZING TECHNIQUES
AND TOOLS

(Courtesy of Y2K Community Project—
www.y2kcommunity.org)

Asset-Based Community Development Institute
http://www.nwu.edu/IPR/abcd.html
Many community organizing groups may find it beneficial to use a process called Community Asset Mapping, developed by John Kretzmann and John McKnight at the Center for Urban Affairs and Policy Research at Northwestern University.

Community building starts with the process of locating the assets, skills, and capacities of residents, citizens associations, and local institutions.

—Kretzmann & McKnight

For a great deal of useful guidance in this area, visit the Institute's Web site. Capacity inventory forms are available on-line.

Kretzmann and McKnight's excellent workbook *Building Communities from the Inside Out* is available from ACTA Publications, 800-397-2282.

Center for Living Democracy
http://www.livingdemocracy.org/

A community-oriented nonprofit organization founded by Frances Moore Lappé and Paul Martin DuBois. The Center is dedicated to building democracy by inspiring and preparing individuals to "solve the problems that most concern them and create the communities that they desire." See in particular the Center's Learning Tools Catalog.

Utne Reader—Y2K Citizens' Action Guide
http://www.utne.com/y2k

Eric Utne printed a million copies of this excellent material and has put the text on-line. It includes important essays about Y2K along with organizing case studies and guidance.

Community Information Resource Center (CIRC)
http://www.azstarnet.com/~circ/index.htm

CIRC is Thomas H. Greco, Jr.'s nonprofit consulting service, networking hub, and information source, connecting people and resources, and fostering the development of healthy communities. The site provides important theoretical and practical perspectives on the role of community in global transformation, with an emphasis on intentional communities, economics, and governance. (HIGHLIGHTS: CIRC News Updates and Transformational Links.)

Coalition for Cooperative Community Economics (3CE)
Bill Ellis
3CE works "to promote a deep cultural transition which will give people in their communities more control over their own lives." 3CE has begun to publish a series of pamphlets on "social innovations which empower people at the grassroots and promote local community self-reliance." Pamphlet #AA lists a number of organizations involved in developing and empowering communities.

STATE RESOURCES

REFERENCE #9
STATE Y2K OFFICES

Alabama
http://agencies.state.al.us/y2k/
ejakers@isd.state.al.us
334-242-3840; FAX: 334-240-3228

Eugene Akers
Information Services Division (ISD)
Chief Information Officer
Department of Finance
64 N. Union St., Suite. 200
Montgomery, AL 36130-2626

Alaska
http://www.state.ak.us/y2000/
Bob_Poe@admin.state.ak.us
phone: 465-5004, fax: 465-5039
State of Alaska Year 2000 Office
410 Willoughby Ave. Suite 103
Juneau, AK 99801

Arizona
http://gita.state.az.us/y2k/index.html
Adranney@gita.state.az.us
340-8538 x215

Arkansas
http://www.dis.state.ar.us/y2k/y2kintro.htm
y2k@mail.state.ar.us
(501)682-4399
State of Arkansas
Year 2000 Project Office
PO Box 3155
Little Rock, AR 72203

California
http://www.year2000.ca.gov/
claudina.nevis@doit.ca.gov
phone:445-5900; fax: 445-6524
Department of Information Technology
Claudina Nevis
801 K Street,
Ste 2100
Sacramento CA 95814

Colorado
http://www.state.co.us/Y2K/year2000@state.co.us
(303)866-3222, (303)866-2168
IMC Year 2000 Project Office
1525 Sherman Street; Suite 100
Denver, Colorado 80203

Connecticut
http://www.doit.state.ct.us/y2k/
peter.sullivan@po.state.ct.us

phone: (860) 566-6246
Year 2000 Program Office
DOIT, State of Connecticut
340 Capitol Avenue—3rd floor
Hartford, CT 06106

Delaware
http://www.state.de.us/ois/y2000/welcom1.htm

Florida
http://y2k.state.fl.us/
Florida.Year2000@laspbs.state.fl.us
Phone: 850/921-2235, Facsimile: 850/921-2483
Year 2000 Project Office
Office of Planning and Budgeting
Executive Office of the Governor
225 Knott Building
111 St. Augustine Street
Tallahassee, FL 32399-0001

Georgia
http://www.year2000.state.ga.us/
mhale@itpc.state.ga.us
(404)657-1350
Information Technology Policy Council
P.O. Box 38391
Atlanta, GA 30334

Hawaii
http://www.hawaiiy2k.com/ "Community Self-Reliance Cooperative"
island@hawaiiy2k.com
The Community Self-Reliance Cooperative
C/O Karlos de Treaux
PO Box 33
Hanalei, HI 96714

Idaho
http://www2.state.id.us/itrmc/2k/default.htm
y2kteam@adm.state.id.us
Phone: (208) 334-3535, Fax: (208) 334-2307

Illinois
None

Indiana
http://www.state.in.us/dpoc/y2k/y2khome.htm

Iowa
http://www.state.ia.us/government/its/century/
paul.carlson@idom.state.ia.us
phone: 281-7117

Kansas
http://y2k.state.ks.us/
Year2000@dadisc1.wpo.state.ks.us
Toll Free: (877) 405-5349
Regular: (785) 368-8300
State Year 2000 Awareness Center
Kansas Department of Administration
Division of Information Systems and Communications
900 SW Jackson RM 751
Landon State Office Building
Topeka, KS 66612

Kentucky
http://www.state.ky.us/year2000/index.htm
year2k@mail.state.ky.us
Phone (502) 564-8715
Department of Information Systems
101 Cold Harbor Drive
Frankfort, KY 40601-3050

Louisiana
http://www.crt.state.la.us/y2kla/y2kmain.htm
raustin@doa.state.la.us
y2k_webmaster@doa.state.la.us
Coordinator J. Renea Austin (225) 342-7105

Maine
http://www.state.me.us/bis/y2k/y2khome.htm
stephanie.parker@state.me.us

Maryland
http://idf.mitretek.org:8080/mdy2k/
y2k@y2k.state.md.u
Office Phone Number: 410-974-7111

Massachusetts
http://www.state.ma.us/y2k/
Y2K@itd.state.ma.us

Michigan
http://www.state.mi.us/dmb/year2000/
buonodonod@state.mi.us
Dan Buonodono, 517-335-5099

Minnesota
http://www.ot.state.mn.us/y2kpage.html
ot-team@state.mn.us
T: 651-215-3878, F: 651-215-3877
Minnesota Office of Technology
First National Bank Building
332 Minnesota Street, Suite E1100
St. Paul, Minnesota 55101-1322

Mississippi
http://www.its.state.ms.us/yr2000/yr2000@its.state.ms.us

Teresa Karnes at (601) 359-2615.

Missouri
http://www.oit.state.mo.us/efforts/y2k/oit1@mail.oit.state.mo.us

Montana
http://www.mt.gov/isd/year2000/index.htm
isdwebinfo@state.mt.us
444-2700 / FAX 444-2701
Information Services Division
125 N Roberts Street
Mitchell Building, Room 229
PO Box 200113
Helena, MT 59620-0113

Nebraska
http://www.das.state.ne.us/das_cdp/rfp/rfp.htm
(402)471-2331
Dept. of Administrative Services
State Capitol, Room 1315
Lincoln, NE 68509

Nevada
server down? www.state.nv.us/doit/y2k/?

New Hampshire
http://www.state.nh.us/das/ditm/y2kpage.htm

New Jersey
http://www.state.nj.us/cio/nj2000.htm
Jack Longworth 633-9773

New Mexico
http://www.cio.state.nm.us/
wnew.htm#Agency_Information_Systems_and_the_Year_

jlarson@gov.state.nm.us
Jody Larson 827-3019

New York
http://www.irm.state.ny.us/yr2000/yr2000.htm
y2koft@oft.state.ny.us
New York State Office for Technology:
Phone (518) 473-5622.

North Carolina
http://year2000.state.nc.us/
yr2000@ncmail.net
(919) 981-2690; (919) 981-5374 fax
Statewide Year 2000 Project Office
Department of Commerce
3900 Wake Forest Road
Raleigh, NC 27609

North Dakota
http://www.state.nd.us/isd/y2k/
(701)328-3190

Ohio
http://www.oy2k.state.oh.us/
Margaret.Theibert@das.state.oh.us
877-925-6446

Oklahoma
None

Oregon
http://y2k.das.state.or.us/home.htm
email: y2kinfo@state.or.us
Phone: (503) 378-4929; Fax: (503) 378-5200
Statewide Year 2000 Project Office

Department of Administrative Services
Information Resources Management Division
155 Cottage St. NE,
Salem, OR 97310

Pennsylvania
http://www.state.pa.us/Technology_Initiatives/year2000/
webmaster@state.pa.us.
val.asbedian@state.ma.us
617/973-0762, 617/727-3766
The Commonwealth of Massachusetts,
Information Technology Division
Room 801,
One Ashburton Place,
Boston, Ma 02108

Rhode Island
http://www.year2000.state.ri.us
spadaros@doa.state.ri.us

South Carolina
http://www.state.sc.us/y2000/
scy2k@oir.state.sc.us
Phone: 803-737-9558
Fax: 803 737-9685
Year 2000 Project Office
Office of Information Resource
300 Gervais Street
Columbia, South Carolina 29201-3042

Tennessee
http://www.state.tn.us/finance/oir/y2k/y2khome.html
rselvage@mail.state.tn.us
(615) 532-5262
Consumer Affairs, Y2K

Suite 660
500 James Robertson Pkwy.,
Nashville, TN 37243

Tennessee
http://www.state.tn.us/finance/oir/y2k/webindex.html
rselvage@mail.state.tn.us
(615) 741-7354 / (615) 741-4589 Fax
Year 2000 Project Office
Office for Information Resources
312 8th. Ave. North; 19th floor
Nashville, TN 37243-15000

Texas
http://www.dir.state.tx.us/y2k/resources/index.htm
andrea.richeson@dir.state.tx.us
(512) 475-2297 / (512) 475-4759 Fax
Year 2000 Project Office
Texas Department of Information Resources
300 West 15th. Street Suite 1300
P.O. Box 13564
Austin, TX 78701

Utah
http://y2k.state.ut.us/
asitmain.cchriste@email.state.ut.us

Vermont
None

Virginia
http://www.cdci.state.va.us/
cdcwebmaster@cdci.state.va.us
804 786-1434, FAX: 804 371-7952
Century Date Change Initiative Project Office

1100 Bank Street, Suite 901

Richmond, VA 23219

Washington

http://www.wa.gov/dis/2000/y2000.htm

Email: year2k@dis.wa.gov

Telephone: (360) 902-2973

Fax: (360) 586-8992

Year 2000 Program Office

P.O. Box 42445

Olympia, WA 98504-2445

West Virginia

http://www.state.wv.us/y2k/default.htm

Wisconsin

http://y2k.state.wi.us/

datcphotline@wheel.datcp.state.wi.us

(608) 224-5058 FAX: (608) 224-4939

Wisconsin Department of Agriculture, Trade & Consumer Protection

10930 W. Potter Rd., Suite C

Milwaukee, WI 53226-3450

Wyoming

http://www.state.wy.us/ai/itd/y2000/index.html

webmaster@www.state.wy.us

U.S. GOVERNMENT Y2K SUPPORT

REFERENCE #10
U.S. SENATORS AND REPRESENTATIVES

Contact Info and Websites

For the House- The Honerable ------------

US House of Reps.

Wash. DC 20515

For the Senate- The Honerable---------

US Senate

Wash. DC 20510

E-MAIL- house.gov/htbin/wrep_findrep

or- house.gov then click lower left to "write your rep."

TO CALL MAIN SWITCHBOARD FOR HOUSE & SENATE—202-224-3121 THE WAIT IS LONG BUT YOU DO EVENTUALLY GET A LIVE OPERATR. WHO IS VERY HELPFUL AND CAN TELL YOU WHO YOUR SENTR. IS IF YOU GIVE HER THE STATE, BUT NEEDS "ZIP CODE" TO GIVE INFO. ON REPRSNTVS.

REFERENCE # 11
U.S. GOVERNMENT Y2K HOTLINE

U.S. GOVERNMENT'S Y2K FREE HOTLINE

New 1-888 Line Provides Free Y2K Information to Consumers

- 1-888-USA-4-Y2K, Assessment Summary Report, Web Information Help Answer Questions about the Year 2000 Computer Problem

The President's Council on Year 2000 Conversion introduced 1-888-USA-4-Y2K, a new free Y2K information line, and other Council initiatives for providing consumers information about the Year 2000 (Y2K) computer problem.

Council Chair John A. Koskinen joined Jodie Bernstein, Director of the Federal Trade Commission's (FTC) Bureau of Consumer Protection, and Sara Cooper, Executive Vice-President of the National Consumers League, at an FTC press conference to launch the information line, which will be supported by the General Services Administration's Federal Information Center (FIC) and the FTC.

"1-888-USA-4-Y2K is a key part of our ongoing efforts to make available information that will help Americans respond appropriately to the Y2K problem as we move through this year," said Koskinen. "We are committed to providing consumers the latest information on how the problem may, or may not, affect government services, banks, household appliances, and other things they depend upon in their daily lives."

1-888-USA-4-Y2K offers free information of interest to consumers in common areas such as power, telephones, banking, government programs, and household products. Information for the line comes from primary sources—government agencies, companies, or industry groups. Prerecorded information, which is available seven days a week, 24 hours a day, is available on the most common topics, and information specialists supported by researchers are available to provide additional information to callers. Information specialists will staff the line from 9 A.M. to 8 P.M. (EST), Monday—Friday.

"Consumers who want to know how computers in the Year 2000 will continue to deliver Social Security checks or how airlines will handle the Y2K problem now have a new tool," said Jodie Bernstein, Director of the FTC's Bureau of Consumer Protection. "The FTC is pleased to work with the President's Council and the FIC to provide this information.

"1-888-USA-4-Y2K will provide timely, accurate information on how computers will be able to deliver goods and services in the Year 2000."

At the end of the month, the FIC will make available a "fax-on-demand" system, to provide callers with printed information on the Y2K problem at the touch of a telephone button.

The Council also announced two other initiatives for providing Y2K information to consumers: the release of its first quarterly summary report on industry assessments of Y2K progress and the creation of a special consumer information area on the Council's Web site.

The quarterly report, the first of four the Council will release in 1999, provides summaries of existing industry assessments for key areas such as communications and finance as well as information on public sector Y2K efforts. These assessments, the bulk of which come from major industry trade associations, are being gathered by the Council's more than 25 working groups; many industry trade associations are in the early stages of gathering information from their members.

"Based on the data we have seen thus far, we are increasingly confident that there will not be large-scale disruptions among banks and in the power and telecommunications industries," said Koskinen. "But one thing is clear: everyone has a lot of work left to do. We are most concerned about organizations that don't have the Y2K problem as a high priority. They are the source of our greatest risk."

Progress among some smaller governments and businesses remains a concern. And despite an increase in activity in other countries, international failures are likely and could have a significant impact upon areas that rely heavily upon cross-border operations.

The Council is working to ensure that the assessments summarized in the report are available in their entirety through its Web site at www.y2k.gov. The next summary report is scheduled for release in April 1999, but individual assessments will be released to the public in the interim as they become available.

The Council has also expanded its Web site, creating a separate area devoted entirely to consumer issues and the Year 2000 problem. This portion of the site contains information similar to that which is available on the 1-888 line, but enables users to go one step further and link directly to the agencies, companies, and industry groups that are the primary sources for much of the existing information on Y2K efforts.

The FTC has three publications for consumers on Y2K: one on consumer electronic products, one on home office equipment, and one on personal finances. These publications are available on-line from the FTC at www.ftc.gov and through the FTC's Consumer Response Center, 202-FTC-HELP. The FTC also has a Business Fact Sheet urging businesses to disclose the Y2K status of their products to their customers.

The President's Council on Year 2000 Conversion, established on February 4, 1998 by Executive Order 13073, is
responsible for coordinating the federal government's efforts to
address the Year 2000 problem. The Council's more than 30
member agencies are working to promote action on the problem and to offer support to public and private sector organizations within their policy areas. Visit the Council via the
Internet at www.y2k.gov.

REFERENCE #12
Y2K FOR KIDS

(Courtesy U.S. Government's Y2K Site)

So What Exactly Is Y2K?

You've probably heard people talking about "Y2K" at home
or on the news; you may have wondered what it meant. Y2K is
shorthand for Year 2000 and is used most often when people
talk about the Year 2000 computer problem.

Why do so many computers have the same problem? Back
in the 1950s, 1960s, and 1970s when computers were first
built, the people who designed the programs that make computers run used only two numbers instead of four to indicate
the year. For example, 1998 was 98, and 1927 was 27. They
did this to save computer space and money. Many of the old
programs are still running computers today. And, out of habit,
many computer programmers continued to use two numbers
instead of four in the 1980s and even in the 1990s.

The Y2K computer problem is found in computers around
the world. Many small computers, called microprocessors, or
computer chips, run machines, such as your VCR and the ele-

vators in our office buildings. Thousands of people have been hired to work on the problem in the government, in the places you shop, in the companies that give you water, heat, and power, and in your schools. The federal government has been working on fixing its Y2K computer problem since 1989. No one is sure how big the problem is, but everyone agrees that most of it can be fixed by the year 2000.

Will Y2K Affect Me?

Y2K could affect you. You might not notice it, but little things may happen. Think about all of the things around you that use computers. You wake up in the morning to an electric clock, watch a videotape in your VCR on your TV, play video games, and heat up your dinner in a microwave oven. All of these machines and many other household appliances work because of the computer chip inside of them. Most businesses use computers every day. Your bank, your grocery store, and your schools use computers. Police stations, fire stations, and hospitals use computers to help people. If all of those computers make small mistakes, there could be a lot of little problems.

These little problems could affect you in many different ways. You may not have electricity for a day or two. Your computer might add numbers wrong if dates are involved. Some stores might not be able to get in your favorite books and games for you and your friends to buy. All in all, though, the Y2K computer problem should not be a disaster. It will not blow up your computer, and it is not likely to cause serious damage in your community. With everyone helping, it might not even cause any little problems.

How Can I Help?

You can help by asking the people around you about the computers they use. Ask your parents if your home computer has been tested for the Y2K problem. Ask your teachers if the computers at school have been tested. If you have a favorite store, have your parents ask the store manager about their computers. By asking people, you make them aware that there might be a problem so that they can fix it in time.

You can also help by preparing for some of the problems you might have. Imagine that you are going to be living in your home without electricity for a few days. Ask your parents to get the things you would need if a storm knocked out your electricity for a day—flashlights, batteries, a battery-powered radio, food, water, candles, and maybe some board and card games. Even if the electricity does not go off, it is always useful to have such things around the house.

If all of us work together, the Y2K computer problem can be fixed.

REFERENCE #13
CONSUMER ALERTS

- Preparing your personal finances for the Year 2000

- Electronic products

- What do consumers need to know about insurance?

- Questions for investors to ask about the Year 2000?

- Information-technology and home-office products

FTC CONSUMER ALERT

Preparing Your Personal Finances for the Year 2000
October 1998
Updated: December 7, 1998
   Do you have a bank account, a credit card, a mortgage, a car loan, or investments? If you do business with a financial services provider, the Year 2000 date change may affect your accounts. Why? The Year 2000 problem... The millennium bug... The Y2K computer glitch... All refer to the inability of some computers and computerized systems to correctly recognize dates after 1999. Y2K problems exist because many computer programs and computer chips recognize only the last two digits of a year on the assumption that the first two digits are 1 and 9. As a result, 98 is read as 1998. This approach works fine until the Year 2000, when 00 may be read as 1900 instead of 2000. This could cause some computer systems to shut down or malfunction.

How Could the Year 2000 Date Change Affect You?

   Many consumer financial services providers, such as banks, mortgage companies, investment firms, and credit card issuers rely on computer systems to perform a variety of date-sensitive functions, including

- Calculating interest and other charges
- Tracking deposit, loan, and lease payments

- Transferring funds electronically

- Producing billing or other periodic statements

Disruptions or errors in these computer functions could create problems with your personal finances, such as:

- Delays in clearing checks

- Billing errors or inaccurate crediting or debiting of trans-actions

- Improper delinquency notices, penalties, or late

- Inaccurate credit reporting

How Can You Protect Your Personal Finances?

Many financial service companies have prepared for the Year 2000. Still, you may want to take the following precautions as the date change approaches to minimize problems or avoid them altogether. Ask your financial service provider about its plans to deal with Y2K. If you're not comfortable with the response, consider doing business elsewhere. Ask your provider what type of backup records are kept in case of an emergency. How would these records be used to identify and correct problems affecting your deposit, loan, or other accounts?

Several months before the date change, get statements from your creditors detailing your payments toward principal, interest, and other charges. Also get a payment schedule showing how your loan balance will decrease until it is paid off.

If you don't normally maintain financial records, as a precaution, you may want to consider doing so in preparation for the Year 2000. That way you'll have proof if something happens to the computerized records. At a minimum, keep a six-month paper trail—three months before and after the date change—on significant transactions, such as mortgages, stocks, and insurance.

Make sure your deposit receipts and periodic statements are accurate. Report discrepancies to your financial services provider(s). Keep canceled checks as proof of payment for at least several months before and after the date change. If you bank by computer, download your transaction records and store them on a backup disk. You also may want to print out downloaded records in case backup disks are contaminated with Y2K problems.

As a precaution, you may want to consider sending payments for mortgages, loans, leases, and other important obligations by certified mail, return receipt requested, for several months before and after the date change. This would give you proof that payments were received on time.

Get a copy of your credit report from one of the three major credit bureaus—Equifax (800-685-1111), Experian (800-682-7654), or TransUnion (800-916-8800)—before and after January 1, 2000. You may be charged up to $8.00 for your report. Check for errors and report them to the credit bureau.

Keep credit card receipts for purchases and cash advances made on or around January 1, 2000. Compare them against your billing statements. Report discrepancies to your card issuer.

If you have a credit card with an expiration date after January 1, 2000, consider carrying a second card that does not have a 2000 date. This may come in handy if a merchant can't process a transaction using the 2000 expiration date. Notify your card issuer if you have problems using your card.

For More Information

Many public and private sector financial organizations provide Y2K information through their Web sites and consumer call centers. To learn more, visit the President's Council on Year 2000 Conversion Web site.

National Banks
Office of the Comptroller of the Currency
Customer Assistance Group
Suite 3710
Houston, TX 77010
(800) 613-6743

State Member Banks of the Federal Reserve System
Consumer and Community Affairs
Board of Governors of the Federal Reserve System
20th & Constitution Avenue, NW
Washington, DC 20551
(202) 452-3693

Nonmember Federally Insured Banks
Federal Deposit Insurance Corporation
Compliance and Consumer Affairs
550 17th Street, NW
Washington, DC 20429
(800) 934-3342

State and Federally Chartered Savings Associations
Office of Thrift Supervision
Consumer Affairs Office
1700 G Street, NW
Washington, DC 20552
(800) 842-6929

Federal Credit Unions
National Credit Union Administration
1775 Duke Street
Alexandria, VA 22314
(703) 518-6330

Other Types of Financial Service Providers Not Categorized Above
(includes finance and leasing companies/retailers/credit bureaus)

Consumer Response Center
Federal Trade Commission
Washington, DC 20580
(202) FTC-HELP (382-4357)
TDD: (202) 326-2502

FTC Consumer Alert!
FTC CONSUMER ALERT:
Electronic Products
October 1998

If you plan to record SuperBowl XXXIV, capture your child's graduation with the class of 2000 on videotape, or use other "household" products containing a microchip, you may want to check with the product manufacturers to find out if the millennium bug will affect them.

The millennium bug is another name for the Year 2000 problem or the Y2K computer glitch. The terms refer to the inability of some computers and computerized systems to correctly recognize dates after 1999. Y2K problems exist because many computer programs and computer chips recognize only the last two digits of a year on the assumption that the first two digits are 1 and 9. As a result, 98 is read as 1998. This approach works fine until the Year 2000, when 00 may be read as 1900 instead of 2000. This could cause some microchip products' systems to shut down or malfunction.

Does This Affect You?

News stories about the Y2K problem are prompting consumers to wonder how—or even whether—certain products will function in the new millennium. Products containing microchips may have Y2K problems if the microchips are programmed to use a calendar function.

Among the consumer products that use microchips are some small and large appliances, heating and cooling equipment, home entertainment audio/video products, photographic equipment, wristwatches, calculators, pocket electronic organizers, thermostats, and security systems.

The good news: Products that display or use only the time of day and/or day of the week—programmable microwave ovens and coffeemakers, for example—are not likely to have Y2K problems. Other products—such as refrigerators and heating and cooling equipment—may have chips that keep track of cycles rather than dates, and also are unlikely to have Y2K problems. Indeed, according to industry groups, few consumer products use a month/date/year calendar function.

That means few consumer products will experience Y2K problems. For example, the Gas Appliance Manufacturers Association reports that a survey of its members confirmed that furnaces, boilers, water heaters, and related products will not fail or shut down due to Y2K problems. If you're not sure whether your product has a calendar function, contact the manufacturer. Many have toll-free telephone numbers and Web sites to answer your Y2K questions.

Still, some consumer products may experience Y2K problems. They include

Some VCR models. On some, you may be able to manually reset the year to 2000. For others, generally pre-1988 models, the time shift function—that is, to record future events—may not work, but you'll be able to continue taping off the air and viewing prerecorded tapes, according to the Consumer Electronics Manufacturers Association (CEMA).

Cameras, camcorders, digital wristwatches, and pocket electronic organizers containing calendar chips. According to CEMA, some camcorder models—those sold before 1988—will display the date incorrectly after the year 2000 but otherwise will function properly.

Monitored security systems with a calendar function. Even if the unit in your home is Y2K compliant, find out if the monitoring company's internal systems are compliant. Do it now, before you are locked in to a one- to three-year contract with a monitoring company.

For More Information

The FTC has several consumer brochures on the Y2K issue. For free copies, contact Consumer Response Center, Federal Trade Commission, Washington, DC 20580; 202-FTC-HELP (382-4357); TDD: 202-326-2502.

CONSUMER BULLETIN

What Do Consumers Need to Know About Insurance?

U.S. DEPARTMENT OF COMMERCE/Office of Consumer Affairs/Washington, DC 20230

The Year 2000 is upon us. As we approach the next millennium, the "Y2K problem," or the "millennium bug," forces us to ask whether our computers will run smoothly or will software programs developed during the past 30-40 years blow up as computers struggle to identify "00" as the Year "2000" or "1900" or another century?

Computers and computer microchips have become so commonplace that we may not even know they are present. Many machines have "embedded chips," microchips that run the machine but are not obvious to the user.

What is your government doing about this problem? The Y2K Council was established by President Clinton on February 4, 1998, to coordinate solutions. The Department of Commerce has joint responsibility with the Federal Reserve in leading the Federal government's efforts to coordinate Y2K conversion in the insurance sector. The Office of Consumer Affairs is preparing a series of Y2K consumer bulletins to show how individual sectors are dealing with the change to the Year 2000. This first bulletin discusses the insurance industry.

Due to the insurance industry's heavy reliance on computer systems, it was one of the first to recognize the Y2K problem. Insurance companies are responsible for their own readiness and also must be concerned about their vendors. Since the industry is regulated by the states, readiness is closely monitored by state insurance regulators as well as the National Association of Insurance Commissioners. Below, we present some frequently asked questions and answers based on discussions with the American Insurance Association.

Consumer Impact

The insurance industry—health, life, automobile, property/casualty—appears ready for the Year 2000. John Koskinen, chairman of the President's Y2K Council, has asked the industry to assess itself to verify this. In addition, insurance regulators in all 50 states have surveyed insurance companies about the status of their Y2K remediation efforts. Most state regulators have approved Y2K endorsements for commercial insurance policies, such endorsements are not likely to be filed for personal lines of insurance, such as homeowners or automobile insurance.

Consumers Want to Know

Consumers: If a product malfunctions because of Y2K problems, will it be covered under existing insurance policies?

Industry: Whether a loss is covered depends upon the circumstances of the loss and the specific language in the insurance policy. It is very important, therefore, that policyholders discuss their coverage with their agent or insurer.

Most insurance policies will not reimburse a policyholder for the cost of repairing a malfunctioning product; therefore, these policies will not cover the cost of repairing a product that malfunctions due to a Y2K defect. On the other hand, if a product malfunction causes damage to other property, or injures a person, most policies will usually take care of these losses. For example, if a home heating system malfunctions and causes a fire in a house, the standard homeowners' policy would cover repair costs for the house. It would make no difference if the malfunction is Y2K-related.

Another example would be an elevator that malfunctions and injures a person riding in it. The commercial liability policies insuring the elevator manufacturer and the building owner may well cover the loss resulting from the injury, but as commercial insurance policies can differ, it is particularly important that business people review their coverage with their agent or broker.

Consumers: The insurance industry is regulated by state insurance commissioners. Will my coverage under insurance policies vary according to where I live?

Industry: Each state has unique insurance laws. However, although these laws and regulations do result in some differences in how policy language is interpreted, for the most part, the differences between what is covered and what is not are usually minor. Of course, whether a loss is covered by your insurance policy will depend upon the type and circumstances of the loss, and the kind of coverage provided by your insurance policy.

It is important to remember that each company can, and often does, create its own policy language, subject to approval of the state insurance commissioner. This is especially true for commercial insurance policies. It is therefore very important that you contact your insurer or agent on any question of coverage.

Consumers: If my car contains components that might malfunction due to Y2K, will my automobile insurance cover them?

Industry: If a malfunctioning automobile part causes an accident, the standard auto insurance policy would cover damage to the vehicle as well as the driver's obligation toward others involved in the accident. To illustrate, if your tires are worn or defective, the standard automobile insurance policy would not cover replacement of tires. However, if the car's bald tires cause an accident, the auto policy would pay for damages that result from the accident. A loss or accident caused by an automobile part that has a Y2K defect is no different. For example, if a Y2K defect in the ignition system causes a fire, the fire damage would be covered under the comprehensive portion of the standard auto insurance policy. Similarly, if the malfunction causes an accident with another car, then the auto policy will pay to take care of your responsibility toward the other driver and passengers, and for the collision damage to your car (that is, if you have collision coverage).

The auto policy would not, however, pay to repair or replace the malfunctioning part itself.

Whether the question concerns auto insurance or any other type of insurance, your insurance company and agent are the best, most reliable sources of information about what your policy covers and what it does not cover.

Consumers: Does my homeowner's policy cover damages if a dwelling catches fire due to a defective microprocessor in my home heating system?

Industry: Homeowner's insurance has two parts, property and liability. While a Y2K loss could theoretically give rise to claims under both property and liability coverages in a homeowner's policy, the chances are remote. Unlike businesses, few homeowners have many date-sensitive applications that are likely, even if they malfunction, to result in damage or injury.

The standard homeowners' insurance policy provides coverage for fire damage. In the unlikely event that a home heating system malfunctioned due to a Y2K defect and caused a house to catch fire, the standard homeowners policy would pay for the fire damage. The homeowners insurance company in turn would have the right to seek reimbursement from the company responsible for the defect.

The same concept applies to auto insurance. If, for example, a Y2K defect in the ignition system caused a fire, the fire damage would be covered under the comprehensive portion of the standard auto insurance policy.

However, insurance policies may differ somewhat in the coverage they provide. Therefore, policyholders are advised to contact their insurer or agent if they have any questions regarding the scope of coverage.

Tips for Consumers

The insurance industry appears well prepared for the Year 2000. But consumers must be forward-looking and follow the industry's advice to contact their insurer or agent with any questions about coverage. Identify all date-sensitive programmable devices such as security systems and contact the companies that manufactured or installed the devices. Request that products be tested for Y2K compliance and where necessary, be repaired or replaced. Your insurer or broker may also be able to recommend resources to help you identify potential Year 2000 problems to prevent losses from occurring.

Contacts for More Information about Y2K

www.aiadc.org
The American Insurance Association
1130 Connecticut Ave., NW, Suite 1000
Washington, DC 20036
phone (202) 828-7100; fax (202) 293-1219

www.naic.org
The National Association of Insurance Commissioners, Support & Services Office
120 West Twelfth Street, Suite 1100
Kansas City, MO 64105-1925
phone (816) 842-3600; fax (816) 471-7004

www.y2k.gov
The President's Council on Y2K Conversion
115 Old Executive Office Building
Washington, DC 20502
phone (202) 456-1414

www.consumer.gov
One-stop shopping for consumers to locate consumer information
provided by an ever-expanding number of Federal government
agencies.
Federal Trade Commission, Consumer Response Center
Washington, DC 20580
phone (202) 326-3128

www.nist.gov/y2k/
Public Inquiries Unit, National Institute of Standards and Technology, U.S. Department of Commerce
Gaithersburg, MD 20899-0001
phone (301) 975-2762; fax (301) 926-1630

For more information about the Office of Consumer
Affairs, consumer bulletins, and other publications, contact:

Office of Consumer Affairs
U.S. Department of Commerce
Room H5718
Washington, DC 20230
Web site: www.doc.gov/oca
E-mail: CAffairs@doc.gov
Voice: (202) 482-5001
Fax: (202) 482-6007 (10/98)

CONSUMER ALERT

Questions for Investors to Ask about the Year 2000 SEC?
September 1997

The "Year 2000 problem" arises because most computer systems and programs were designed to handle only a two-digit year, not a four-digit year. When the year 2000 begins, these computers may interpret "00" as the year 1900 (e.g., 1997 is seen as "97") and either stop processing date-related computations or will process them incorrectly. To fix the problem, test their systems, test interactions with other systems as year 2000 compliant—all before the stroke of midnight on December 31, 1999.

While the government is monitoring this problem, there are no guarantees. The best advice we can give anyone concerned about the year 2000 problem is to ask questions.

As a Customer of a Brokerage or a Shareholder of an Investment Company, Ask Your Broker or Money Manager...

- What is your firm doing to become year 2000 compliant?

- How can I be satisfied that your firm will be ready on time?

- If your firm is not ready, how could I be affected?

- Assuming that your firm will be ready, what is being done to make sure that the exchanges, clearing agencies, and other market participants are also ready?

- Are there provisions to test operations with the exchanges, clearing agencies, and other market participants before 2000? Will your firm be participating in any industry-wide tests?

- What will happen if I want to sell some stock in December 1999 or early January 2000 and your firm or some other market participant is having computer problems and my sale is delayed or possibly can't be executed at all on the day I placed the order? What will your firm do for me in that situation?

- Is your firm's research department evaluating companies' compliance with year 2000 and the effect their compliance might have on their bottom line before you make buy and sell recommendations?

- How can I be assured that my interest and dividend payments will not be affected on January 2000?

As an Investor or Shareholder in a Public Company, Ask the Company or Your Broker or Financial Adviser Recommending the Investment...

- What is the company doing to prepare its computers for the year 2000?

- What will be the effect of the year 2000 problem on the company?

- Is the year 2000 only an internal operational problem for the company, or will it have an effect on the company's products and/or services?

- What is the company's schedule for fixing and testing your systems? Can you send me a copy of the company's schedule?

- How do the company's costs in addressing the year 2000 problem affect its bottom line? Do these costs have a material financial effect? Can I see something in the company's recent reports or other public statements in which the company discusses its approach to the year 2000 problem?

- Even if you don't believe the costs or potential effects of the year 2000 are material, can you tell me how much the year 2000 problem will cost the company?

- Have any of the company's officers or members of the board bought personal liability insurance specifically for year 2000 problems?

- As a manufacturer or supplier of [computer equipment, software, medical equipment, computer services,...], are you concerned about the potential liabilities associated with the company's products or services? What is your best assessment of corporate exposure to legal actions arising from equipment or software failures associated with the company's products or services?

Office of Investor Education and Assistance

U.S. Securities and Exchange Commission at
Mail Stop 2-13
450 Fifth Street, N.W.
Washington, D.C. 20549
Phone: (202)-942-7040
Fax: (202)-942-9634
E-mail: help@sec.gov
Call 1-(800)-SEC-0330 and ask for our publications:
Invest Wisely: Advice From Your Securities Industry Regulators
Invest Wisely: An Introduction to Mutual Funds
http://www.sec.gov/consumer/y2kaskit.htm
Last update: 06/16/98

FTC CONSUMER ALERT

Information-Technology and Home-Office Products
October 1998

Whether you use a personal computer (PC) to run a home-based business, keep track of the family finances or play com-

348 The Complete Y2K Home Preparation Guide

puter games, the Year 2000 date change may affect you. The terms Year 2000 problem, millennium bug, and Y2K computer glitch refer to the inability of some computers and computerized systems to correctly recognize dates after 1999.

Y2K problems exist because many computer programs and computer chips recognize only the last two digits of a year on the assumption that the first two digits are 1 and 9. As a result, 98 is read as 1998. This approach works fine until the Year 2000, when 00 may be read as 1900 instead of 2000. This could cause some computer systems to shut down or malfunction.

News stories about the Y2K problem are prompting consumers to wonder how—or even whether—certain products will function in the new millennium. Products containing microchips may have Y2K problems if the microchips are programmed to use a month/date/and year calendar function. Products that display or use only the time of day and/or day of the week are not likely to have Y2K problems.

If you're not sure whether your product has a calendar function, or if you simply want more information about Y2K and your "information technology" and home-office products, contact the manufacturer. Many have toll-free telephone numbers and Web sites to answer your Y2K questions.

You also can buy inexpensive testing programs for your hardware, operating systems, and more popular software applications or find free testing tools online. It's a good idea to check with the manufacturer or publisher before attempting to fix your computer.

Information technology and home-office products that may experience Y2K problems include:

Computer Hardware: All PCs have a calendar function. That is, they maintain a system date, which is used by operating systems and other software programs for date stamping files or for processing, storing, or displaying dates or events. Your computer retrieves the date and time when you turn it on. More specifically, a PC contains a real time clock chip to keep track of the current date and time. The date and time are established through the real time clock chip and the start-up software.

Many manufacturers are providing free software upgrades if the upgrade will help your PC handle the Y2K transition. You may have to buy and install a new start-up chip for older PCs and you may want to hire a professional to do the installation.

Computer components, such as monitors, modems, sound cards, display or graphics cards, TV-tuner cards, and peripheral equipment like backup drives, also may contain embedded chips. These items may not use a calendar function, but you may want to contact the manufacturer to be sure. For components included in the purchase of your system, contact your computer manufacturer; for components purchased separately, contact the manufacturer of the item.

Computer Software: Many off-the-shelf software programs are date-sensitive. That is, they process, store, or display dates. For example, dates may be used for date-stamping and record keeping; for retrieving or sorting files and records; for calculations, comparisons, projections and forecasts; or for triggering specific actions. Date-sensitive software includes: operating systems, such as DOS, OS/2, Windows-based systems, and Macintosh systems used by Apple computers, databases and spreadsheets; accounting, financial and tax software; contact or project manager programs; utilities, such as file managers, personal information managers, uninstallers, backup programs and anti-virus software; and fax, e-mail or other communication programs.

Operating Systems: Most recently issued operating systems should be able to handle the Year 2000 date change. Some may require you to download and install a software upgrade. Most publishers are providing information about the Y2K-readiness of their operating systems, and any software upgrades, through their Web sites and toll-free telephone numbers. Apple Computers has stated that the McIntosh operating system will not experience Y2K problems.

Specific Purpose Software Programs: Whether other date-sensitive software can handle Y2K problems varies by program and, often, by version. Some software publishers are providing free updates or patches—mainly for newer versions.

Customized data applications—created by users or third parties—using date-sensitive commercial programs also may require Y2K modifications. This depends, in part, on how dates were entered and stored in such applications. Check with the program's publisher or with software retailers to determine whether any data conversion software to help this process is available. It's also important to consider how much a particular program interfaces with others, and to confirm the Y2K status of those programs to prevent intermingling of compliant and non-compliant date data.

Home-Office Products

While scanners, copiers and printers may contain embedded chips, they generally don't have calendar functions and should not have Y2K problems. However, if you've added transaction-logging components with date-stamping capabilities to such equipment, check with the equipment's manufacturer to learn whether the added component will cause Y2K problems.

Fax machines have calendar functions. According to manufacturers, most current models won't have Y2K problems. Some older models, while they'll continue to function, may date stamp incoming and outgoing faxes with the wrong dates. Contact the manufacturer for more information.

To Learn More

The FTC offers consumer brochures on the Y2K issue. For free copies, contact: Consumer Response Center, Federal Trade Commission, Washington, DC 20580; 202-FTC-HELP (382-4357); TDD: 202-326-2502.

REFERENCE #14
RED CROSS ON Y2K

What You Should Know

For more than 100 years, the American Red Cross has been at the cutting edge of disaster relief activities, helping people prevent, prepare for, and cope with disasters and other emergencies. That's why your Red Cross has published the following information about "Y2K"—its potential effects and what you can do to be prepared.

Frequently Asked Questions

What is "Y2K" and why are people concerned?

The Year 2000 technology problem, or bug, as it is sometimes called, was created in the early days of computers, when memory in computers was scarce and expensive. Programmers took shortcuts whenever possible to save space. Instead of using a four-digit code for year dates, a two-digit entry was used. This practice persisted, long after the need for saving space was eliminated. The two-digit code also was used in embedded chips, which exist in many devices that control processes, functions, machines (like cars), building ventilation systems, elevators, and fire and security alarm systems, which are part of our everyday lives.

When the year 2000 comes, programs that have been coded with two-digit year codes will not distinguish between the years 2000 and 1900. If the program includes time-sensitive calculations or comparisons, results are unpredictable. No one knows what problems may occur, how widespread they may be, or how long they will last. The good news is that federal, state, and local governments; banks and other financial institutions; retail businesses, and every other group affected by this problem have been working to resolve it, and a great deal of progress has been made.

When could Y2K problems happen?

Most people anticipate Y2K problems may happen December 31, 1999, at midnight. Many experts predict that the problem is more likely to be a persistent one over a few years rather than a single "crash." For example, there may be a computer-based problem with other dates, such as April 9, 1999, which is the 99th day of the year, or on 9/9/99. In the past, a computer program, and some experts believe that when all nines show up in a date sequence, some computer systems could read it as a program termination command. There also is some concern regarding fiscal year 2000 dates in those organizations with fiscal years that start earlier than December 31, 1999. Also, the year 2000 is a leap year, and the leap year date 02/29/00 may be a problem for some computer programs as well.

What kinds of things could happen as a result of Y2K problems?

The President's Council on Y2K Conversion, established by the White House, as well as a special Senate Committee, have focused their attention on defining the scope of the Y2K problem. Hearings have been conducted by the United States Senate Special Committee on the Year 2000 Technology Problem and have focused on the following eight areas:

- Utilities and the national power grid
- International banking and finance
- Health care
- Transportation
- Telecommunications
- Pension and mutual funds
- Emergency planning
- General business

The potential effect of the Y2K technology problem on any of these areas is unknown, and the situation continues to change as federal, state, and local governments; industries; businesses; and organizations, as well as the general public, take actions to reduce the problem. Experts who spoke at the

Senate hearings believe that there may be localized disruptions. For example, in some areas, electrical power may be unavailable for some time. Manufacturing and production industries may be disrupted. Roads may be closed or gridlocked if traffic signals are disrupted. Electronic credit card transactions may not be processed. Telephone systems may not work.

Because no one can be certain about the effects of the Y2K problem, the American Red Cross has developed the following checklist for you. These are some easy steps you can take to prepare for possible disruptions. All of these recommendations make good sense, regardless of the potential problem.

WHAT YOU CAN DO TO BE PREPARED

Y2K Checklist

Check with manufacturers of any essential computer-controlled electronic equipment in your home to see if that equipment may be affected. This includes fire and security alarm systems, programmable thermostats, appliances, consumer electronics, garage door openers, electronic locks, and any other electronic equipment in which an "embedded chip" may control its operation.

❏　Stock disaster supplies to last several days to a week for yourself and those who live with you. This includes having nonperishable foods, stored water, and an ample supply of prescription and nonprescription medications that you regularly use.
See Your Family Disaster Supplies Kit for suggestions.

❏　As you would in preparation for a storm of any kind, have some extra cash on hand in case electronic transactions involving ATM cards, credit cards, and the like cannot be processed. Plan to keep cash in a safe place, and withdraw money from your bank in small amounts.

❑ Similar to preparing for a winter storm, it is suggested that you keep your automobile gas tank above half full.

❑ In case the power fails, plan to use alternative cooking devices in accordance with manufacturer's instructions. Don't use open flames or charcoal grills indoors.

❑ Have extra blankets, coats, hats, and gloves to keep warm. Please do not plan to use gas-fueled appliances, like an oven, as an alternative heating source. The same goes for wood-burning or liquid-fueled heating devices that are not designed to be used in a residential structure. Camp stoves and heaters should only be used out of doors in a well-ventilated area. If you do purchase an alternative heating device, make sure it is approved for use indoors and is listed with the Underwriters Laboratories (UL).

❑ Have plenty of flashlights and extra batteries on hand. Don't use candles for emergency lighting.

❑ Examine your smoke alarms now. If you have smoke alarms that are hard-wired into your home's electrical system (most newer ones are), check to see if they have battery backups. Every fall, replace all batteries in all smoke alarms as a general fire safety precaution.

❑ Be prepared to relocate to a shelter for warmth and protection during a prolonged power outage or if for any other reason local officials request or require that you leave your home. Listen to a battery-operated radio or television for information about where shelters will be available.

❑ If you plan to use a portable generator, connect what you want to power directly to the generator; do not connect the generator to your home's electrical system. Also, be sure to keep a generator in a well-ventilated area—either outside or in a garage, keeping the door open. Don't put a generator in your basement or anywhere inside your home.

❏   Check with the emergency services providers in your community to see if there is more information available about how your community is preparing for any potential problems. Be an advocate and support efforts by your local police, fire, and emergency management officials to ensure that their systems will be able to operate at all times.

The American Red Cross helps people prevent, prepare for, and respond to emergencies. We're in your neighborhood every day, providing disaster preparedness information and teaching classes in first aid and other lifesaving skills, to help keep families like yours safer. For more information, please contact your local American Red Cross.

Disasters happen anytime and anywhere. And when disaster strikes, you may not have much time to respond. A highway spill or hazardous material could mean evacuation. A winter storm could confine your family at home. An earthquake, flood, tornado, or any other disaster could cut water, electricity, and telephones—for days.

After a disaster, local officials and relief workers will be on the scene, but they cannot reach everyone immediately. You could get help in hours, or it may take days. Would your family be prepared to cope with the emergency until help arrives?

Your family will cope best by preparing for disaster before it strikes. One way to prepare is by assembling a Disaster Supplies Kit. Once disaster hits, you won't have time to shop or search for supplies. But if you've gathered supplies in advance, your family can endure an evacuation or home confinement.

Prepare Your Kit

Review the checklist below. Gather the supplies that are listed. You may need them if your family is confined at home. Place the supplies you'd most likely need for an evacuation in an easy-to-carry container. These supplies are listed with an asterisk(*).

There are six basics you should stock for your home: water, food, first aid supplies, clothing and bedding, tools and emergency supplies, and special items. Keep the items that you would most likely need during an evacuation in an easy-to carry container—suggested items are marked with an asterisk(*). Possible containers include

- A camping backpack
- A duffle bag

Water

Store water in plastic containers such as soft drink bottles. Avoid using containers that will decompose or break, such as milk cartons or glass bottles. A normally active person needs to drink at least two quarts of water each day. Hot environments and intense physical activity can double that amount. Children, nursing mothers, and ill people will need more. Store one gallon of water per person per day. Keep at least a three-day supply of water per day (two quarts for drinking, two quarts for each person in your household for food preparation/sanitation).*

Food

Store at least a three-day supply of nonperishable food. Select foods that require no refrigeration, preparation or cooking, and little or no water. If you must heat food, pack a can of sterno.

Select food items that are compact and lightweight.

*Include a selection of the following foods in your Disaster Supplies Kit:

Ready-to-eat canned meats, fruits, and vegetables

First Aid Kit

Assemble a first aid kit for your home and one for each car.

❑ Assorted sizes of safety pins

❑ Cleansing agent/soap

❑ Latex gloves (2 pairs)

❑ 2-inch sterile gauze pads (4-6)

❑ 4-inch sterile gauze pads (4-6)

❑ Nonprescription drugs

❑ 2-inch sterile roller bandages (3 rolls)

❑ 3-inch sterile roller bandages (3 rolls)

❑ Scissors

❑ Tweezers

❑ Needle

❑ Moistened towelettes

❑ Antiseptic

❑ Thermometer

- ❏ Tongue blades (2)
- ❏ Tube of petroleum jelly or other lubricant
- ❏ Nonprescription Drugs
- ❏ Aspirin or nonaspirin pain reliever
- ❏ Antidiarrhea medication
- ❏ Syrup of Ipecac (use to induce vomiting if advised by the Poison Control Center)
- ❏ Laxative
- ❏ Activated charcoal (use if advised by the Poison Control Center)

Tools and Supplies

- ❏ Mess kits, or paper cups, plates, and plastic utensils*
- ❏ Emergency preparedness manual*
- ❏ Battery-operated radio and extra batteries*
- ❏ Flashlight and extra batteries*
- ❏ Cash or traveler's checks, change*
- ❏ Nonelectric can opener, utility knife*
- ❏ Fire extinguisher: small canister ABC type
- ❏ Tube tent
- ❏ Pliers
- ❏ Tape
- ❏ Compass
- ❏ Matches in a waterproof container
- ❏ Aluminum foil

❑ Plastic storage containers

❑ Signal flare

❑ Paper, pencil

❑ Needles, thread

❑ Medicine dropper

❑ Shut-off wrench, to turn off household gas and water

❑ Whistle

❑ Plastic sheeting

❑ Map of the area (for locating shelters)

Sanitation

❑ Toilet paper, towelettes*

❑ Soap, liquid detergent*

❑ Feminine supplies*

❑ Personal hygiene items*

❑ Plastic garbage bags, ties (for personal sanitation uses)

❑ Plastic bucket with tight lid

❑ Disinfectant

❑ Household chlorine bleach

Clothing and Bedding

*Include at least one complete change of clothing and footwear per person.

❑ Sturdy shoes or work boots*

❑ Rain gear*

❏ Blankets or sleeping bags*

❏ Hat and gloves

❏ Thermal underwear

❏ Sunglasses

Special Items

Remember family members with special requirements, such as infants and elderly or disabled persons

*For Baby**

❏ Formula

❏ Diapers

❏ Bottles

❏ Powdered milk

❏ Medications

*For Adults**

❏ Heart and high blood pressure medication

❏ Insulin

❏ Prescription drugs

❏ Denture needs

❏ Contact lenses and supplies

❏ Extra eye glasses

Entertainment

❏ Games and books

Important Family Documents

Keep these records in a waterproof, portable container:

❏ Will, insurance policies, contracts deeds, stocks and bonds

❏ Passports, social security cards, immunization records

❏ Bank account numbers

❏ Credit card account numbers and companies

❏ Inventory of valuable household goods, important telephone numbers

❏ Family records (birth, marriage, death certificates)

Store your kit in a convenient place known to all family members.

Keep a smaller version of the Disaster Supplies Kit in the trunk of your car. Change supply every six months so it stays fresh. Replace your stored food every six months. Rethink your kit and family needs at least once a year. Replace batteries, update clothes, etc.

Ask your physician or pharmacist about storing prescription medications.

REFERENCE #15
FEMA AND Y2K

FEMA (Federal Emergency Management Agency) Urges Local Communities, Emergency Services Sector and Public to Get Ready Now for Y2K

Washington, January 6, 1999—Federal Emergency Management Agency (FEMA) officials are urging the emergency management, fire and emergency services communities and the public to get ready now for Y2K.

"It is very important that counties, municipalities, school districts and other organizations that have not yet begun to work on Y2K issues, start now," FEMA Deputy Director Mike Walker said. "While some failures will be minor annoyances, some may have more serious consequences."

The Y2K issue is worldwide and refers to electronic and computer system problems that may occur because of the inability of date-sensitive devices to compute "2000" when systems move from 1999 to the Year 2000 (Y2K). Virtually all systems that rely on computers or electronic devices that refer to date and time may be affected by Y2K in one way or another. This includes power, dispatch and communications systems, 911 systems, microcomputers, and much more.

In a recent FEMA survey of state emergency management directors concerning Y2K issues at the state and local levels, the directors reported that although Y2K fixes are well underway in state-level emergency preparedness offices, the emergency service systems of many counties and municipalities remain untested.

"Generally states and the larger local governments are aware of and making some progress toward resolving Y2K issues, however, many smaller local governments as well as some state and territorial governments seem not to be aware of the problem," Walker said.

"Clearly the most serious potential for problems is at the local level, and this is what we are concerned about."

In February and March, FEMA will conduct Y2K Consequence Management workshops around the country to identify critical issues, assess vulnerabilities, review contingency plans and consider policies and decisions that need to be taken to deal with possible Y2K consequences. Participants will include state Y2K emergency coordinators, emergency managers and state fire marshals as well as regional representatives of FEMA's Federal Response Plan partners.

Many states also reported that they have not developed contingency plans specifically for Y2K problems; instead they plan to address problems under existing emergency plans or they expect to have their systems Y2K compliant in time. Most states expressed some level of concern over the possibility of power failures, especially where power is provided by smaller utilities. Other areas of concern cited by the states include limited or lack of resources to assess, test and validate systems and fixes for Y2K problems.

"Every community, every organization and every individual has an obligation to learn more about their vulnerabilities and take action to prevent potential problems before they occur."

Walker said. "Potential problems need to be identified and addressed now."

As chair and coordinator of the Emergency Services Sector (EES), FEMA is one of 34 sector coordinators working with the President's Council on Y2K Conversion, headed by Presidential Advisor John A. Koskinen. The EES group is working to make sure that all segments of the nation's emergency management community operate normally through the cross-over period from 1999 to the Year 2000 and beyond.

Updated: January 6, 1999

We also must be ready for the 21st century from its very first moment, by solving the so-called Y2K computer problem. (Applause.)

We had one member of Congress stand up and applaud. (Laughter.) And we may have about that ratio out there applauding at home, in front of their television sets. But remember, this is a big, big problem. And we've been working hard on it.

Already, we've made sure that the Social Security checks will come on time. (Applause.) But I want all the folks at home listening to this to know that we need every state and local government, every business, large and small, to work with us to make sure that this Y2K computer bug will be remembered as the last headache of the 20th century, not the first crisis of the 21st. (Applause.)

REFERENCE #16
DISASTER PREPAREDNESS
FOR PEOPLE WITH DISABILITITES

Being prepared for emergencies can reduce the fear, panic, and inconvenience that surround a disaster.

Check for hazards in the home.

During and right after a disaster, ordinary items in the home can cause injury or damage. Anything that can move, fall, break, or cause fire is a home hazard. Check for items such as bookcases, hanging pictures, or overhead lights that could fall in an earthquake or a flood and block an escape path.

Be ready to evacuate.

Have a plan for getting out of your home or building (ask your family or friends for assistance, if necessary). Also, plan two ways; some roads may be closed or blocked in a disaster.

Have disaster supplies on hand.

- Flashlight with extra batteries.

- Portable, battery-operated radio and extra batteries.

- First aid kit and manual.

- Emergency food and water.

- Nonelectric can opener.

- Essential medicines

- Cash and credit cards

- Sturdy shoes.

Maintain a list of the following important items and store it with the emergency supplies. Give a copy to another family member and a friend or neighbor.

- Special equipment and supplies, e.g., hearing aid batteries

- Current prescriptions names and dosages

- Names, addresses, and telephone numbers of doctors and pharmacist

- Detailed information about the specifications of your medication regime

- Create a self-help network of relatives, friends, or co-workers to assist in an emergency.

- If you think you may need assistance in a disaster, discuss your disability with relatives, friends, and co-workers and ask for their help. For example, if you need help moving or require special arrangements to receive emergency messages, make a plan with friends.

- Make sure they know where you keep emergency supplies. Give a key to a neighbor or friend who may be able to assist you in a disaster.

- Contact your local emergency information management office now.

- Many local emergency management offices maintain registers of people with disabilities so they can be located and assisted quickly in a disaster.

- Wearing medical alert tags or bracelets to identify your disability may help in case of an emergency.

- Know the location and availability of more than one facility if you are dependent on a dialysis machine or other life-sustaining equipment or treatment.

If you have a severe speech, language, or hearing disability:

- When you dial 9-1-1, tap space bar to indicate TDD call.

- Store a writing pad and pencils to communicate with others.

- Keep a flashlight handy to signal whereabouts to other people and for illumination to aid in communication.

- Remind friends that you cannot completely hear warnings or emergency instructions. Ask them to be your source of emergency information as it comes over their radio.

- If you have a hearing ear dog, be aware that the dog may become confused or disoriented in an emergency. Store extra food, water, and supplies for your dog.

Planning for Evacuation

People with disabilities have the same choices as other community residents about whether to evacuate their homes and where to go when an emergency threatens. Listen to the advice of local officials. Decide whether it is better to leave the area, stay with a friend or go to a public shelter. Each of these decisions requires planning and preparation.

If you need a wheelchair:

Show friends how to operate your wheelchair so they can move you if necessary. Make sure your friends know the size of your wheelchair in case it has to be transported.

Updated: June 16, 1998

Electric Power Industry Y2K Assessment Issued FEMA and the Year 2000 Initiative

Washington, January 12, 1999—Yesterday the President's Council on Year 2000

Conversion received its second report on the nation's electric power industry's preparations for Y2K conversion. John Koskinen, Assistant to the President and Chair, President's

Council on Year 2000 Conversion, issued the following statement:

STATEMENT OF JOHN A. KOSKINEN

Assistant to the President and Chair, President's Council on Year 2000 Conversion

January 11, 1999

I applaud NERC (North America Electric Reliability Council) for its leadership in developing this second assessment of the electric power industry's Y2K readiness. NERC and its partner organizations are performing a valuable public service by providing all of us important information about the status of the electric power industry's work in dealing with the Y2K problem as well as the challenges the industry still must face to be ready for the Year 2000.

There is no evidence at this time that the Y2K problem will create national failures in electric power service. Indeed, the industry is making significant progress in preparing critical systems for the Year 2000, and is taking an aggressive approach to contingency planning.

But much work remains. It is vital that each of the more than 3,000 power companies in the United States be prepared to meet their obligations to customers throughout the Year 2000.

Periodic assessments of industry and government Y2K progress such as that provided today by NERC are crucial to the country's efforts to prepare for the century date change.

Assessments help to promote action on the problem by providing industry members with benchmarks for progress. In the case of the electric power industry, such assessments also help those who rely on electric power to engage in more realistic contingency planning efforts, which will become increasingly important as we approach January 1, 2000.

The Council looks forward to receiving additional information from NERC on the readiness of the electric power industry.
Updated: January 12, 1999

REFERENCE #17
PRINCIPLES AND OBJECTIVES
FOR NUCLEAR NONPROLIFERATION
AND DISARMAMENT

Draft decision proposed by the President

Reaffirming the preamble and articles of the Treaty on the Nonproliferation of Nuclear Weapons, Welcoming the end of the cold war, the ensuing easing of international tension and the strengthening of trust between States.

Desiring a set of principles and objectives in accordance with which nuclear nonproliferation, nuclear disarmament and international cooperation in the peaceful uses of nuclear energy should be vigorously pursued and progress, achievements and shortcomings evaluated periodically within the review process provided for in article VIII (3) of the Treaty, the enhancement and strengthening of which is welcomed,

Reiterating the ultimate goals of the complete elimination at nuclear weapons and a treaty on general and complete disarmament—under strict and effective international control,

The conference affirms the need to continue to move with determination towards the full realization and effective implementation of the provisions of the Treaty, and accordingly adopts the following principles and objectives:

1. Universality

2. Universal adherence to the Treaty on the Non-Proliferation of Nuclear Weapons is an urgent priority. All States not yet party to the Treaty are called upon to accede to the Treaty at the earliest date, particularly those States that operate unsafeguarded nuclear facilities. Every effort should be made by all States parties to achieve this objective.

Nonproliferation

3. The proliferation of nuclear weapons would seriously increase the danger of nuclear war. The Treaty on the Nonproliferation of Nuclear weapons has a vital role to play in preventing the proliferation of nuclear weapons. Every effort should be made to implement the Treaty in all its aspects to prevent the proliferation of nuclear weapons and other nuclear explosive devices, without hampering the peaceful uses of nuclear energy by States parties to the Treaty.

Nuclear disarmament

4. Nuclear disarmament is substantially facilitated by the easing of international tension and the strengthening of trust between States which have prevailed following the end of the cold war. The undertakings with regard to nuclear disarmament as set out in the Treaty on the Nonproliferation of Nuclear Weapons should thus be fulfilled with determination. In this regard, the nuclear-weapon States reaffirm their commitment, as stated in article VI, to pursue in good faith negotiations on effective measures relating to nuclear disarmament.

5. The achievement of the following measures is important in the full realization and effective implementation of article VI, including the programme of action as reflected below.

- The completion by the conference on Disarmament of the negotiations on a universal and internationally and effectively verifiable comprehensive nuclear Test Ban Treaty no later than 1996. Pending the entry into force of a Comprehensive Nuclear Test Ban Treaty, the nuclear-weapon States should exercise utmost restraint;

- The immediate commencement and early conclusion of negotiations on a nondiscriminatory and universally applicable convention banning the production of missile material for nuclear weapons or other nuclear explosive devices, in accordance with the statement of the Special co-

ordinator of the conference on Disarmament
and the mandate contained therein;

• The determined pursuit by the nuclear-weapon
States of systematic and progressive efforts to reduce nuclear weapons globally, with the ultimate
goal of eliminating those weapons and by all
States of general and complete disarmament under strict and effective international control.

Nuclear-Weapons-Free Zones

6. The conviction that the establishment of Internationally recognized nuclear-weapon-free zones, on the
basis of arrangements freely arrived at among the
States of the region concerned, enhances global and
regional peace and security is reaffirmed.

7. The development of nuclear-weapons-free zones, especially in regions of tension, such as in the Middle East,
as well as the establishment of zones free of all weapons
of mass destruction should be encouraged as a matter
of priority, taking into account the specific characteris-
tics of each region. The establishment of additional
nuclear-weapons-free zones by the time of the Review
conference in the year 2000 would be welcome.

8. The cooperation of all the nuclear-weapon States and
their respect and support for the relevant protocols is
necessary for the maximum effectiveness of such
nuclear-weapon-free zones and the relevant protocols.

Security Assurances

9. Noting United Nations Security Council resolution 984 (1995), which was adopted unanimously on 11 April 1995, as well as the declarations by the nuclear-weapon States concerning both negative and positive security assurances, further steps should be considered to assure nonnuclear-weapon States party to the Treaty against the use or threat of use of nuclear weapons. These steps could take the form of an internationally legally binding instrument.

Safeguards

10. The International Atomic Energy Agency (IAEA) is the competent authority responsible to verify and assure, in accordance with the statute of the IAEA and the Agency's safeguards system, compliance with its safeguards agreements with States parties undertaken in fulfillment of their obligations under article III (1) of the Treaty, with a view to preventing diversion of nuclear energy from peaceful uses to nuclear weapons or other nuclear explosive devices. Nothing should be done to undermine the authority of the IAEA in this regard. States parties that have concerns regarding noncompliance with the safeguards agreements of the Treaty by the States parties should direct such concerns, along with supporting evidence and information, to the IAEA to consider, investigate, draw conclusions and decide on necessary actions in accordance with its mandate.

11. All States parties required by article III of the Treaty to sign and bring into force comprehensive safeguards agreements and which have not yet done so should do so without delay.

12.IAEA safeguards should be regularly assessed and evaluated. Decisions adopted by its Board of Governors aimed at further strengthening the effectiveness of IAEA safeguards should be supported and implemented and the IAEA's capability to detect undeclared nuclear activities should be increased. Also States not party to the Treaty on the Nonproliferation of Nuclear Weapons should be urged to enter into comprehensive safeguards agreements with the IAEA.

13. New supply arrangements for the transfer of source or special fissionable material or equipment or material especially designed or prepared for the processing, use or production of special fissionable material to non-nuclear-weapon States should require, as a necessary precondition, acceptance of IAEA full-scope safeguards and internationally legally binding commitments not to acquire nuclear weapons or other nuclear explosive devices.

14. Nuclear missile material transferred from military use to peaceful nuclear activities should, as soon as practicable, be placed under IAEA safeguards in the framework of the voluntary safeguards agreements in place with the nuclear-weapon States. Safeguards should be universally applied once the complete elimination of nuclear weapons has been achieved.

Peaceful Uses of Nuclear Energy
15. Particular importance should be attached to ensuring the exercise of the inalienable right of all the parties to the Treaty to develop research, production and use of nuclear energy for peaceful purposes without discrimi-

nation and in conformity with articles I, II as well as III of the Treaty.

16. Undertakings to facilitate participation in the fullest possible exchange of equipment, materials and scientific and technological information for the peaceful uses of nuclear energy should be fully implemented.

17. In all activities designed to promote the peaceful uses of nuclear energy, preferential treatment should be given to the nonnuclear-weapon States party to the Treaty, taking the needs of developing countries particularly into account.

18. Transparency in nuclear-related export controls should be promoted within the framework of dialogue and cooperation among all interested States party to the Treaty.

19. All States should, through rigorous national measures and international cooperation, maintain the highest practicable levels of nuclear safety, including in waste management, and observe standards and guidelines in nuclear materials accounting, physical protection and transport of nuclear materials.

20. Every effort should be made to ensure that the IAEA has the financial and human resources necessary in order to meet effectively its responsibilities in the areas of technical cooperation, safeguards and nuclear safety. The IAEA—should also be encouraged to intensify its efforts aimed at finding ways and means for funding

technical assistance through predictable and assured resources.

21. Attacks or threats of attack on nuclear facilities devoted to peaceful purposes jeopardize nuclear safety and raise serious concerns regarding the application of international law on the use of force in such cases, which could warrant appropriate action in accordance with the provisions of the Charter of the United Nations.

The Conference requests that the President of the Conference bring this decision, the Decision on Strengthening the Review Process of the Treaty, the Decision on the Extension of the Treaty and the Final Declaration of the Conference to the attention of the heads of State or Government of all States and seek their full cooperation on these documents and in the furtherance of the goals of the Treaty.

Index

Are you ready for Y2K?
Year 2000 Preparation Video

A look at how to prepare
your home and family!
- Food Storage
- Water Treatment
- Money & Finances
- Water Storage
- Heating & Lighting
- Health and Safety

FEATURING

preparedness expert
James Talmage
Stevens, author of
*Making the Best Of
Basics: A Family Preparedness Handbook*
and *Don't Get Caught With Your Pantry Down*!

Visit our Y2K web mall at: www.readyfory2k.com

ORDERING DETAILS ON PREVIOUS PAGE